THE CATALOG OF
WORLD ANTIQUES

THE CATALOG OF
WORLD A

A fully illustrated collector's guide to styles and prices

by William C. Ketchum, Jr.

Photography by Chun Y. Lai

NTIQUES

The Rutledge Press
New York, New York
rP

To the staffs of Phillips and Plaza galleries,
whose assistance helped make this book possible.

Design by Allan Mogel
Edited by Jay Hyams

Copyright 1981 in all countries of the
International Copyright Union by The Rutledge
Press. All rights reserved.

Published by The Rutledge Press, A Division of W. H. Smith
Publishers Inc., 112 Madison Avenue,
New York, New York 10016
First Printing 1981.
Printed in Italy by Mondadori, Verona.

Library of Congress Cataloging in Publication Data

Ketchum, William C., date.
The catalog of world antiques.

Bibliography: p.
Includes index.
1. Antiques—Catalogs.   I. Lai, Chun.   II. Title.
III. Title: World antiques.
NK1125.K47   745.1'075   81-5232
ISBN 0-8317-9499-2   AACR2

Page 1: Decanter set in electroplated silver and blown glass; Germany, late 19th century; $275–350. The bottles have silver labels and stoppers.

Pages 2–3: Massive sculpture of a tiger in bronze on a base of gilt wood; Japan, late 19th–early 20th century; $1,200–1,600.

Pages 4–5: Okimono of sumo wrestlers and attendant in carved ivory; Japan, 19th century; $160–210. The attendant has a bucket of water.

Pages 6–7: Tinsel painting on glass; United States, mid-19th century; $200–250. Tinsel and reverse-glass painting were popular female pursuits around the middle of the century.

Contents

Introduction

This book is intended to fill a recognized need among collectors for a fully illustrated guide to the most popular areas of world antiques and collectibles. This, of course, implies coverage of a very large area within which there is substantial variation not only in age but in the nature of the objects discussed. Some are very old, others are quite recent, and some are not even categorized as antiques or collectibles but as primitive art. Nevertheless, all share the common characteristic of being highly collectible. Over the past decade, collectors, both here and abroad, have expanded their interests to include not only such traditional areas as silver, furniture, and Oriental rugs, but also such newer areas as toys, Art Deco accessories, and pre-Columbian artifacts.

As they have broadened their tastes and multiplied their interests, these enthusiasts have often found that the existing books on antiques and art were not sufficient for their purposes, either through lack of enough large, detailed photographs or because of the absence of information on the current availability and prices of items they were seeking. It is the goal of this book to provide such collectors with a general price and identification guide to the major areas of world antiques and collectibles. Since the fields involved are so extensive and since many of the older items are seldom available to the average collector, emphasis here is on those items that collectors can actually find rather than on those items that most of us can see only in museums. In line with this policy, the prices quoted are those obtained at auction or sought by dealers and are given as a range, for even the

Opposite: Tazza in pilque-à-jour enamel; Sweden, late 19th–early 20th century; $2,300–3,000. Pieces in the plique-à-jour technique resemble fine stained glass. Right: Figure of the deity Fukurokujin in biscuit and glazed porcelain; from the Kutani pottery, Japan, 20th century; $450–600. Kutani is one of Japan's best-known sources of pottery and porcelain. Far right: Washkuk polychrome wooden carving; Polynesia, late 19th century; $150–200. Primitive art of this quality is a good investment.

9

Opposite: *Primitive painting of a gentleman; England, 19th century; $250–325. Bannister-back armchair; United States, late 18th century; $950–1,150. Sheraton desk; United States, 1800–20; $1,500–2,000. Reverse-painted mirror; probably England, 1870–80; $200–275. Two pieces of porcelain; China; $275–425 each. Brass student lamp; United States; 1890–1900; $300–375. Right: Vase in blue-frosted Sabino glass with molded representation of two parrots; France, 1925–35; $650–800. Far right: Trumpet-shape vase with etched-glass overlay; marked "Daum Nancy," France, early 20th century; $1,200–1,600.*

same piece rarely obtains the same price twice—a fact that somehow eludes those who tout the virtues of the one-price guides based on but a single transaction.

The various sections of this catalog are arranged in a generally chronological order so that the reader may observe, for example, the historical development of silver styles and their correlation with architectural forms and motifs, and within each such category examples are given from various sources and maufacturers in the major silver-making countries. In some cases this leads to the illustration of a broad range of objects. Such is the case with furniture, which was made throughout Europe and North America as well as in most other areas of the world, though from a collector's point of view the most important non-Western furnishings are those of China. In some areas most of the pieces shown and discussed come from a relatively small number of countries, simply because most available examples come from these sources. The chapter on toys is a good example, for few collectible toys of any age can be found outside Western Europe, Japan, and the United States. The reader should bear in mind that "collectible" is the key word here: a museum or a specialized toy collector might well own rare toys from Africa, South America, or Southeast Asia, but few typical collectors could hope to find—or afford—these items, and to include them would not be consistent with the purpose of this book.

The prices quoted here are for undamaged specimens in average condition. This is an important distinction, for in many categories damaged examples or examples in especially fine condition can fetch prices that vary considerably from the norm. Sophisticated quilt collectors, as an example, regularly pay a premium for pieces that have the original sizing, for it is proof that the items have never been used or even washed. The same is true with certain toy collectors, for whom a nineteenth-century example with "like-new" paint is justification for payment of a price that may double the market cost for an ordinary piece that is otherwise identical. In such areas as glass and pottery, chips or cracks, even though relatively minor or skillfully repaired, will result in sharp value reductions among the knowledgeable. New collectors should be aware of these nuances. Such distinctions mean that anyone who pays a high price for a damaged item will often find that he or she cannot recoup the investment on a resale, much less make a profit. Furthermore, those who buy things that are in extremely fine condition will usually see their investments increase steadily in value. Another consequence of the prejudice against damaged goods is the increasing problem of extremely skillful repairs—particularly in the areas of fine glass and pottery—which are intentionally concealed from the buyer. Few sophisticated collectors in these fields go anywhere today without the blacklight that is so critical in determining whether or not a piece is truly without blemish.

The factor of the antique as investment cannot be ignored today—it is a fact of life in the collecting world. With good examples of everything from sixteenth-century paintings to twentieth-century art glass bringing prices that are not only far more than anything previously realized but that also seem likely to be bested within months or even weeks, collectors must not only use care in buying but in selling as well. The general

Above: Rocking horse of fabric stuffed with horsehair mounted on a painted wooden base; United States, 1850–70; $750–900. Right: Bronze head in the 14 th-century Ife style; Nigeria, 19th century; $550–700. Some of the world's most interesting bronzes come from Africa. Far right: Automaton in the form of a seated Pierrot, or clown, with a bisque head and extremities and a cloth body; Europe, 20th century; $300–400.

trend of prices in all areas is up, but as a rule the rarer or finer example will not only increase in value more rapidly but will also, in the event of a recession, hold its market worth. Buying antiques for profit is, of course, a gamble just like the stock market, but several recent studies have indicated that the risk is actually less with a piece of Tiffany glass or a rare Swiss watch than with even a blue-chip stock.

The investor-collector who hopes to profit in the world antiques market deals with a much broader and more fluctuating field than does the enthusiast of Americana. In the first place, the field is infinitely broader. In the second, the competition is worldwide. Few Europeans are interested in American antiques and collectibles outside the narrow fields of quilts, Shaker furniture, Indian artifacts, and, perhaps, one or two other areas. When one ventures into the field of world antiques one encounters collectors from nearly every continent. Near Eastern merchants pursue Oriental rugs, Japanese businessmen buy old masters and nineteenth-century

Above: *Friction toy in the form of a locomotive made of iron and wood; Germany or the United States, 1880–1910; $150–200.* Right: *Geisha doll with musical instrument and bisque head; Japan, 20th century; $65–90. The Japanese are among the world's foremost makers of dolls.*

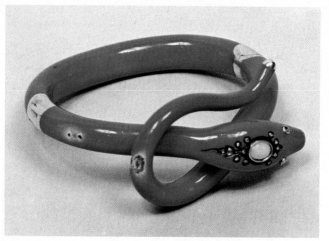

Left: Brooch in plique-à-jour enamel and gold; Spain, early
20th century; $250–300. Above: Pendant in openwork gold
enameled in red, green, and white with reverse side set with
an emerald and coral, turquoise, and diamond slivers; India,
late 19th century; $500–600. Right: Victorian bangle bracelet
in enamel and gold in the form of a snake set with rose-cut
diamonds and an opal; Europe, late 19th century; $1,000–1,300.
In part due to the Egyptian Revival, Victorians were fascinated
with snake forms. Opposite: Musical toy with three singing
birds in a brass cage; Switzerland, 20th century; $450–600.
When wound up the birds produce a remarkably accurate bird song.

bronzes. Dutch collectors reclaim their old clocks and pewter which we purchased and brought to this country decades ago. The renewed European and Japanese interest in collecting and in antiques as an investment coupled with the present unfavorable balance of American trade and currency value has brought new and knowledgeable collectors into the field. One must now know not only the trends in New York and Los Angeles but also those in Geneva, Tokyo, and Paris.

This catalog will help the collector to spot trends and to evaluate potential investments as well as to enjoy and appreciate his acquisitions, but it alone is not enough. More in-depth information is necessary in the field or fields of one's own choice, and to that end I have included a bibliography for each chapter. By reading one or more of the books listed in each category the collector should be able to obtain the detailed background information necessary to guide his or her choices.

However, reading is only part of the process of acquiring knowledge in these areas. It is also wise to make regular visits to museums, particularly those with permanent collections or exhibitions touching on your fields of interest. Also helpful are attendance at antiques shows and regular visits to antiques shops, especially those run by dealers who specialize in only a few areas and are, as a consequence, more likely to know their wares. The museum visits will provide information and the opportunity to view examples arranged by experts. The shows, shops, and auctions will provide a guide to what is available in the field and the prices being asked. Remember, knowledge is power in the antiques and collectibles field, and the knowledgeable collector will, in most cases, be the wisest and most successful buyer. He or she will also usually have the most fun!

14

1

Furniture

Most collectors think of antique furniture in terms of those pieces made and used in Europe, North America, and China. Although furnishings from other areas exist, they are for the most part either limited in type and number or are clearly derivative of pieces made in the three major centers.

The most sophisticated and varied furniture has come from Europe, where cabinetworkers were active as early as the Greek and Roman eras and where certain stylistic progressions make it possible to recognize and date specific examples. The earliest of these pieces were made in Egypt, Greece, and Rome before or soon after the dawn of the Christian Era. In all three cultures furniture was a luxury intended for a limited number of people. Chairs were low but elaborately carved and painted and were usually of the gothic, or scissors, form, not unlike a modern folding camp stool. Tables and couches were also low, since eating was customarily done while reclining. Few examples from these eras now exist. Tombs and other archaeological sites have yielded a few specimens, and the forms of others can be learned from surviving wall paintings.

Following the collapse of the Western Roman Empire, last of these great civilizations, Europe entered the Dark Ages, a period of great turmoil and dislocation during which many of the furniture-making skills developed by the ancients were lost. From approximately A.D. 500–1100 war, famine, and disease ravaged the Continent, and the few cabinetmakers active during this period (which is known as the Romanesque) worked crudely with the crudest of implements. Though surviving writings make reference to beds, chests, and chairs, and paintings show these to have been simple pieces decorated with rough floral patterns in a vaguely remembered Roman manner, all is now lost. No furniture has survived from the Romanesque period.

By the early thirteenth century conditions had greatly improved in western Europe. Strong if localized central governments were beginning to appear, and towns were growing up about the castles of the feudal lords. The church emerged as a powerful force, and as its influence grew so did its holdings. The Gothic age (1200–1400) saw the building of Europe's first great churches and the beginning of a traditional relationship between architecture and furniture design. Furniture form and decoration mimicked architectural motifs. Though this pattern has continued to the present day, it was especially evident during the Gothic era. The churches built during that period had pointed arches, pillars, and flying buttresses, and these were imitated in contemporary furnishings.

More profound changes were taking place in furniture construction. At the beginning of the period furniture makers were still making furniture by nailing together slabs of wood that had been roughed out with a broadax. By the fourteenth century they were framing their pieces—fitting thin wooden panels into a slotted framework, a stronger as well as a more attractive design.

Moreover, traditional carved decoration was supplemented with painting and gilding as the craftsmen were affected by contemporary illuminated manuscripts.

European furniture design from the fifteenth century on can be divided into several more-or-less clearly distinct eras of design, each of which gave rise to a specific type of furniture. The first of these periods is the Renaissance (1400–1550). Unlike the Gothic, which was largely northern European in inspiration, Renaissance design arose in Italy as a mixture of surviving classical (Roman) concepts and Near Eastern importations. The period was one of great intellectual and spiritual ferment. The Italian city states were rising from the ashes of the long-defunct Roman Empire, and in their rich and populous communities craftsmen began to make new types of furniture.

The Renaissance had a profound effect on Europe, partly because its concepts developed at a time when communications on the Continent were improving. Travelers from Italy carried the new design ideas to France and from there to Spain and nothern Europe. Francis I of France eagerly adopted the new mode, while England's Henry VIII imported Italian designers. In Spain a mixture of Gothic and Renaissance ideas led to the massive, iron-bound tables and nail-decorated chairs for which the country became famous.

So great was the impact of the Renaissance that some people, no doubt, assumed it was an immutable style. But such was not the case. A pattern of change was emerging in which each dominant mode would be replaced by a succeeding one, and by the middle of the sixteenth century a new style was evolving in France. Weary of the classical symmetry of Renaissance pieces, French designers began to create pieces that emphasized decoration rather than overall form. Characterized by exaggerated size, asymmetrical balance, and lavish carving, furniture of the baroque (1550–1700), as the period was called, was inlaid in marble, gilded and bronzed, and often crowned with elaborately carved eagles, lions, and blackamoors.

During this period the wealth and trade of Europe were increasing enormously. Asia and the Americas were being opened to trade, and the wealth of these areas was flowing into Continental coffers. Homes were ceasing to be fortresses and were becoming palaces, and new furnishings had to be designed for changing living conditions. The *cassone* vanished, to be replaced by console tables and clothes presses such as the large *kas* of Holland. The French developed the commode, a double-drawer chest on legs, and the upholstered sofa, while Flemish designers introduced caned chairs of almost thronelike proportions. In Germany and England desks, daybeds, wing chairs, and high chests appeared.

The baroque, too, was destined to pass. The sheer massiveness and exaggerated decoration of many pieces were annoying to some, while others sought an even less symmetrical style. This

17

appeared in the form of the rococo (1700–1770), a lighter and more naturalistic mode that took its inspiration from the lines of natural forms and was characterized by the cabriole leg, a gothic-shaped support somewhat resembling an animal leg.

Rococo decoration was less elaborate than that of the previous period. Painting, gilding, and inlay in precious woods and metals were all practiced but with a subtlety that had previously been lacking. However, there were those who longed for something even more severe, more classic. English designers had modified the mode to emphasize wood grain and patina rather than gilding or sculptured surfaces, and by the final quarter of the eighteenth century they had introduced yet another style, this one based on classical sources uncovered during the excavations at the ancient Italian towns of Pompeii and Herculaneum.

The neoclassic (1770–1810), as this mode came to be called, was characterized by plain surfaces, minimal carving, and rectangular form, the latter, of course, a distinct break with previous periods. Veneer became popular, and line inlay was customary, as was the use of gilt bronze, or ormolu, for drawer pulls, feet, and decorative accents. Initially inspired by the architect Robert Adam and guided by the cabinetmakers George Hepplewhite and Thomas Sheraton, English furniture makers momentarily wrested stylistic dominance from the French.

The rise of Napoleon Bonaparte quickly shifted the balance of power back to France, at least as far as continental Europe was concerned. Napoleon approved of the classic—indeed, he saw parallels between the Roman Empire and the one he was forging in Europe. But Napoleon did not favor the liberal interpretations adopted by the English designers. Instead the emperor wanted exact copies of Greek and Roman furnishings or pieces that adhered as closely as possible to authentic examples from those periods. As a consequence, furniture of the period he dominated (the Empire, 1810–1840) is characterized by massive shapes, heavily carved feet, arms, and pedestals, and the liberal use of gilt bronze. Except in the very best examples, there is a certain "clunkyness" about Empire furnishings that has put them in disfavor with collectors even to the present day. For this reason alone they represent one of the best investments in the antiques world.

Napoleon's schemes were brought to an abrupt end at Waterloo, and the furniture style he fostered gradually fell from favor, though it lingered in Italy and in Germany, where it was known as the Biedermeier. By 1840 no single, unifying design concept governed European manufacture. Instead, manufacturers, left to their own devices, began to produce a variety of revival styles, mimicking every mode from the Gothic to the rococo. This highly eclectic period is known as the Victorian (1840–1910) because it roughly coincided with the reign of the English queen during whose reign the factory system at last took over furniture manufacture.

In the second half of the nineteenth century a reaction to the less aesthetic aspects of the Victorian set in. English designers began to construct plain oak furnishings, modeled in part on their conception of ancient Gothic design. This style is referred to as Arts and Crafts. In France a combination of naturalism and reverence for the legendary forms of the rococo period led to the development of Art Nouveau.

The Arts and Crafts and Art Nouveau modes coexisted for a relatively short period of time (1880–1910), and they shared the stage with the still popular Victorian style. Yet even another style was rising. In Italy Carlo Bugatti, in Belgium Victor Horta, in Germany Marcel Bruer, all were experimenting with new designs and materials, especially with the idea of adopting factory materials, such as steel, plastics, and synthetic textiles, to the manufacture of furniture.

The modern movement, as it came to be called, was already well under way in Germany and Austria by the time of the First World War, but in France another, though related, style arose: Art Deco. Drawing on a mixture of Oriental color and essentially rococo design, blended with acceptance of machine construction, Deco designers moved reluctantly into the twentieth century.

By and large this progression of styles held true as well for those areas under the political and economic power of the Western nations. In North America, colonial styles were at first mixed, reflecting the preferences of the first settlers. Thus, French-speaking areas of Canada followed French fashions, and the diverse groups that settled the American colonies, such as the Dutch, Spanish, French, and Swedish, left their imprints. However, by the late eighteenth century American style was essentially English, and it continued to be so throughout the next century, only asserting its independence with the rise of industrial design in the 1900s.

The only other major design center for furniture was China, and things were quite different there. We cannot be sure when the Chinese first began to use furniture, but it appears that chairs were introduced (probably from the West) prior to A.D. 400. By the Ming period (1368–1644) a substantial variety of furniture types existed. These fell into two categories. In the colder northern areas of the country household activities centered around the *kang*, a heated and elevated platform in one area of the house. Here there were low tables and cupboards of rich hardwoods, but no chairs, since most activities took place with the participants sitting or lying on the floor.

In the warmer regions of the south there was no need for the *kang*, and it became first a platformlike bed and later a couch. Chairs were common in the south, as were stools and benches and tables, especially large round ones that became a family gathering place just as the *kang* was in the north. Cupboards became taller in the south and were often crowned by large hatboxes.

Unlike the case in Europe the design of these furnishings was established at a very early period and continued unchanged, so that the kind of stylistic progression that took place in Europe did not take place in China. Therefore a Chinese chair from the sixteenth century looks very much like one produced a hundred years ago.

Most Chinese furnishing are made of highly polished hardwoods (not the teak and camphorwood employed in tourist pieces) and are quite modern in appearance—so much so that they fit beautifully in modern homes, Eastern or Western. From the point of view of the collector, however, very few pieces more than one hundred years old are available on the market. In fact, war and civil unrest have taken a heavy toll of Chinese pieces.

While inlaid chests may be found in Southeast Asia, Japan and Korea are the other major sources of Asian furniture. Both produced fine, brass-bound chests known as *tansu* as well as cupboards (often built-in); neck rests; low tables, which frequently were built around braziers for warmth and cooking convenience; and simple chairs of the scissors type. Like the Chinese examples, these are well made in traditional designs of highly polished hardwoods.

Furniture, whatever its source, is and will remain one of the most important areas of collecting. Unlike many antiques, most pieces are immediately usable, and, unlike contemporary furnishings, which lose 70 percent of their value upon purchase, earlier pieces will in most cases continue to increase in value.

Double headrest in carved and painted hardwood; Africa, early 20th century; $175–225. Headrests of wood or clay took the place of the pillow in many African and Asiatic societies. ▼

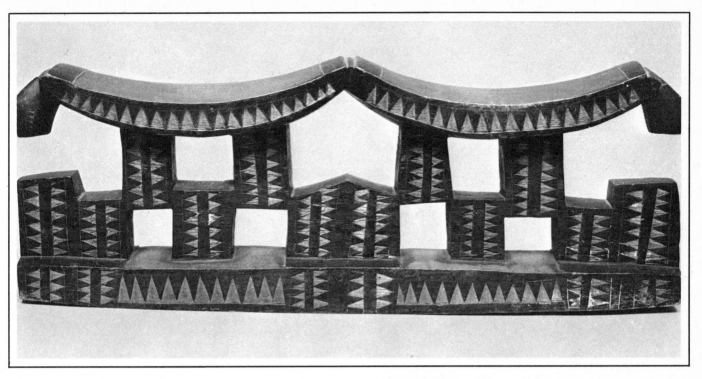

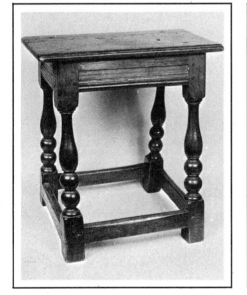

Stool in woven rush and reed; Africa, 20th century; $50–65. Seats such as this have been made for centuries in northern and central Africa. They are both attractive and functional. ◀

Stool in carved wood in the form of a human figure supporting a seat; Africa, late 19th century; $200–300. Early African stools are relatively uncommon. ▼

▲ *Stool in turned and shaped oak; England, 18th century; $200–300. Called joint stools, these small seats often doubled as low tables.*

◀
Chow table in mahogany in the Oriental manner; probably Europe, late 19th–early 20th century; $150–200.

Regency style marking bench (one of a pair) in mahogany with curule base and upholstered top; England, ▼ 19th century; $300–400 the pair.

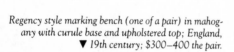

Stool in turned ash with reed seat; from a Shaker ▲ community, United States, mid-19th century; $900– 1,100 the set of 6. Early American stools are often quite plain in appearance.

Ebonized footstool with bamboo turnings and brass-studded leather top in the Egyptian Revival style; France, late 19th century; $120–160. ▼

▲ Footstool in pine with old red paint; United States, mid-19th century; $65–85. Pieces such as this were often made at home by amateur cabinetmakers.

20

▶ Louis XVI style turned footstool with needlepoint top; France, early 20th century; $90–110. Needlepoint was a popular turn-of-the-century pastime.

◄ Armchairs; United States, late 18th century. Left: Turned spindle back; $65–80. Right: Turned ladder-back; $225–275. Both chairs have rush seats.

▶

Side chair (one of a pair) in oak with turned spindles and stretchers and carved back; England, early 18th century; $600–800 the pair. English oak is still underpriced.

Massive armchair in turned oak in triangular form; Germany, 19th century; $200–275. This piece is in a 17th-century form; reproductions of this sort have long ▼ been popular on the continent.

Side chair in carved oak with floral ▲ motif on seat and back; Switzerland, 19th century; $125–175. Chairs of this sort were made throughout the mountain regions of central Europe.

Love seat in carved and turned butternut with textile ▲ pillows; Italy, early 20th century; $200–275.

▶ Pair of Victorian ballroom chairs in black lacquer and papier-mâché with mother-of-pearl inlay and upholstered seats; Europe, mid-19th century; $300–450 the pair.

Chippendale style corner chair in mahogany with shaped crestrail and pierced splats; England, late 18th century; $650–800. ◀

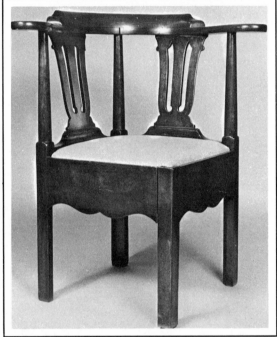

Hepplewhite style armchair in painted and gilt wood with needle-point seat and back; England, late 18th century; $1,100–1,500. A good example of a "high style" chair. ▼

▲ Bowback Windsor armchair in maple with a shaped pine seat; United States, late 18th century; $2,000–2,400. Windsors are the most unique and desirable American chair form.

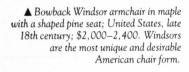

▶ Victorian fancy chair (one of a set of 4) in walnut with open-carved backs and cane seats; Italy, late 19th century; $550–750 the set.

22

Side chair in hardwood inlaid with pewter with vellum seat and back and decorated with textile tassels; by ▼ Carlo Bugatti, Italy, ca. 1900; $1,200–1,700.

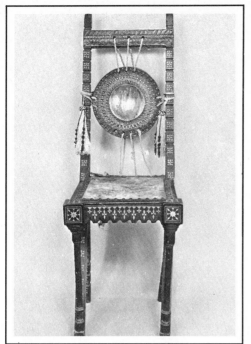

◄
Bentwood platform rocker with cane seat and back; Austria, early 20th century; $300–450. Even without the label of the famous bentwood manufacturer, Thonet, this is a desirable piece.

◄
Renaissance Revival style upholstered armchair; England, late 19th century; $175–225. Note the machine-cut decoration typical of Victorian makers.

▲ *Unusual rocker in painted ash and maple; United States, 1840–50; $700–800. Painted furniture is very popular with many collectors and is increasing in value.*

Slipper chair in carved and stenciled wood upholstered ▲ in velvet; Europe, late 19th century; $175–250.

23

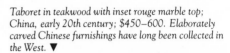

Taboret in teakwood with inset rouge marble top; China, early 20th century; $450–600. Elaborately carved Chinese furnishings have long been collected in the West. ▼

Upholstered side chair of the type known as a Marlborough in oak and ▲ *textile; England, 19th century; $100–135.*

Rocker in turned and bentwood ash and elm with old ▲ *paint; England, late 19th century; $90–110. This is a child's rocker.*

Art Deco style armchair in mahogany and mahogany ▲ *veneer upholstered in leather; France, 1925–35; $700–850. Art Deco furnishings are making a comeback with collectors.*

Folding tripod table with engraved brass top and carved ▲ *hardwood legs; India, early 20th century; $135–170. India is noted for its brasswork, and the top of this piece is really a large brass tray.*

French Provincial style table in softwood; France, 19th century; $250–325. A plain but appealing piece. ▼

Art Nouveau style table with bamboo turnings and inlaid wooden top; by Emile Galle, France, late 19th century; $1,500–2,100. ▼

Table in red and black lacquerwork with removable top and folding base; India, early 20th century; $300–400. The detailed decoration on this piece is of high quality. ▶

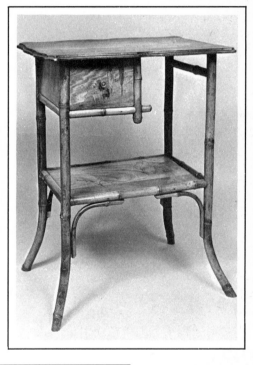

Taboret in teakwood with inset marble top and carved keyfret frieze; China, late 19th century; $400–500. ▼

◀
Work table in pine and maple with old green paint; United States, early 19th century; $650–750.

Country Chippendale two-drawer stand in walnut with ivory escutcheons and turned wooden pulls; England, early 19th century; $250–325. ▶

Miniature drop-leaf table in pine; United States, 1880–1900; $175–200. On the table is a milk-glass fairy lamp; United States, ca. 1900; $150–185. While some miniature furniture served as salesmen's samples, most pieces were ornamental. ▼

Unusual trestle table with gallery and scalloped skirt; United States, early 19th century; $750–850. The purpose of this table is uncertain. It may have been a type of planter or even a sorting ▼ table.

One-drawer stand in satinwood and mahogany with cross-banded top and inlaid body; Europe, early 19th century; $750–900.

Pedestal table in carved fruitwood with rope-carved shaft and base ▲ and inlaid top; England, mid-19th century; $350–500.

Regency style octagonal pedestal table in amboyna wood and burl elm with inlaid top and base and four ormolu lion's-paw feet; England, ca. 1815; $750–900. ▼

Empire style pedestal table with ebonized finish and inlaid checkerboard top; United States, mid-19th century; $350–425. ▼

Art Deco style center table in hardwood and hardwood veneers; France, 1930–40; $225–300. Though influenced by machine production, Art Deco manufacturers often produced well-made, hand-crafted pieces. ▼

Empire style three-column table in mahogany with ▲ ormolu mounts and gray marble top; France, early 19th century; $400–500.

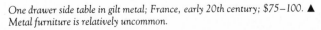

One drawer side table in gilt metal; France, early 20th century; $75–100. ▲
Metal furniture is relatively uncommon.

◀ *Tilt-top table in mahogany; England, early 18th century; $700–1,000.*

Library table with shaped skirt and stretcher inlaid in pewter and covered in part with cowhide and copper-clad legs and inset with ivory; by Carlo Bugatti, Italy, ca. 1895; $4,500–6,000.
▶

Empire style hinge-top table in ▲ mahogany with ormolu mounts and top that opens to reveal an interior storage area; France, early 19th century; $750–950.

Miniature lamp stand in cherrywood; United States, 1830–40; ▲ $400–500. Atop the stand are a pair of English Staffordshire porcelain "spaghetti dogs"; 1850–60; $90–110 each.

Queen Anne tilt-top candlestand in mahogany with ▲ top banded in fruitwood; England, early 18th century; $600–750.

Bible box in oak with carved decoration and wrought-iron hinges; England, 17th century; $250–350. Bible boxes, often with slanted lids, served as the first desks. ▼

Octagonal-form dumbwaiter with brass molding and three tiers joined by lyre-▲ shaped supports with cutout decoration; England, mid–19th century; $750–900.

Fern stand in mahogany; France, 1925–35; $85–125. ▲
Accessories such as this are among the most appealing of Art Deco furnishings.

▶

Lap desk in mahogany with domed tambour
front, brass fittings, and glass ink bottles and
sander; England, 19th century; $550–700.

Lady's desk in mahogany with inlay and brass fittings; ▲
England, early 19th century; $1,300–1,600. Small
desks such as this were often found in the bedroom.

Lady's desk in oak; England, late 19th century; $450–600. ▲
English Art Nouveau was considerably more restrained than the
Continental version.

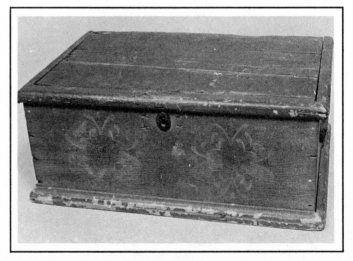

Six-board chest in tulip wood painted red and blue; ▲
Austria, mid–19th century; $150–200. Small storage
chests are found in most Western countries.

Large footed storage chest in pine and maple grain-▲ painted in brown and yellow; United States, mid–19th century; $650–725. Original paint does much to enhance the value of such a piece.

Traveling chest in softwood bound in iron with leather handles; Germany, late 19th century; $75–100. ▼

▲ Massive campaign chest in oak with copper fittings; England, 1890–1900; $1,200–1,700. Arts and Crafts pieces such as this are beginning to draw collector attention.

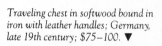

▶
Dressing case in rosewood with velvet-lined interior and lower drawer; Germany, early 19th century; $200–275. An attractive and well-outfitted traveling vanity.

Side-locking ten-drawer Wellington chest in burr elm; England, ca. 1810; $750–900. ▼ An unusual storage chest in a rich grain.

Cupboard in pine with glass doors and original red and blue paint; United States, early 19th century; $950–1,100. A country piece from the state of Maine. ▼

Louis XV style commode with kingwood marquetry with an ▲ elaborately shaped carcass, white marble top, and ormolu fittings; France, 19th century; $3,400–4,000.

Bureau-top dresser mirror in mahogany; United States, 1820–30; ▲ $385–455. A handy portable mirror in the Federal style.

Child's chest of drawers in mahogany with shaped skirt and ▲ splashboard; United States, mid–19th century; $225–275.

◀ *Mirrored sideboard in rosewood; France, early 20th century; $1,200–1,700.*

▲

Empire style mirrored bureau in bird's-eye and tiger maple; United States, ca. 1830; $2,500–2,900. An unusual piece in the popular figured maple.

▲ *Bookshelves in bamboo and wood; Europe, late 19th century; $150–200. Bamboo furniture was quite popular at the turn of the century.*

Spice chest in oak with brass pulls; England, mid–19th ▲ century; $175–235.

Art Nouveau style cabinet in butternut with brass fittings; ▲ France, late 19th–early 20th century; $1,500–2,000. Good Art Nouveau pieces are accelerating in price.

Pedal-operated portable keyboard in rosewood on stand; France, mid–19th century; $250–350. ▼

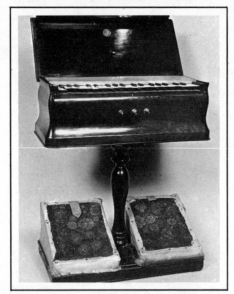

Tambour-front desk-top file in walnut ▲ and brass with inlaid brass stringing and hardware; England, late 19th century; $175–250.

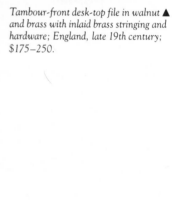

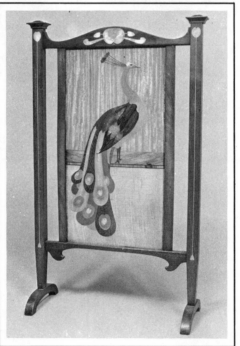

Plant stand in oak with copper inserts; England, early 20th century; $60–85. ▼

Art Nouveau style fire screen in mahogany ▲ with fruitwood inlay and tapestry panel; Belgium, late 19th century; $350–500.

Circular console stand in giltwood in the form of a ▲ winged caryatid supporting a circular top; France, late 19th century; $200–300.

Hanging wall cabinet in pine with decoration in black on red ground; United States, mid–19th century; $175–250. ▼

Victorian folding wall pocket in walnut decorated with porcelain knobs; Canada, late 19th century; $45–60. Everything from dried flowers to newspapers might be tucked into a storage space like this. ◄

Hanging shelf in carved and painted softwood; central Europe, late 19th cen- ▲ *tury; $55–70. Pieces such as this were made by many mountain craftsmen.*

Miniature desk in mahogany with inlay in fruitwood; England, late 19th cen- ▲ *tury; $200–275. Though a miniature, this piece could also serve as a storage box atop a desk or table.*

2

Silver

From the earliest times and in every part of the world where it is found in any quantity, silver has been worked and treasured. Its beauty and its relative scarcity have seen to that. Objects made from the precious metal have been found in the tombs of the pharaohs, in the ruins of pre-Columbian civilizations, and in the burial mounds of ancient Japan.

For the collector, these precious baubles are of academic interest only: little of the truly ancient material appears on the market, and when it does prices are prohibitively high. There is a substantial quantity of eighteenth- and nineteenth-century silver available, and it forms the bulk of most collections.

The absence of older pieces is explained not only by the passage of time but also by the nature of silver and the social and economic roles it has traditionally played. Like gold, but unlike most other natural substances, silver is inherently valuable, even in an unworked state. Therefore, silver vessels can be melted down—to facilitate hiding or transporting them during times of crisis—without any great loss of value.

Furthermore, silver has enjoyed for a long time a social status that sets it apart from the baser metals. It has shared with gold the role of royal metal. In some lands the ownership of silver has been restricted to certain classes; in others even the working of the metal has been limited to particular groups. It was not until the seventeenth century that European silver vessels were made in any great variety or in sufficient quantity to allow for ownership by the general public. This situation resulted not only in the production of a relatively limited number of forms, such as master salts, nefs, and massive drinking cups, the use of which was traditionally associated with the ruling classes, but, for better or ill, it also identified silver with the secular or ecclesiastical overlords. This had its disadvantages, as in seventeenth-century England when the ascent of the puritanical followers of Cromwell was followed by the mass destruction of silver associated with the fallen monarchy. A similar situation arose in France following the revolution of 1789.

The value of silver fluctuates widely over time as social and economic conditions change, and this, too, leads to the loss of plate. A current example is the wholesale melting of American silver, some of which is of historic importance, which has followed the dramatic rise during the past three years in the value of silver bullion.

The unique qualities of the precious metals, including their customary use in coinage, have long required governmental supervision. In some lands, such as ancient Persia and Egypt, this took the form of direct control of production. Since the Middle Ages western European governments have delegated this role to groups of craftsmen organized in guilds. The role of the guild was twofold: to supervise the quality of silver objects sold on the market and to train competent silversmiths.

The supervision of quality is of prime importance. Like gold,

silver in its natural state is quite soft: easily worked, it is not a medium from which durable vessels can be made. This problem can be solved by the addition of base metals, such as copper, a process known as alloying. Alloys make the silver harder, but they also make it less pure and, therefore, less valuable. Moreover, some people reasoned that if a little of an alloy is a good thing, a lot is even better. Rulers found it necessary to establish laws governing the smallest amount of silver permissable in alloying. Traditionally, the allowable percentage has been fixed at 80 percent bullion or better. In Europe and North America the standards were even higher, with the so-called sterling standard requiring that an object be 92.5 percent pure. National coinage was permitted to be 10 percent base metal, and silverware conforming to this rule is customarily referred to as "coin silver."

The duty of the silver guild was to examine all objects of silver made within its jurisdiction to determine that they conformed to national requirements and to reject them if they did not. In Europe and the British Isles elaborate systems of marking approved pieces to indicate their place of origin, maker, and date of manufacture were established, and these often allow the collector to learn much about a specific item. In China reign marks served a similar purpose, and American makers, although they were under no specific requirement to do so, often applied their names and marks to their wares.

The second function of the guilds was to oversee the training of new silversmiths. Apprentices were required to undergo a seven-year training period, at the successful conclusion of which they became journeymen, qualified to work in the shop of a guild member. Some went no further, but others eventually became masters of their craft and guild members in their own right. Though the formal requirements may vary, nearly every society that works gold or silver has established some form of apprentice system.

The apprentice system resulted in a substantial uniformity in the methods of working and decorating silver. The nature of the metal itself led to even greater uniformity. Silver can be melted and then cast, or it can be raised, a process involving the hammering of pieces into shape with the use of various tools and wooden forms. Decoration consists of one or more of the following: repoussé, the creation of raised designs on the surface by hammering from the interior; piercing or cutting patterns through the metal; chasing, which involves hammering decorative patterns into the surface without piercing it; and engraving, in which the surface of a piece is scratched or scraped away in certain areas.

Until late in the eighteenth century silversmiths throughout the world, no matter how their work might differ stylistically, worked in much the same way, utilizing the methods described above. This was greatly changed through Western ingenuity, which developed not only a new method of working silver but also new types of silver. English craftsmen perfected the process of spinning, whereby a sheet of silver was pressed against a wooden form attached to a turning lathe. By this means a skillful workman could shape a bowl or plate far more quickly than by the traditional methods of raising or casting. The specter of industrialization had raised its head.

Even more revolutionary was the development of Sheffield plate. In 1742 Thomas Boulsover of Sheffield, England, discovered that by heating two thin sheets of silver and a thicker one of copper and then running all three through heavy roller presses, with the copper in the middle, it was possible to create a metallic "sandwich," which looked like solid silver and felt like solid silver, but which was, in fact, composed primarily of base metal.

Then, in 1840, the Birmingham silversmith George Elkington carried the process a step further by patenting the method of electroplating silver that had been developed a few years earlier by one John Wright. Wright had discovered that passing an electric current through a solution of silver cyanide in which a copper bar was emersed would cause the silver to be deposited evenly on the bar. To the casual observer, the resulting piece appeared to be solid bullion. Electroplating was cheaper and faster than the Sheffield method, and by the 1870s it had largely replaced it, assuring a vast supply of inexpensive silver plate.

Collectors and students of Western silver—that which was produced in Europe and North America—soon recognize that there are distinctive stylistic differences among the pieces made over a long period and that these differences, like those in the field of furniture, generally follow the lead provided by architectural forms and motifs. The relationship is particularly evident in silver of the Gothic era (the twelfth to the fifteenth centuries), a period marked by the construction of northern Europe's great cathedrals. As the towered edifices, with their fretwork and rose windows, spread over the land, the decorative devices employed by their architects were mimicked in silver design. Like the new buildings, Gothic silver was massive and ornate. Jewel-encrusted master salts, as bulky as miniature cathedrals, dominated the tables of the powerful, separating, through their placement on the board, the chosen from the rest. Great flagons and bizarre centerpieces, known as nefs, were also made, but since most people still ate with their hands, the variety of silver was quite limited.

The Gothic never greatly affected southern Europe, particularly Italy, where centuries of turmoil and civil strife had failed to completely obliterate the memory of Rome's grandeur. It is not surprising that as the sixteenth century dawned the emerging mercantile states of the Italian peninsula began to shape a new style: the Renaissance.

Based on a liberal interpretation of classical remains overlaid with Eastern elements acquired in trade, Renaissance design incorporated the columns and pilasters of ancient Rome, the classical lines of Greek urns, and the vines and leaves of the Near East in a style that, while basically architectural, had a fluidity and grace often lacking in the Gothic.

Within fifty years of its appearance in Italy the new mode had swept over Europe. France, whose monarch employed Benvenuto Cellini (1500–1571), one of the era's greatest craftsmen, was first to be affected, but Spain and Portugal, their coffers bulging with the stolen ores of South America, were also quick to adopt the Renaissance style. Northern Europe followed more slowly, for there the Gothic had a social and religious base lacking in the south.

But even as it was gaining grudging acceptance in the northern climes, the Renaissance was on the wane in Italy. By the second half of the sixteenth century the formality of Renaissance design was submerged in the more elaborate style known as Mannerism. Eschewing simplicity, the Mannerist designers covered their beakers, bowls, salts, and tankards with cast human and animal figures and employed everything from jewels and enamel to stoneware and even coconut shells to achieve their effects.

The Mannerist style reached its apex in Germany, where the great centers were at Augsburg and Nuremberg, and in Holland. At the beginning of the seventeenth century Dutch silver designers combined classic grotesques, scrolls, and lobed ornaments with newly arrived oriental elements to create the baroque, a mode that emphasized elaborate floral patterns and heavy embossing. As the new style spread across Europe new forms appeared, such as the teapots and caddies required for a beverage that was rapidly becoming the rage.

The baroque and its Dutch exponents did not long maintain their artistic dominance. By the beginning of the eighteenth century French designers had modified the style into one that featured chasing and engraving rather than casting; by 1730 they had replaced this style, the regency, with the rococo, a curvilinear, asymmetrical mode that emphasized organic, rocaille (rockwork) shapes.

Like the baroque, the rococo spread to England and, eventually, to North America, where colonial craftsmen created forms patterned after those popular in Europe. There is relatively little early American silver, because shortages of raw materials and trade restrictions severely limited production until well into the 1800s.

By the middle of the eighteenth century European silver once more began to undergo a stylistic revolution. A reaction to the elaboration of prior styles combined with design concepts based on archaeological discoveries at the cities of Pompeii and Herculaneum led to the development of a plainer and more geometrical style; the neoclassic. Broad, unadorned surfaces and restrained engraving replaced the rich shapes of an earlier generation.

As the nineteenth century dawned neoclassic shapes became heavier and the decoration more pronounced; by 1830 the style had largely vanished to be replaced by a melange of form and decoration that came to be known collectively as the Victorian. An eclectic rehashing of previous styles, Victorian design is not particularly original. It is, however, often quite spectacular and finely made. Moreover, this era, which saw the flowering of electroplate, was the first in which silver truly became available to everyone, and large quantities of plated silver remain.

The stylistic progression just described did not take place outside Europe and its colonies. Elsewhere, as in China, Japan, and the Near East, designs were traditional and more or less fixed for centuries until disrupted by the coming of Westerners. Furthermore, in the Far East bronze was always preferred to silver, and little silver was produced, except in the form of jewelry and religious figures until trade with the West led to the making of export pieces, often in a European style.

Despite recent price fluctuations, silver remains an exciting and potentially profitable field for the collector. Most enthusiasts will find themselves limited to European and American pieces from the eighteenth through twentieth centuries, but the choice here is wide, and good buys remain, especially in the fields of Sheffield and electroplate. Collectors seeking older and more expensive examples should note that faking, from the striking of false makers' marks to the outright reproduction of entire pieces, is not unknown. Unless one is quite sophisticated, top-quality silver should not be purchased without the aid of an expert.

Plaque in embossed silver; by Johann Schuch, Augsburg, Germany, 1677–1715; $3,000–3,600. This piece indicates the high quality of early German silver. ▼

Bowl on stand in silver (part of a set of 5 pieces); Germany, late 19th century; $3,000–3,750 the set. Matching serving sets were a popular Victorian conceit. ▲

Covered cup in silver in the form of a pineapple with floral finial and figural base; Germany, 1720–80; $550–650. Fanciful examples such as this were popular on the Continent during the 18th century. ▶

Left: Muffinier in silver with fluted body and pierced cover; Germany, early 19th century; $250–325. Right: Basket in silver with swagging and pierced decoration; Augsburg, Germany, late 18th century; $400–500. ▲

Sweetmeat basket in silver with applied openwork border and scroll feet; Germany, early 19th century; $150–200. ◀

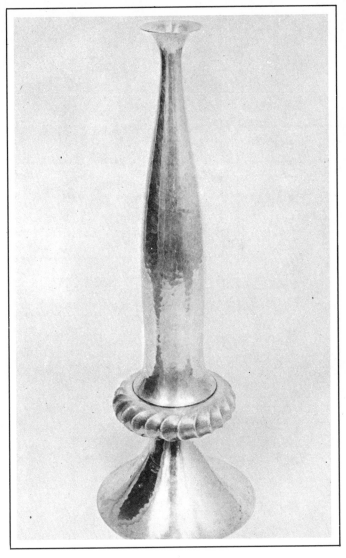

Bowl in silver with embossing and elaborate openwork decoration; France, 1840–70; $200–275. This small but elaborate bowl is typical of much French Victorian silver.

◄ *Art Deco bud vase in silver with hammered finish; Germany, 1925–35; $300–375. Though long ignored by collectors, Deco silver is now attracting a growing audience.*

Dish in embossed silver with inset gold coin; Belgium, 1866–91; $250–325. The use of coins as decorative motifs in silver and glass was common during the 1800s. ▲

Art Nouveau dish in silver in butterfly shape with stamped ▲ and raised decoration; Austria, 1900–10; $300–375.

Victorian kettle in silver on stand; Italy, 1880–1900; $950–1,150. Heated by alcohol spirits, such kettles warmed tea or coffee water. ▼

Vase in silver in baluster shape with repoussé decoration; Portugal, 1860–90; $450–550. ▼

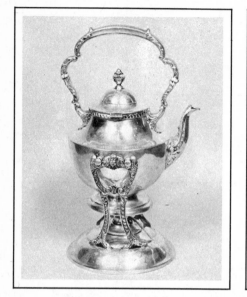

Rococo kettle in silver on spirit stand; Italy, mid-19th century; $1,200–1,600. This florid piece is part of a 7-piece suite valued at $7,000–8,000. ▲

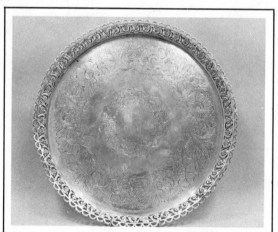

▲ *Salver in silver; Oporto, Portugal, 1853–62; $1,800–2,200. Salvers were frequently intended as presentation pieces to be given as gifts or in honor of a special occasion.*

Reliquary in silver gilt; Moscow, Russia, 1802; $1,500–1,750. The detailed decoration of this piece includes repoussé work, stamping, piercing, and applied work. ►

Icon in silver gilt depicting the Mother of God of Iverskaya; Moscow, Russia, 1908–17; $140–175. Small religious objects such as this are common among eastern European silver.

Tankard in silver with engraved and punched decoration; Russia, 1820–30; $600–750. The clean lines of this vessel mark it as being of the neoclassic style. ▼

◀ *Nut dishes in silver filigree with swing handles; Russia, mid-19th century; $400–500.*

▶ *Rococo teapot in silver; Hungary, ca. 1870; $800–1,000. The massiveness and the naturalistic form of this piece are characteristic of late Victorian silver.*

41

Kitchen pepper in silver; attributed to Samuel Welles, London, England, ca. 1756; $600–675. English silver has been produced in large quantities and many different styles and is a great favorite among collectors. ▶

Lamp base in silver; by Georg Jensen, Copenhagen, Denmark, ca. 1919; $4,000–4,500. Electric lamp bases in silver are quite uncommon. ▼

Fork-and-spoon serving sets in silver; by Georg Jensen, Copenhagen, Denmark, 1920–30. Left: ▼ *$150–175. Right: $120–145.*

Ladle in silver with embossed shell decoration; Lucerne, Switzerland, ca. 1856; $150–180. ▼

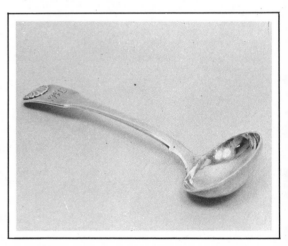

◀

Art Nouveau tazzas in silver; by Georg Jensen, Copenhagen, Denmark, ca. 1924; $1,600–1,900. Jensen, who worked both in Denmark and the United States, became one of the 20th century's most popular silver makers.

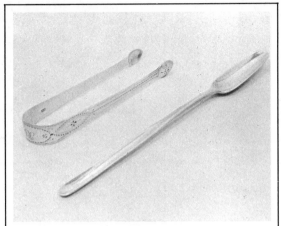

Silver; London, England. Left: Bright-cut sugar tongs; by Gabriel Wirgman, ca. 1792; $120–135. Right: Marrow scoop; attributed to John Lambe, ca. 1783; $280–330. ◄

Wine taster in silver; England, early 19th century; $180–210. In the French style. ▼

◄
Flatware in silver (from a set of 77 pieces); Sweden, 1930–40; $3,000–3,500 the set.

Buckles in silver; by G. Wintle, London, England, ca. 1795; $500–600. Though once common, early silver buckles are infrequently seen today. ▼

▲
Two-handled cup in silver; by Nathan Smith and Company, Sheffield, England, ca. 1803; $500–575.

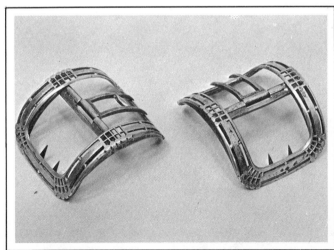

43

Beer mug in silver with engraved and tooled decoration; by Charles Fox I, London, England, 1819; $1,500–1,800. This handsome piece is in the neoclassic style.

Tea caddy spoons in silver; London, England. Left: In shell pattern; ca. 1831; $80–95. Right: In Old English form; attributed to Thomas Wallis II and Jonathan Hayne, ca. 1815; $120–150.

Open sauce tureen in silver; attributed to Robert Garrard I, England, ca. 1817; $650–750. The heavy lion mask and paw feet mark this piece as of the late neoclassic or Empire period.

Neoclassic swing-handle cake basket in silver; by Robert Hennell, London, England, 1785; $500–650. Note the openwork gallery-style foot.

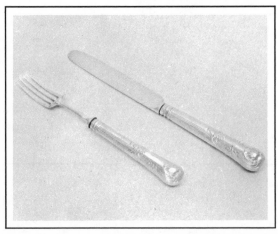

Dessert knife and fork in silver (part of a 12-piece set); by A. Haddfield, Sheffield, England, 1827; $350–425 the set.

Victorian salver in silver with shell and leaf motifs as well as scroll-form bracket feet; by William Brown, London, England, 1827; $800–900. ▶

Creamer in silver with reeded borders and bright-cut decoration; London, England, 1793; $250–300. In the neoclassic style. ▲

Saltcellars in silver with blue-glass liners; by David and Robert Hennell I, London, England, ca. 1766; $250–300. ▲

◀ *Open sugar, coffeepot, and teapot in silver; England, ca. 1760; $3,500–4,000. Continental influence is evident here in the overall repoussé decoration and snake or gooseneck spouts.*

Tea service in silver (part of a 4-piece set); by William Bateman II, London, England, 1834–36; $6,000–6,500. Bateman is a well-known silversmith. ▶

Victorian compotes in silver; Sheffield, England, 1870–75; $2,000–2,600. Massive pieces such as these represent a substantial investment in both time and silver by the craftsman. ▼

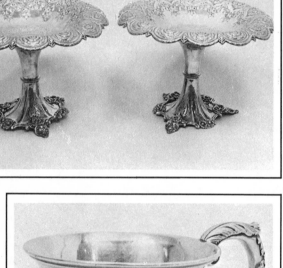

Fish slice in silver with bright-cut and openwork decoration; by Peter, Ann, and William Bateman, London, England, 1801; $350–425. The Batemans are one of England's most famous silver-making families. ▼

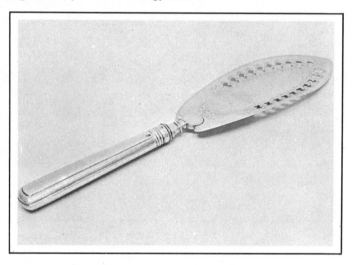

▲
Child's mug in silver with raised foliate decoration and an inscription from 1890; London, England, 1828; $400–475. Old silver was often inscribed with dates when passed from one generation to the next.

Victorian grape shears in silver; by George Adams, London, England, 1855; $375–450. ▼

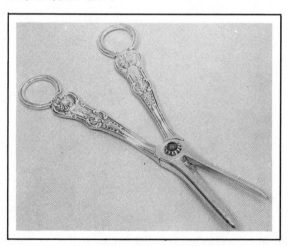

Victorian beer mug in silver with repoussé decoration; Sheffield, England, 1893; $350–400. ▶

Victorian serving trowel in silver with ivory handle and engraved decoration; London, England, 1874; $300–400. This is a dedication or presentation piece. ▼

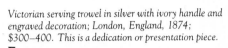

Victorian saltcellars in silver; by Robert Harper, London, England, 1874; $215–265. ▼

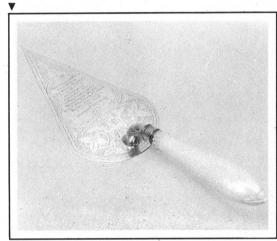

Victorian pepperettes in silver; Birmingham, England, 1888; $150–185. ▼

Presentation flatware in silver gilt; by Robert Garrard I, London, England, 1857–58; $675–775. Flatware is less commonly given as a presentation piece than bowls or salvers. ▲

Federal style mustard pot in coin silver; by N. Harding & Company, Boston, Mass., 1830–40; $175–225. Early American silver tends to be plainer than contemporary European examples. ▶

◀ Victorian card case in silver with foliate decoration; by Nathaniel Mills, Birmingham, England, 1842; $175–235. In the 19th century every gentleperson had visiting cards, which were often carried in a silver card case.

Art Deco "Cymric" bowl in silver with repoussé and enamel decoration; by Liberty & Company, London, England, 1910; $300–350.

Art Deco butter cooler in silver; by Liberty & Company, London, England, 1912–13; $325–400. During the late 19th and early 20th centuries, Liberty exports had a wide influence on European taste. ▲

Federal style pedestal saltcellars in silver; by George B. Sharp, Philadelphia, Pa., ca. 1848; $260–340. These simple but elegant pieces are in the best American tradition.

Serving pieces in silver; United States, 19th century; $30–70 each. Left to right: Shell-shaped sugar spoon, by Salisbury & Company; cream ladle, by W. S. Smith; salt spoon, by Palmer & Bachelders; cheese scoop and engraved fish slice. ▶

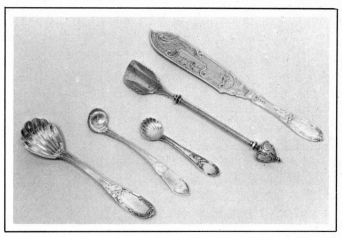

Mugs in silver; New York, N.Y. Left: By John W. Faulkner, ca. 1830; $200–275. Right: By William Gale & Son, ca. 1855; $100–135. ▼

Centerpiece bowl in silver with applied cast decoration; by Ball, Black and Company, New York, N.Y., ca. 1865; $1,500–1,750. ▼

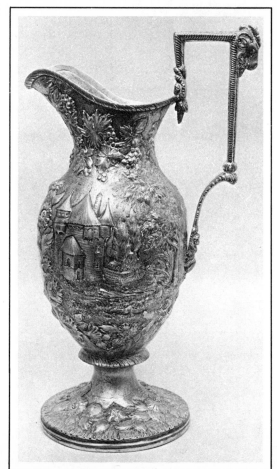

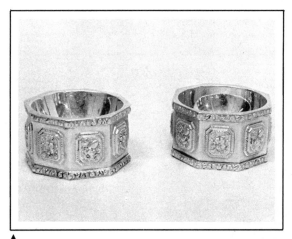

▲
Renaissance Revival style trencher salts in silver; attributed to Leonard & Wilson, Philadelphia, Pa., ca. 1850; $150–185.

◀
Ewer in silver with repoussé and chased decoration; by S. Kirk and Son, Baltimore, Md., ca. 1850; $2,500–3,000.

Milk pitcher in silver in the baluster form; by John L. Westerwelt, Newburgh, N.Y.; ca. 1850; $350–400.
▼

▲
Coffee set in silver; by Gorham, Providence, R.I., ca. 1860; $2,500–3,000. Elaborate handles and finials highlight this Victorian set

◀
Serving or candy dish in silver in the shape of a swan; by Gorham, Providence, R.I., late 19th century; $200–250.

Salver or serving tray in silver with pierced border and engraved decoration; by Gorham, Providence, R.I., late 19th century; $750–850. Gorham has long been one of the major names in American silver. ▼

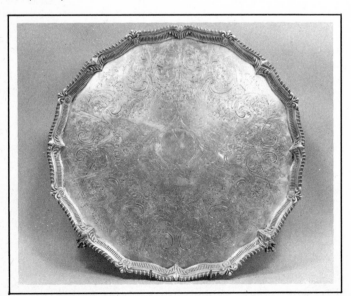

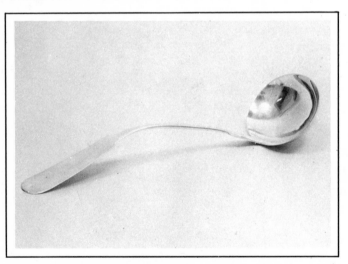

▲
Ladle in silver; by Wood & Hughes, New York, ca. 1870; $225–275. This serving piece is in the traditional fiddle style.

Serving dish in silver in the form of a heart with elaborate pierced decoration; by Gorham, Providence, R.I., late 19th century $250–300. ▶

Teaspoons in silver with unusual acorn-shaped bowls and twist stems; United States, late 19th century; $150–185 the set. ▼

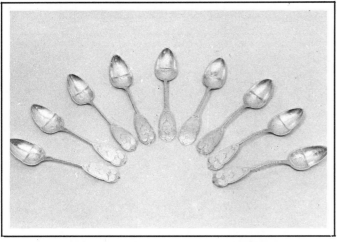

Sugar bowl and creamer in silver with overall repoussé decoration; by William B. Durgin, Concord, N.H., ca. 1887; $2,300–2,700. ▼

Centerpiece in silver with sculpted Indian heads in bronze and gilt interior; by Tiffany & Company, New York, N.Y., ca. 1896; $10,000–12,000. Tiffany was one of the world's leading silver makers during the later 19th and early 20th centuries. ◀

Bowl in sterling silver; by Tiffany & Company, New York, N.Y., ca. 1920; $600–700. This piece is a reproduction of a bowl made by the 18th-century silversmith Joseph Conyers. ▶

Demitasse set in silver; by Tiffany & Company, New York, N.Y., ca. 1899; $550–650. ▲

Chamber candlestick in silver in the Arts and Crafts style; by Dominick & Haff, United States, ca. 1884; $700–800. ▼

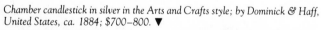

Candlesticks in sterling silver with hammered surface decoration; United States, early 20th century; $125–175 the pair. ▲

Sugar bowl and creamer on matching tray in silver; by Preisner, United States, 1930–40; $140–180. ▼

◄ *Water pitcher in silver; by Tiffany & Company, New York, N.Y., ca. 1923; $400–550.*

Four-light candelabras in Sheffield plate; England, 1855–75; $500–600 the pair. The Sheffield "silver sandwich" was the first practical way of producing inexpensive silverware. ▼

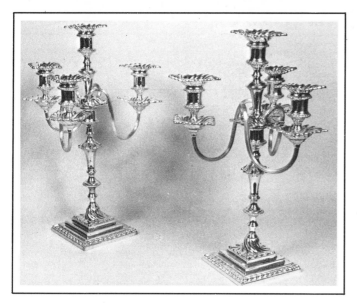

Water pitcher and tray in silver; Mexico, early 20th century. Pitcher; $700–800. Tray; $1,800–2,100. ▲

►

Coffee set in silver in bamboo pattern; by Bisanda, Japan, 1920–30; $1,700–2,200. The Japanese made and exported a substantial quantity of silver during the early 20th century.

Teapot in electroplated silver with engraved decoration; England, 1860–70; $135–175. Electroplated silver has begun to attract collector attention, and prices are rising, particularly for the better items. ▶

Wine coolers in Sheffield plate with original base-metal inserts; England, 1810–20; $1,600–2,000 the pair. Good early Sheffield brings good prices. ▶

Taper stick and tray in silver with matching crystal inkwells; England, 1840–50; $350–425 the set. ▼

Candlesticks in Sheffield plate in the Corinthian pattern; England, ▲ 1850–60; $250–325 the pair.

Water jug on stand in electroplated silver; Connecticut, late 19th century; $300–375. These rather ostentatious pieces were frequently given as commemorative gifts. ▶

Art Deco tea set in electroplated silver; United States, 1930–35; $300–400. ▼

▲ *Presentation fireman horns in electroplated silver; United States, late 19th century. Left: $250–300. Right: $425–500. Often given to retiring members of the fire department, these pieces are primarily of interest to firefighting buffs.*

Art Nouveau card tray in electroplated silver; United States, 1880–1900; $800–900. The sculptural quality of this piece brings a premium price. ▶

3

Virtu and Cloisonné

One of the most challenging tasks for the craftsman is to work within a confined space, and in both the East and the West objects have appeared which though small in size are often gigantic in the artistic abilities they reflect. In the East there are the netsuke and inro of Japan and the carved snuff bottles of China. In the West there are virtu and cloisonné.

Virtu encompasses a wide variety of boxlike containers, personal seals, smoking paraphernalia, and the like. These items are diverse in form but are all characterized by a high degree of craftsmanship exercised within a remarkably small area—often no more than a few square inches. The earliest virtu date from the late seventeenth century, when the newly acquired vice of snuff-taking necessitated both boxes for its storage and mills to grind the raw tobacco. Among the wealthy these items soon assumed a social role as gifts to be given to friends or bestowed upon faithful retainers, and goldsmiths vied with each other to create the most attractive examples.

While the work of the French goldsmiths was generally considered the finest in this field, especially during the eighteenth century, Swiss, German, English, and Austrian craftsmen also excelled at the art. Though many different objects were produced, boxes of various sorts were always most common. Among the most typical were the necessaire and the patch box. The necessaire, a small casket divided into compartments, was used to carry writing materials or toilet articles when traveling or visiting. Usually four to nine inches tall, the exterior of the necessaire might be enameled or made of semiprecious stones mounted in gold, and its interior compartments contained cut-glass scent bottles, a powder box, thimbles, scissors, writing tablets, and the like. A similar but unfitted box was called an etui.

Patch boxes were smaller than necessaires and were often made of porcelain or earthenware elaborately glazed and gilded. Patch boxes were made to hold the tiny cloth patches or beauty spots favored by seventeenth- and eighteenth-century beauties. French records refer to patch boxes, which were called *boite a mouches* (*mouches* being the word for "fly"), as early as 1647, and they were made throughout the eighteenth century—often from designs by famous contemporary artists.

Other small containers include scent boxes for perfume, spectacle cases, vanities, and pin boxes. By far the most important form was the snuffbox, the style and decoration of which often indicated the owner's rank in the complex social structure of the eighteenth century. Many snuffboxes were given as gifts. These presentation boxes were of two types: highlighted by a miniature portrait (often of the donor) set in jewels; or with an engraved top, usually bearing the recipient's coat of arms, and a base marked with the arms of the city or individual making the presentation.

The acceptable decoration for snuffboxes varied over the course of time. In the late 1600s the finest examples were mi-

nutely embossed and engraved, and various alloys were introduced to vary the hue of the gold. Engraving reached its height in the early 1700s, especially in France, and new techniques appeared, including the making of boxes carved from stone in various animal forms and the use of polychrome enamels. By the end of the century the Swiss had introduced miniature painting, and other craftsmen began to employ such exotic materials as mother-of-pearl and tortoiseshell. After 1800 the buyers of snuffboxes included more of the rising middle class, and materials became less costly and design more ordinary, with engine-turned cases and silver replacing handwork and gold.

With changed social and living habits, particularly the popularization of cigarette smoking, the snuffbox gradually vanished from the social scene. Other small containers were made, however, including the decorated enamel boxes that were manufactured in England as early as 1830 and were known, curiously enough, as potlids, and the vanity cases that developed from the necessaire and its successor, the abalone-shell-encased perfume dispenser.

Some of the most remarkable of these creations came from the shops of the Russian designer Peter Carl Faberge (1846–1920). Faberge's most famous pieces are the jewel-encrusted Easter eggs he made for the Russian royal family. These beautiful creations often contained fanciful surprises, such as music boxes. The Faberge firm made other items, including covered jars; buckles; miniature animals; and the traditional Russian drinking cups, the *kovshi* and *charki*, which were often used as presentation pieces in the manner of the snuffbox.

Although some collectors regard Faberge as the last true maker of virtu, the making of tiny rare objects did not end with him. Late-nineteenth- and twentieth-century designers responded to changing tastes, especially the new roles being assumed by women, with a variety of innovative objects, including cases for visiting cards, cigarette boxes and cases, lighters, office utensils, and personal jewelry. Among the best known of these creative manufacturers are Rene Lalique (1860–1945) who excelled in glass and Louis Comfort Tiffany (1848–1933).

There was interest in miniaturized art in the Orient, too. During the Edo period (1615–1867) Japanese artisans began to decorate the netsuke, the toggles that attached to the sash of the traditional kimono; and the inro, the small, compartmented boxes often suspended from the kimono's sash and used to carry personal items, such as medicines, perfumes, seals, and a supply of ink. Both these items are quite small: netsuke are rarely more than two and a half inches long, and inro usually measure about three by two by one inch. Yet Japanese artists created masterpieces on these tiny surfaces.

Netsuke are carved in one of four traditional shapes: as animal or human figures; in a flattened, round form similar to a rice cake; as masks based on designs from the No or Kabuki plays; and as a round device embellished by the addition of a metal mirror. Most netsuke were carved from woods such as cherry or ebony, but these might be painted, lacquered, or inlaid with mother-of-pearl or semiprecious stones. Examples can also be found in ivory, horn, porcelain, and even native seashells or nuts.

Many of the characters depicted on the netsuke are taken from the history and folklore of Japan, and many of the artists' names (they often signed their work) have become household words among collectors of the art form.

Inro, too, were frequently marked by their creators, who included such renowned artists as Korin (1658–1716) and Zeshin (1807–1891). Inro are larger than netsuke and therefore provide a more ample space for the artist. In most cases they are decorated in lacquer laid down over the wooden core, though examples covered in cloth, metal, silk, or paper are also encountered. The customary finish is lacquer, however, and the goal of the artist is to create a miniature painting—a seascape or a delicate rendition of a misty morning, for example—upon his tiny canvas. How well this can be done is reflected in the great popularity of inro among both Eastern and Western collectors. Good examples may bring thousands of dollars, and interest in all types is growing.

Chinese snuff bottles are equally well known. Seldom more than three inches high, they are more or less bottle-shaped and have a tiny stopper with a spoon attached for removing the snuff. Unlike most Chinese arts, the making of snuff bottles is a relatively late innovation. They were known as early as the reign of Kang Hsi (1662–1722), but the majority date from the 1800s.

Being of a recent vintage does not diminish the charm of these remarkable creations. Some are carved from jade, quartz, or other semiprecious stones in the form of humans, animals, or mythological creatures; others are of glass or porcelain. The glass examples are sometimes so skillfully colored and carved or molded that they resemble jade, agate, or crystal so closely only an expert can tell the difference. The porcelain examples are decorated in underglaze in the same manner as traditional ceramics of the period. Thus, it is possible to find china snuff bottles to match a set of *famille rose* or underglaze-blue dinnerware!

Other snuff bottles are carved from amber, made from milk glass, or made from a clear crystal enameled on the interior to create a particularly jewellike surface effect. Many of the pieces bear reign or makers' marks, but as is the case in many areas of Chinese arts, these should be taken with a grain of salt. This is especially true today, for many inferior bottles are being made in Hong Kong and elsewhere for sale in the West. These may be offered as antiquities, but they are seldom very old, and, most important, they usually do not measure up to the high standards set by the artisans of the nineteenth century.

Another extremely appealing and delicate art form is ena-melware. Enamel is a hard, glasslike compound that can be colored with mineral oxides and will adhere well to various metals. The art of enameling was known in the Near East centuries ago and reached a high level of sophistication in Europe as early as the thirteenth century, when important manufactories specializing in enameled religious objects, such as crucifixes and reliquaries, flourished at Limoges in France and Cologne in Germany.

Though variations exist, there are three general types of enamel work: champlevé, cloisonné, and plique-à-jour. In the first method, channels or depressions in a design are cut into the metal surface (usually copper or bronze) leaving narrow, raised walls between them. Liquid enamel is then poured into these recesses and fused by firing in an oven. After firing, the enamel is polished to a jewellike surface.

Cloisonné enamel is created in a different manner. Thin ribbonlike bands of metal are soldered to the metal surface in whatever design the artisan chooses to make. These tiny metal walls then serve as the dividers between the various colored enamels. Cloisonné work reached a particularly high level in nineteenth-century Japan and China. Japanese artisans specialized in detailed floral pieces, usually jars or vases, that could be completely covered with enameled decoration or could consist of a pictorial representation on a soft-toned enamel background.

The technique of plique-à-jour was first utilized in the fourteenth century. It is similar to cloisonné except that the narrow metal walls—the cloisons—are attached not to a metal vase or plate but to a sheet of metal. After firing this sheet of metal can be removed, leaving a finished work that looks very much like stained glass. Plique-à-jour is fragile and hard to make, but extremely beautiful.

Finally, there is the process of enamel painting in which the liquid enamel is used much as one would handle oils or watercolors. In the usual case a dark enamel ground is first laid over the entire object. Then the design or subject is painted on in lighter colors. In some cases an undercoating of silver or gold foil may be utilized to give additional brilliance to the final product.

Enamelwares are readily available to collectors. In the late nineteenth century substantial numbers of high-quality reproductions of Limoges pieces were turned out in Europe (the originals are practically unobtainable), while Chinese and Japanese pieces are always available, as are some examples from India and the Near East. It should also be noted that during the late nineteenth and early twentieth centuries artisans working in the so-called Arts and Crafts style also became interested in enamels and turned out everything from jewelry to such mundane things as ashtrays and compacts. Some of these are of substantial merit as are the later Art Deco enamels.

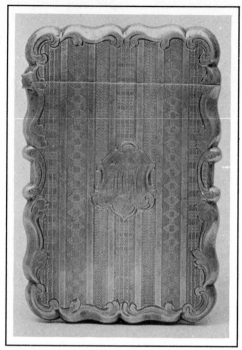

Visiting-card case in sterling silver with scalloped edges and engraved decoration; United States, 1870–90; $80–110.

Snuffbox in embossed silver; Amsterdam, late 18th century; $125–150. Some of the finest decorated snuffboxes came from Holland.

George III snuffbox in silver with engraved and picked decoration; by Thomas Phipps and Edward Robinson, London, 1798; $250–300.

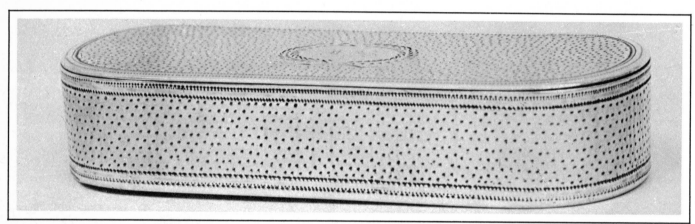

Vinaigrette in silver in the form of a drinking mug with engraved decoration; England, late 18th century; $175–250. This unusual piece is only 3 inches high.

Virtu in silver; Birmingham, England. Left: Patch box in bright cut; by Jospeh Taylor, ca. 1810; $100–120. Center: Nutmeg grater in bright cut; by Samuel Pemberton, ca. 1800; $120–150. Right: Vinaigrette; by Samuel Pemberton, ca. 1792; $75–90.

Pillbox in silver with embossed decoration in the shape of a flower basket; Holland, early 19th century; $110–135. ▼

Octagonal pillbox in engraved silver; Holland, 1800–20; $100–135. Boxes such as this were often given as favors or tokens of respect at formal balls. ▼

Vinaigrettes in silver; Birmingham, England. Left: Engine-turned watchcase form; by J L, ca. 1817; $250–350. Right: Pierced and engraved book shape; by Ledsam, Vale and Wheeler, 1830; $275–325. ▲

Snuffbox in undecorated silver with gold-wash interior; by Thomas Wilmore, Birmingham, England, 1796; $175–250. ▼

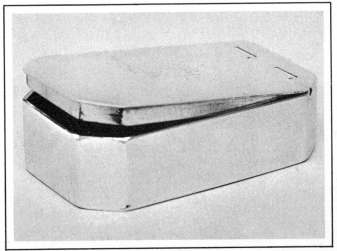

Cigarette case in gold and silver with engraved decoration; France, late 19th century; $300–400. The presence of gold adds value to an otherwise ordinary piece. ▲

Rectangular box in silver with complex engraving; Europe, late 19th century; $70–95. ▶

Late Victorian visiting-card case in silver with engine-turned chevron design; Europe, late 19th–early 20th century; $100–125. Pieces such as this were produced in large numbers for many Victorians carried visiting cards. ▼

Nutmeg grater in silver in the shape of a walnut; United States, early 20th century; $75–90. This is the type of object retailed by Tiffany in New York. ▼

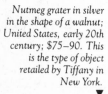

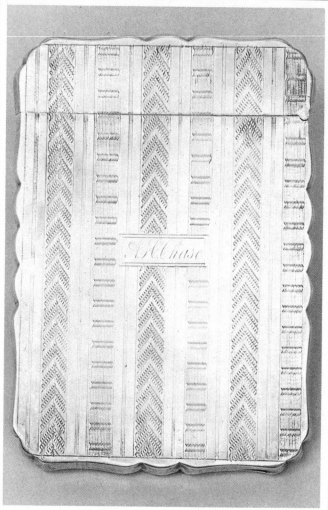

Pillbox in engine-turned silver in the shape of a bucket; Holland, mid-19th century; $80–100. Engine turning made possible the production of inexpensive small decorative boxes. ▲

George III vinaigrette in silver in the form of a purse; by John Lawrence & Company, Birmingham, England, 1819; $275–350. ▲

Personal seal in blue sodalite mounted in silver; St. Petersburg, Russia, ca. 1896; $100–150. Silver is often combined with cut or carved stone in vertu. ▼

Snuffbox in silver and brass with embossed decoration; France, late 19th century; $60–75.

Compact in sterling silver with engraved representation of a cat, the eyes of which are set with rubies and which wears a ruby-and-diamond bow tie; Germany, ca. 1920; $350–425. ▼

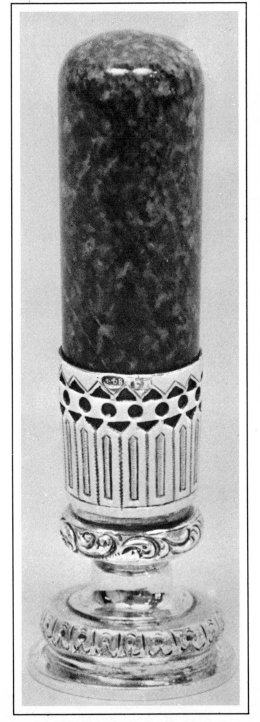

Music box in parcel gilt silver; Germany, ca. 1900; $2,000–2,500. Opening the lid of this tiny box makes a bird rise and sing. ◄

Circular box in engraved brass with ivory cameo insert; China, 1890–1910; $70–85. ▼

Snuffbox in lacquer and mother-of-pearl; Japan, late 19th century; $125–165. Some of the most sophisticated snuffboxes are the oriental lacquer examples. ▼

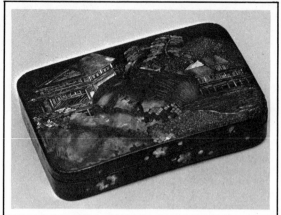

Cigarette box in brass with green cloisonné inlay; China, 1910–20; $40–50. Intended for export, small brass objects such as this were produced in large quantities by the Chinese during the early 20th century. ▼

Islamic miniature drinking horn in brass with engraved decoration; Near East, early 19th century; $60–75.

Box in silver embellished with figure of a Foo dog; Japan, early 20th century; $85–115.

▲
Cigarette box in tin with painted decoration; Spain, mid to late 19th century; $275–350. The value of this piece is enhanced by a concealed interior pornographic picture — a not uncommon Victorian device.

◀
Box in enamel and silver gilt with scene of a chariot race; Germany, ca. 1920; $500–600. Like many enamel or porcelain boxes, this one is a miniature work of art.

▲
Oriental style inkstand in papier-mâché; signed by Wilkerson, England, late 19th century; $165–200. A good imitation of lacquer ware.

Rectangular box in lacquer and mother-of-pearl inlay; Japan, late 19th century; $75–90.
◀

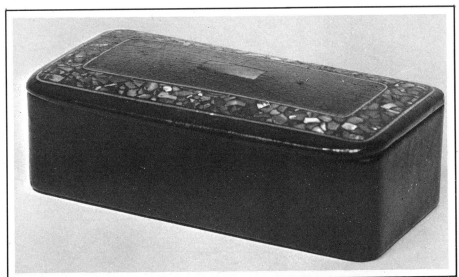

George III snuff mull in silver-mounted cowrie shell; England, ca. 1800; $175–225. Exotic shells and mother-of-pearl have long been popular virtu materials. ◀

Box in mother-of-pearl and silver with interior mirror and two compartments; France, ca. 1750; $700–1,000. Delicate objects such as this rarely survive for over 200 years. ▼

Perfume dispenser in abalone shell with brass scroll-work base and crystal perfume bottles; France, late 19th century; $110–150. ▼

Standish with two inkstands and quill drawer in mother-of-pearl and brass; Europe, 1870–90; $125–160.

Visiting-card case in enamel and silver; Vienna, Austria, late 19th century; $175–250.

Box in polychrome porcelain with gilt-metal mounts and scenes of explorers and their ships; France, 1750–70; $1,100–1,400.

Patch boxes; France, mid-19th century. Left: In porcelain and gilt metal in an 18th-century style; $60–75. Right: In faience in the 18th-century manner with gilt-metal mounts: $75–90.

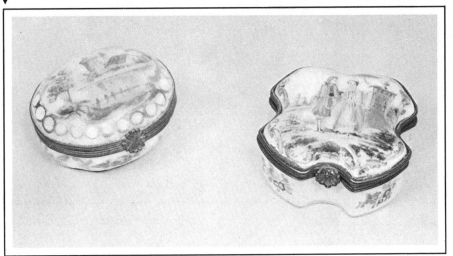

Art Deco cigarette case in tortoiseshell and silver; Europe, 1920–30; $125–150.

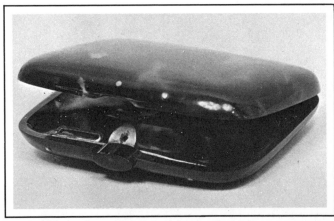

Regency tea caddy in tortoiseshell with silver ball finial and two interior tea wells; England, 1820–30; $300–400.

Case in tortoiseshell with brass hasp; Europe, late 19th century; $75–100. Due to shortages and restrictive laws, tortoiseshell objects are becoming scarce.

Covered box in porcelain entitled "Master of the Hounds"; by Pratt, England, mid-19th century; $85–115. Among collectors these pieces are known as potlids. ▼

◄ Miniature horn in highly detailed porcelain with brass fittings; Austria, 1850–70; $225–275. A fine example of European enamel work.

Necessaire in enamel; probably Germany or Austria, mid-19th century; $750–900. This box is fitted with various compartments and has two glass bottles with enamel covers. ▼

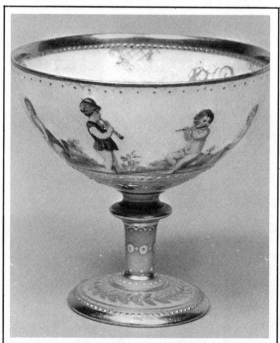

Miniature cabinet jar in Sèvres-type porcelain; France, late 19th century; $150–200. ▲

Miniature stemmed cup in porcelain with polychrome decoration; Dresden, Germany, 20th century; $25–35. ▲

Perfume vial in carved alabaster; Egypt, period of the New Kingdom (1150–1100 B.C.); $400–500. The creation of tiny but beautiful stone objects has a long history.

Double dish stand in porcelain and brass; France, 20th century; $20–30. Objects of this sort are in the nature of souvenirs.

Oval box in green nephrite mounted in gold; Russia, 1908–17; $700–1,000. A plain but sophisticated piece.

Footed cup in sterling silver, ivory, and enamel; Sweden, late 19th century; $125–175.

So-called Mary Gregory pin box in jet glass and brass with enamel decoration; probably Bohemia, late 19th century; $60–75. Though often attributed to a decorator at the Sandwich, Mass., glassworks, most pieces decorated in this manner are of European origin.

Objects in carved spinach jade; China, late 19th–early 20th century; $120–160 the set. Left: Matchbox case. Center: Spill vase. Right: Personal seal. ▶

Cigarette box in pink rhodonite and silver plate and ashtray in rhodonite; Europe, early 20th century; ▼ *$75–100 the set.*

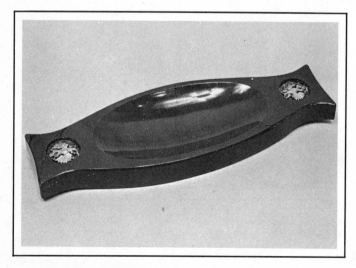

Boat-shape ashtray in troitsk with gold double-headed ▲ *eagles inset at each end; Russia, early 20th century; $200–250. Troitsk is a hard, green stone.*

Oval box in turquoise mosaic with brass fittings and ▲ *gilt-metal interior; India, early 20th century; $50–65.*

Screen in carved jade in teakwood stand; China, 20th century; $120–160. ▼

◄ *Figure of a man with fruit in carved ivory; China, 20th century; $25–30. Pieces such as this are commonly found in stores selling Oriental goods. They are frequently of substantial artistic quality.*

▲

Rhinoceros in carved ivory; India, early 20th century; $40–55. Though Chinese and Japanese works are best known, ivory carving has long been practiced in many parts of Asia and Africa.

Inkwells in carved stone; Europe, early 20th century. ▲
Left: Jadeite; $35–45. Center: Tigereye; $60–75.
Right: Blue john; $45–60.

▶
Okimono in carved ivory in the form of a samurai with two boys; Japan, late 19th century; $230–290. Complex carving such as this takes many hours.

▶
Netsuke in carved ivory in the form of two turtles; Japan, 19th century; $125–150. Seldom more than 2 inches long, netsuke represent remarkable examples of miniature ivory carving.

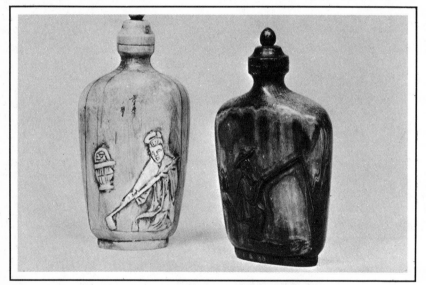

▲
Snuff bottles in carved hardstone; China, late 19th–early 20th century. Left: In light stone, a woman working in field; $70–95. Right: In dark stone, a man fishing; $55–75.

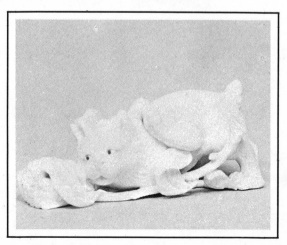

Okimono in carved ivory of a cat annoyed by a fly; ▲
Japan, 19th century; $250–300.

Counter box (with game counters) in finely carved export ivory; China, early 19th century; $90–120. ▲

Blotter in carved pink serpentine and brass; China, 20th century; $55–75. The elephant motif is common on Chinese export wares. ▼

Left: Compact in enamel on silver; Austria, ca. 1920; $100–150. Right: Compact in black enamel and gold set with rose-cut diamonds; France, 1925–35; $1,000–1,500. ▼

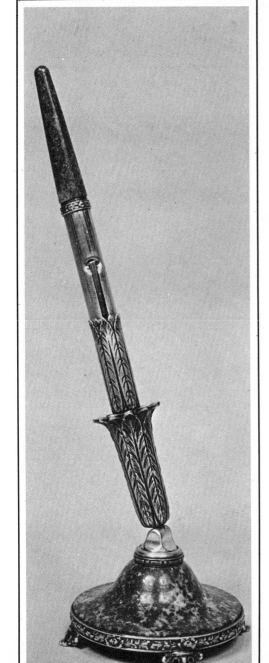

▲

Snuff bottles in enamel; China, early 20th century. Left: $90–120. Right: $80–110. The Chinese have long produced snuff bottles in several different mediums, including glass.

Inkwell in the form of a houseboat in carved pink quartz and cast brass; China, 20th century; $100–150. ◄

Fountain pen and stand in lapis lazuli, silver, and silver gilt; Europe, early 20th century; $135–185. ◄

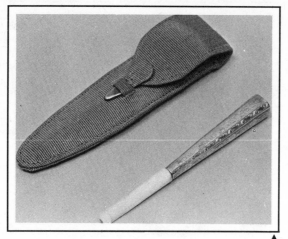

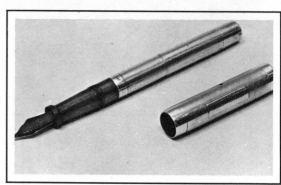

Fountain pen in gold with overall engine-turned decoration and Masonic symbol in enamel; United States, 20th century; $150–200. ▼

Cigarette holder in gold and ivory with fitted case in silk; probably United States, 20th century; $200–250. ▲

Compact in polychrome enamel on silver with three interior compartments; Germany, 1910–25; $400–475. ▼

Cigarette box and case in black lacquer and Coquille D'Oeuf enamel; by Dunhill, Paris, 1930–40; $250–350 for the case (a signed piece); $175–250 for the box. ▲

Mirror and powder box in enamel and brass; Europe, 20th century; $130–175 the pair. ▲

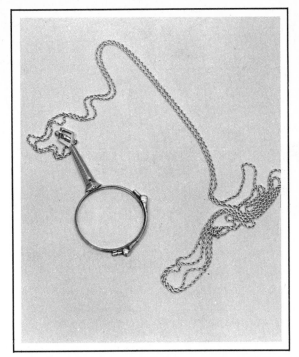

Lorgnette in engine-turned gold with rope-twist gold chain; Italy, late 19th century; $550–700.

Round compact in silver with chain and loop; Europe, 20th century; $55–70.

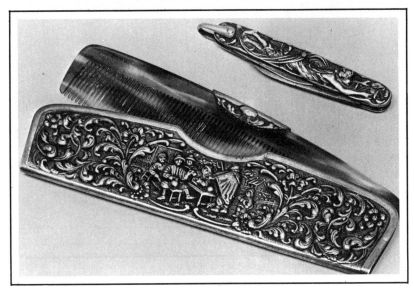

Left: Comb in silver; Switzerland, early 20th century; $40–60. Right: Pocketknife in silver; Switzerland, late 19th century; $45–65.

Paperweight in alabaster; United States or England, early 20th century; $35–50.

Oval box in cloisonné on brass with scene of Mt. Fuji; Japan, early 20th century; $120–165. A well-done piece. ▼

Napkin rings in cloisonné on brass; China, early 20th century. Left: $45–60. Right: $60–75. ▼

Boxes in brass and enamel; Persia, early 20th century. Left: $60–75. Right: $55–65. Enamel and cloisonné work was widely practiced in the Islamic world. ▼

▲ *Covered rose jar in blue cloisonné; Japan, 20th century; $50–65.*

▶
Teapot in cloisonné on brass with good quality floral design; China, late 19th–early 20th century; $75–95. Chinese cloisonné is among the most common and inexpensive.

Covered jar in cloisonné with brass finial; China, 19th century; $125–150. ▼

Ovoid vase in enamel on copper; marked Faure, Limoges, France, 20th century; $550–700. A choice example of modern European enamel work by a recognized master. ▼

One of a pair of cabinet vases in cloisonné; China, 1960–70; $75-100 the pair. Good quality cloisonné is still coming out of China and Taiwan. ▼

◄ *Pair of ovoid bottleneck vases in cloisonné with a deep-blue ground and polychrome decoration; Japan, 19th century; $375–500 the pair.*

Octagonal lidded box in cloisonné; Persia, late 19th century; $90–120. ▼

Ink pot on stand in cloisonné on brass; Italy, late 19th–early 20th century; $110–150.

4

Jewelry

Objects of personal adornment are found in every culture and every period of man's development. It is likely that such items first served as religious symbols or marks of official status, and those functions are still important in certain primitive societies. However, in Europe, which has been the world's major producer of jewelry, the baubles—even in Greek and Roman times—have been perceived as an adjunct to dress.

Until the Victorian era jewelry design followed clothing styles. The lack of a dominant or unifying style during the Victorian era accompanied by the tremendous increase in jewelry manufacture and use during that period led to a proliferation of forms and the use of a variety of materials never before seen. Therefore, most jewelry collectors concentrate on objects produced during the past one hundred fifty years.

This approach is sound, for not only are there relatively few available pre-1800 examples, but the variety and imagination exhibited by nineteenth- and twentieth-century jewelry has never been equalled. Nevertheless, it is important to know something of the earlier work.

Beadwork may be the earliest form of jewelry, and stone or ceramic beads have been found in ancient tombs and ruins from Peru to Egypt and China. Moreover, the custom of wearing beaded bracelets, necklaces, and even clothing continued well into the modern era. The Indians of North America are renowned for their beaded belts, bags, and clothing, and bright trade-bead jewelry is still an attraction to the tourist in Africa.

Other forms of jewelry appeared at an early period. Carved jade rings and bracelets have been found in Chinese tombs dating to the second century B.C., and elaborately worked gold and silver objects, such as face masks, bracelets, and amulets, have come from such diverse sources as ancient Persia, Ireland, and Scandinavia. It is evident from the skill with which even the earliest of these pieces were created that the art of jewelry design is very ancient. It is also clear, however, both from existing records and from the circumstances under which most early examples were found, that in early cultures the ownership of jewelry was limited to a very small number of individuals.

As late as the sixteenth century jewelers, both by training and by guild affiliation, were identical to goldsmiths, the artisans whose social status was highest and the craftsmen whose work was most closely related to that of the architect and cabinetmaker. In fact, most jewelry of the Gothic and Renaissance periods was based on architectural motifs, and it is possible to see an identity in design between a sixteenth-century brooch and a picture frame or fireplace surround of the same period.

During the Renaissance era in particular a background in goldsmithery was regarded as the best training for the sculptor or painter. The cast and chased gold jewelry of the 1650s often resembles miniature sculpture. But even at this time jewelry design was closely tied to prevailing clothing styles. For example, necklaces and breast ornaments, which were common during the early 1500s, began to disappear toward the end of the century as women began to favor high ruffled collars which, of course, left no room for the display of such jewelry.

Political factors also played a part in jewelry design. During the seventeenth century Europe was ravaged by war and economic unrest, and men, whose main business was now warfare, abandoned almost all jewelry other than gold chains (which were appropriately enough worn as though they were supporting a sword), while both sexes favored somber black garments. Jewelry at this time was often a form of political expression, with men and women indicating their preference among various contending parties or factions by wearing brooches or rings, such as the badges that adorned the breasts of supporters of the Spanish Inquisition.

Such expressive use of personal adornment has a long history. In the Middle Ages men and women wore posy rings to convey their affection and heraldic jewelry, such as the White Deer of Richard II, to indicate their allegiance to a certain noble or royal family. During times when death of young and old, from fire or famine or disease, was all too common, mourning jewelry was worn for years at a time. Such pieces were of jet and gold or of the intricately woven hair of the deceased—a gloomy sort of tribute that remained popular well into the 1800s.

Straitened circumstances aside, jewelry design did not long remain in the somber, rigid stance of the early 1600s. By the middle of the century Spanish styles and ideas were giving way to those of the Dutch and French, which were based on an emerging interest in naturalism and involved the translation of floral motifs to jewelry forms. Flowing forms such as the floral spray became popular, and gems, which were for the first time available in quantity, became the feature of a piece of jewelry rather than being merely an added attraction to a massive gold or silver bauble. This innovation was due not only to the influx of gems from newly exploited sources in Africa and South America but also to innovations in gem cutting. The rose cut, which involved giving a stone a flat base and between sixteen and twenty-four facets, had been developed during the 1500s, but the mastery in the succeeding century of the brilliant cut, with its fifty-eight gleaming facets, made precious stones so spectacularly attractive that they dominated jewelry design until well into the eighteenth century.

The rise of the gemstone marked a change in the role of the jeweler. He now became a cutter and setter of gems rather than a goldsmith, a transition that led to both a decline in the jewelers' status and to the mass production of jewelry.

Another important milestone in the history of jewelry was reached in 1674 when an Englishman, George Ravenscroft (1618–1681), invented flint glass, a lead and calcined flint-based glass that was more brilliant as well as softer and more dense than any glass previously known. Flint glass could be cut to look like diamonds or, if colored, other gems, and its availability led to the growth, during the late eighteenth and early nineteenth centuries, of an extensive market in paste, or imitation jewelry.

This demand for the artificial was partially inspired by another innovation of the 1700s, the preference for two types of jewelry: lighter, more whimsical pieces, often based on classical themes, to be worn during the day; and heavier, gold and gem-encrusted pieces that were reserved for the evening. Daytime adornment tended to feature paste as well as semiprecious stones, such as garnet and rose quartz. These stones were often set in silver or pinchbeck, an alloy of zinc and copper invented by Christopher Pinchbeck (1670–1732) that served as a gold look-alike. Also popular during the period was cut-steel jewelry composed of metal that was cut and polished so that it resembled tiny diamonds. Cut-steel buckles, brooches, and earrings form an interesting category for the collector.

By the early nineteenth century the combination of improved production methods and a vastly increased buying public had wrought great changes in the jewelry industry. As more and more people could afford to own personal adornment (a situation facilitated by the development of synthetic materials and mass-production methods) the variety of jewelry styles became overwhelming.

In the first quarter of the century interest in the artifacts of ancient Egypt, Greece, and Rome led to a series of revivalist styles, featuring everything from pins in the form of the imperial Roman eagle to brooches adorned with stylized Egyptian heads. At a later date a renewed enthusiasm for the rococo inspired lush, naturalistic designs, and events such as the opening of the gold mines of California and the discovery of the diamond hoards of South Africa triggered wholesale modifications in public taste.

In part this situation reflected the fact that the world was drawing closer together. Improved methods of communication and transportation insured that the newest London or Paris fashion was public knowledge within a few days in Moscow or San Francisco. These changes were also part of the breakdown in previously unified taste that marked the Victorian era in every field from architecture to dress. The jewelers' market, which had been confined to a tiny group of the very wealthy, had suddenly expanded. Their new customers wanted everything, and they wanted it immediately. The jewelers tried to comply.

The old standbys, precious metals and gemstones, were, of course, put to maximum use. Evening, or formal, jewelry became extremely lavish, with suites, or parures, of matching pieces mandatory at any event of consequence. Some of these sets of rings, necklaces, belts, earrings, and the like were quite extraordinary; many have been lost over the years due to neglect and changing taste, which dictated that out-of-style pieces be melted down or sold in order that they might be replaced with something in the newest mode.

The preference for valuable substances did not preclude the Victorian taste for something different. Cameo cutting, a skill known in ancient Rome, was brought to the fore once more, and portrait cameos cut in hard stones such as agate or onyx became especially popular for such things as rings, brooches, and pendants. While most cameos were light in color, lava cameos in gray or brown were also popular, as were the ceramic imitations first favored in the eighteenth century by the English potter Josiah Wedgwood.

Other substances were utilized. Coral was particularly preferred, for this pinkish material was thought to have the power to ward off evil. During the second half of the century coral bracelets, necklaces, and earrings, often set in gold or combined with diamonds and other gemstones, were a common sight in the Victorian parlor. Also seen were jet, amber, ivory, jade, and such esoteric items as Scottish pebble jewelry fashioned from highly polished stones. Jet was especially popular, for its black surface suited the gloomy side of the nineteenth-century persona. But the Victorians were on the whole a happy lot, and both men and women sported a variety of love tokens, lockets filled with the hair of loved ones, and bright-green jade trinkets carved in China for export to the West.

Most of such jewelry was made for women. Wives and daughters of the new middle class had little to do other than attend an almost endless series of social events, each of which required its own particular dress and adornment. Since diamonds were by custom reserved for married women, unmarried girls wore colored gems or semiprecious stones, thus assuring that every woman of status would go through several sets of jewelry during her lifetime. Men did not do too badly, though. Every man of consequence had a watch, chain, and bar, as well as such oddities as cufflinks, rings, tiepins, and the studs required for formal evening wear.

The proliferation of jewelry forms and materials continued throughout the Victorian era and into the twentieth century. Designers associated with the Arts and Crafts and Art Nouveau movements created pieces appropriate to those styles with the lush Art Nouveau jewelry of Louis Comfort Tiffany and his associates proving particularly outstanding. In Europe the major figure in the epoch was Rene Lalique of France, who combined glass and diamonds, pot metal and gold, and such unusual materials as carved horn and ivory to create ornaments that were remarkably ahead of their time.

As the present century advanced, though, the Art Nouveau motifs of grotesque insects, flowering plants, and voluptuous women were gradually supplanted by a new vocabulary—that of the Art Deco. Deco jewelry tended to be geometric in form, understated in design, and showed a distinct preference for enamel surfaces, often framed in silver. Enamel had been used in jewelry design as early as the sixteenth century, but it had fallen somewhat out of favor in the succeeding years. The Art Deco designers, however, used bold panels of red and black enamel to create an exciting and contemporary surface; their pieces are now attracting serious collector attention.

Other areas of the world had their jewelry. China and Japan produced large quantities of carved jade and ivory, though little gold or silver until the nineteenth century, when Western demand justified its production. Bronze was the favorite metal in these countries, and it was also popular in Africa, where the Ashanti people made massive bronze bracelets. In other areas, such as Polynesia and South America, native materials that might vary from gold to bronze to such mundane substances as seashells and edible nuts were used in the creation of personal ornaments. Unlike the case in Europe, the designs of such pieces remained remarkably static over long periods of time, reflecting both the innate conservatism of the societies and the traditional social role that jewelry played in these areas.

Necklace in translucent shell and twisted fiber; Philippines, late 19th–early 20th century; $150–200. ▶

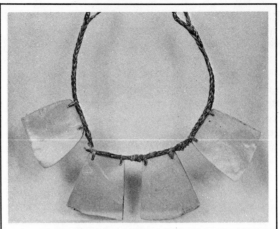

Necklace of shell, fiber, and tusk in the form of a stylized figure; Ramu River area, Melanesia, late 19th century; $200–250. Artisans in primitive cultures employ a wide variety of materials in jewelry making. ▼

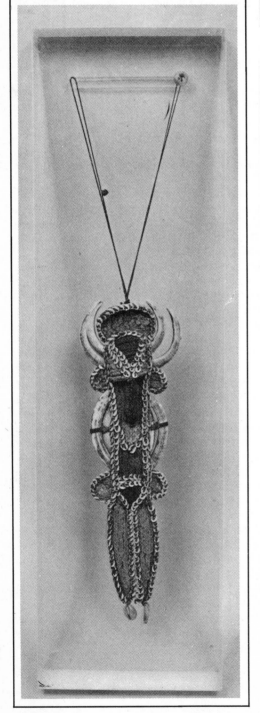

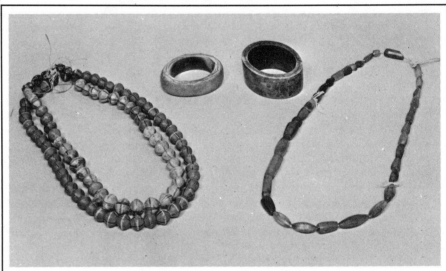

Jewelry; Africa, early 20th century. Left: Necklace of ceramic trade beads; $60–90. Center: Bracelets of carved ivory; $35–50 each. Right: Necklace of cut carnelian; $50–75. ▲

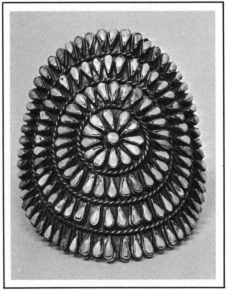

◀

Bracelet in turquoise and silver cluster; by Zuni, United States, early 20th century; $250–325. This bracelet may have been worn on the upper arm.

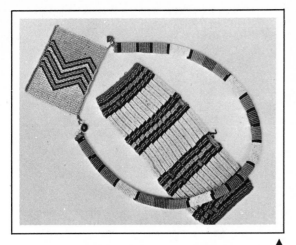

Beaded jewelry in red, white, and green; by Zulu, Africa, early 20th century. Left: Arm band; $100–135. Right: Collar; $150–225.

Bracelet/rattle in silver; Japan, late 19th century; $135–185. The rattle is concealed within the ball clutched between the dragons' mouths.

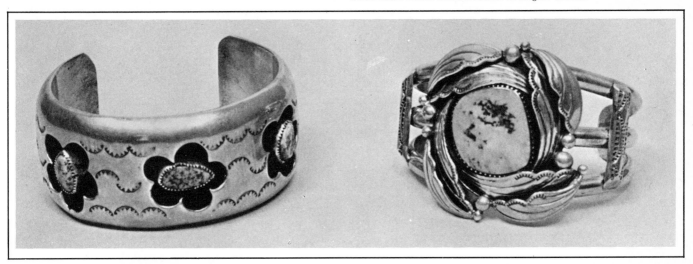

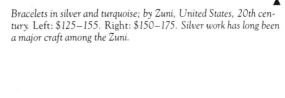

Bracelets in silver and turquoise; by Zuni, United States, 20th century. Left: $125–155. Right: $150–175. Silver work has long been a major craft among the Zuni.

Bangle bracelet in jadeite; China, early 20th century; $100-150. Chinese and Japanese manufacturers have produced many Western-style jewelry pieces in jade—their traditional medium.

Bracelet in black and orange agates strung on an elastic band; Scotland, late 19th century; $75–100. Semiprecious stones such as agate, quartz, and garnet are frequently employed in less expensive jewelry.

Bracelet in silver gilt with with large amethysts in foliated frames; Austro-Hungary, mid-19th century; $175-250. ▶

Bracelet in gold, turquoise, and pearl; Europe, early 20th century; $400–500. The delicate filigree work on this piece reflects skilled craftsmanship. ▼

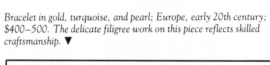

Bangle bracelet in white gold, diamond, ruby, and enamel with lion's-head finials; Europe, early 20th century; $1,600–2,000. An archaic form for a relatively modern piece. ▲

▶
Bangle bracelet in coral and gold; England, late 19th century; $125–175. English jewelry is somewhat less common than Continental examples.

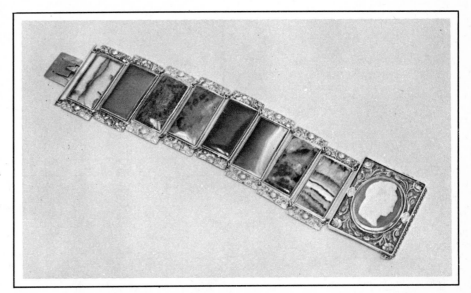

Bracelet in gold and agate with clasp in the form of an agate cameo depicting a warrior's head; by Capparoni, Italy, late 19th century; $2,000–2,500. ▼

Cuff bracelet in gold and onyx featuring a carved onyx cameo depicting a blackamoor whose headband is set with a diamond and rubies and other rubies appear on his necklace; Italy, 19th century; $2,000–3,000. ▲

Flexible-link bracelet composed of three rows of enamel flowers set with pearls spaced by two rows of rubies edged with gold links; Europe, 20th century; $2,500–3,000. ▼

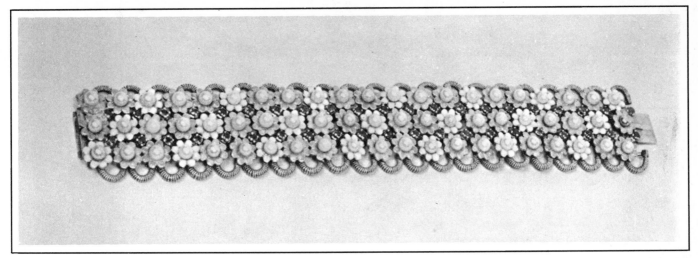

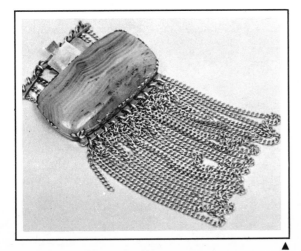

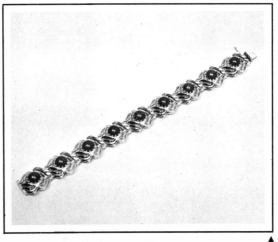

Bracelet festooned by 11 gold chains connected by a rectangular clasp set with a large agate plaque; Austria, mid-19th century; $500–650.

Link bracelet in gold decorated with glass beads and a blue enamel border; Italy, late 19th century; $450–500.

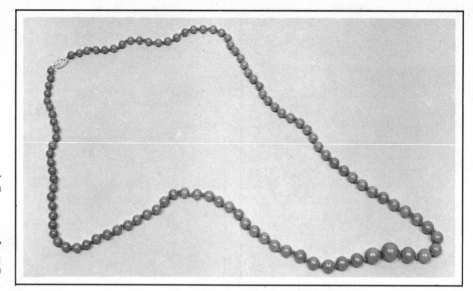

Strand of pink coral beads with gold filigree clasp; Asia (probably the Philippines), 20th century; $500–650. These beads are of particularly high quality. ►

Necklace of peach pits carved in the form of Buddhas; China, mid-19th century; $75–100. This is probably a prayer necklace. ▼

◄ Strands of beads carved from natural substances; Europe, late 19th century. Left: Lapis lazuli with a white gold clasp; $450–600. Right: Baltic amber; $300–400.

Necklace in liquid silver embellished with turquoise and shell beads; Mexico, early 20th century; $125–175. ▼

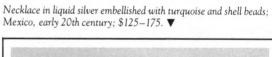

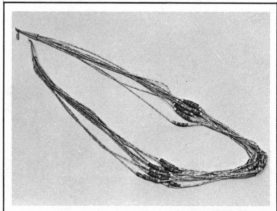

Necklace of opals and crystal rondelles with a white gold clasp; Europe, late 19th–early 20th century; $750–1,000. Opals are not usually found in a necklace.

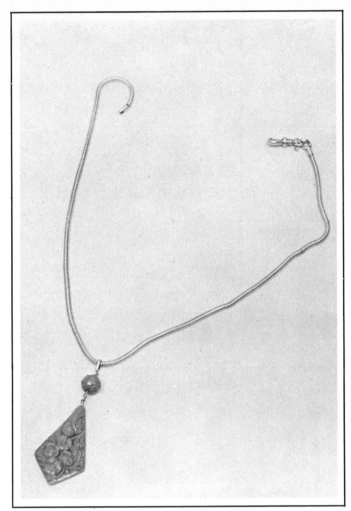

Pendant necklace with faceted black onyx set with portrait photograph in gold frame; Europe, late 19th century; $350–500. ▼

Art Deco choker in gold combined with a Victorian kite-shaped pendant in coral in a foliate design; United States, early 20th century; $225–300. It is not unusual to find jewelry of different periods combined in a single piece.

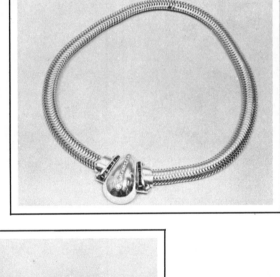

Choker in gold set with small diamonds and rubies; Germany, 1925–35; $1,800–2,500. ▶

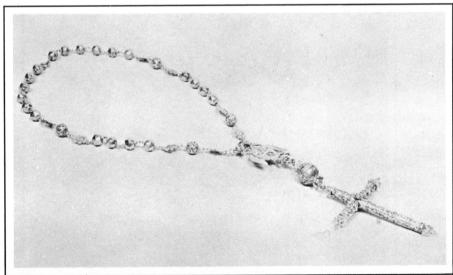

Pendant necklace of filigreed gold beads supporting a massive gold slab and a wirework cross surmounted by a double eagle; Austro-Hungary, mid-19th century; $1,750–2,000.

Locket pendant in gold with chain, the front of the locket set with four small pearls; England, late 19th century; $350–500. ◄

Necklace in gold set with graduated and carved white shell cameos depicting young Greek men and women; France, late 18th century; $3,500–5,000. ▲

Mosaic jewelry; Italy, late 19th–early 20th century. Left: Brooch; $35–50. Right: Pendant in the form of a cross with gold link chain; $100–130. ▼

Brooch and clip-on earring set in gold and turquoise; Italy, early 20th century; $750–900. This matching set is highlighted by Florentine-style carving. ▶

◄

Bottom center: Brooch in gold and coral in the Etruscan Revival style; Italy, mid-19th century; $225–300. Left, right, and top center: Brooch and matching earrings in carved jade and silver; China, 1920–25; $75–100 the set.

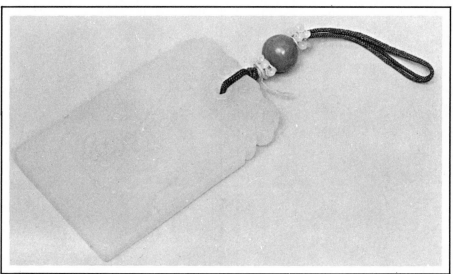

►

Pendant in carved white jade cut with a foliate motif on a blue textile cord set with a coral bead and several small glass beads; China, 1915–25; $100–125.

Brooch and earrings in sterling silver; by Georg Jensen, Sweden, early 20th century; $150–200 the set.

▲

Pendant in mottled green and brown jade inscribed with decorative motifs set with an interior gold ring and gold pendant loop; China, late 19th century; $225–275.

▲

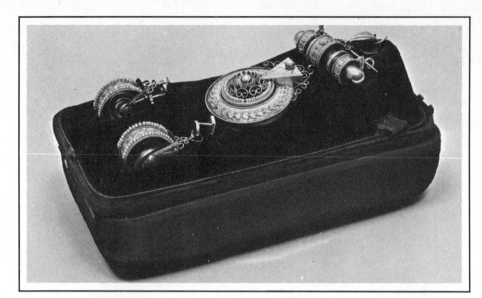

Brooch and earring demi-parure in gold in the Etruscan Revival style; France, mid-19th century; $1,100–1,500. All the pieces are set with seed and half pearls. ▶

Brooch/pendant in jade, diamond, and gold embellished with a stylized swan with diamond-set eye and pearl cluster crown; France, late 19th century; $800–950.

Charm in ruby and chrysoprase in the form of a Buddha mounted on an openwork gold altar; Europe, early 20th century; $350–500.

Brooch in turquoise and diamond in the form of a turtle; France, 1845–55; $350–450. This is a small but interesting piece.

Brooch in diamond, ruby, and chalcedony on a gold base in the Egyptian Revival style; England, early 20th century; $4,000–5,000. The Egyptian Revival style was very popular during the 1920s.

Art Nouveau brooch in the form of a butterfly with ruby eyes, red and green enamel wings, and set with many diamonds; Europe, late 19th century; $2,200–2,600.

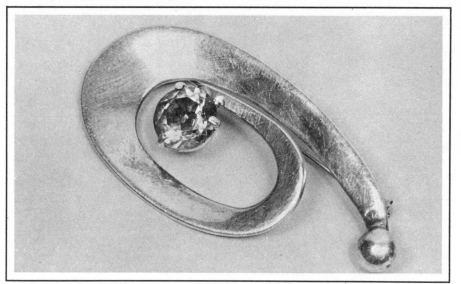

◄ Brooch in silver in free-form Art Deco style set with a round amethyst; Mexico, 1925–40; $75–100. Though often interesting, Mexican jewelry is undervalued.

Portrait locket brooch in silver; by Georg Jensen, Inc., United States, early 19th century; $120–155. This square locket has room for two pictures. ▼

Brooch in openwork silver set with two pieces of black glass; France, mid-19th century; $125–165. This piece looks surprisingly modern. ▲

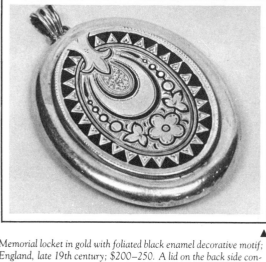

Memorial locket in gold with foliated black enamel decorative motif; England, late 19th century; $200–250. A lid on the back side conceals space for a picture of the departed. ▲

Locket in gold in the Victorian manner set with numerous pearls concealing frames for two portraits; Europe, late 19th century; $275–350. ▲

Brooch in gold set with 7 cabochon diopsides and 16 diamonds; by Celino, Italy, early 20th century; $1,500–2,000.

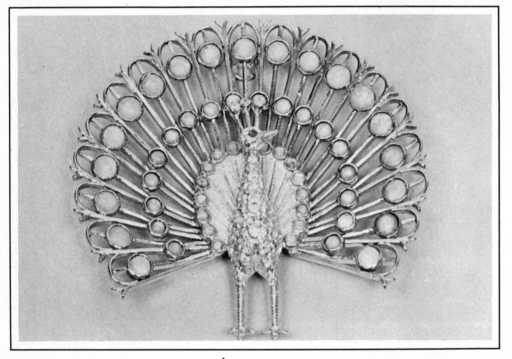

Pendant in gold in the form of a peacock set with a ruby eye, numerous small diamonds, and 53 opals; France, early 20th century; $1,200–1,600.

Coin pendant based on a 1781 coin set within a gold open Greek-key border; Austria, 18th century; $350–500. Coin pendants were and still are a popular form of jewelry. ▶

Cameos in carved shell; Italy,
early 19th century. Left:
$100–150. Right: $90–125.
Cameos were produced in large
quantities during the 1800s,
especially in Italy.

Cameo brooch in shell depicting a hunter on horseback and a lion
mounted on a gilt-metal frame; Europe, mid-19th century;
$80–120.

Cameo in lava depicting a Roman lady mounted on a white-metal
frame; Italy, 19th century; $120–170. Lava cameos are dark-gray
in color.

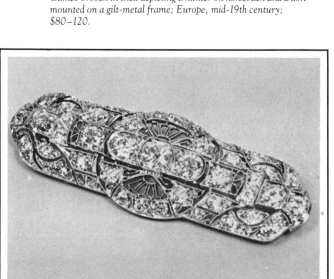

Oval bar brooch in platinum set with nearly 3 carats in diamonds;
by Fougeray, France, early 20th century, $2,000–2,700.

Brooch in pietra dura with a white, green, and gold flower on a black ground in an elaborate gold frame; Italy, late 19th century; $175–250. ◀

Miniature portrait brooch in oil paint on a tortoiseshell plaque with filigreed silver-gilt frame; Holland, late 19th century; $250–300. ▶

Miniature portrait brooch in oil paint on enamel in a gold frame; by A. Golay Leresche, Geneva, Switzerland, ca. 1920; $650–800. Miniatures are a specialized area of painting. ▼

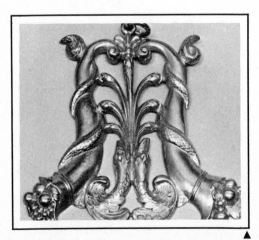

Pendant in silver gilt in Georgian mode; by Benjamin Smith, England, ca. 1821; $650–800. The design is two snakes coiled about cornucopias.

Miniature portrait brooch in enamel, pearl, and turquoise; France, early 20th century; $200–275.

Earrings in gold set with coral half-beads in a filigreed and beaded mount; Europe, late 19th–early 20th century; $650–800. These earrings were part of a suite that also included a pendant necklace. ▲

Brooch in gold set with a black enamel band and a solid gold key; Russia, ca. 1896; $225–300. This is a rather unusual piece. ▼

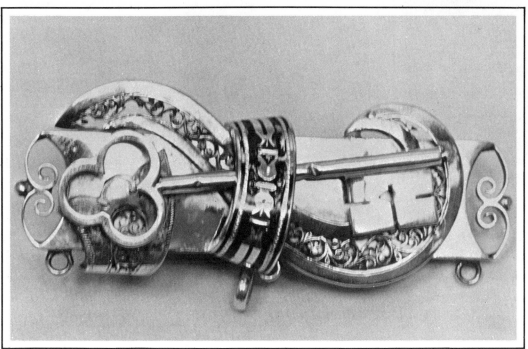

Earrings in jadeite and gold; China, 20th century; $100–135. These pieces are typical of those produced for export by the Chinese during the period 1920–45. ▲

Pendant in white gold filigree set with a large center diamond surrounded by smaller diamonds and sapphires; Europe, 19th century; $350–400. ▲

Lady's ring in gold set with a large domed carved coral embellished with turquoise beads and a border of pear-shaped lapis lazuli; Italy, early 20th century; $550–700.
▼

Lady's figural ring in the form of a dragonfly in coral and gold with enamel wings and tail in blue and green; Spain, early 20th century; $150–200.

◄
Daguerreotype ring in gold with an oval hinged lid set with a jasper plaque that conceals space for a small photograph; United States, late 19th century; $350–500.

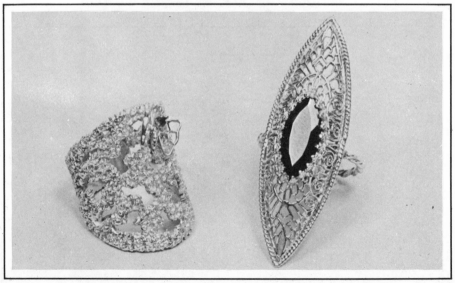

▲
Lady's rings in gold filigree openwork; Europe, late 19th century. Left: With a tiny ruby-set butterfly; $135–185. Right: With a navette-shape garnet; $175–250.

Lady's ring in platinum set with many
small diamonds on a foliate mount;
France, ca. 1910; $2,500–3,000.
Pieces like this were usually reserved for
evening wear. ◀

Lady's ring in gold set with a large step-cut topaz; England, late 19th
century; $200–275. ▼

▶
Lady's ring in gold set
with a large carved green
tourmaline; Germany,
20th century; $100–
135. This piece reflects
the influence of modern
design on jewelry.

▲
Lady's ring in gold frame
with large cabochon em-
erald bordered by many
small diamonds, a row of
round sapphires, and an-
other row of rubies; Eng-
land or United States,
20th century;
$4,500–5,000.

Lady's ring with white gold mount, emerald-cut aqua-
marine, and many small diamonds; Europe, early
20th century; $700–1,000. ▲

◀
Lady's ring with platinum frame centering a large ca-
bochon emerald surrounded by many small diamonds;
France, 1920–30; $3,500–4,750.

93

Men's cufflinks in rock crystal set with tiny diamonds forming the numeral five; by Rozet & Fischmeistre, Vienna, Austria, early 20th century; $1,000–1,200. This set was probably intended for presentation on a birthday or other special occasion. ▼

Belt of carved silver gilt links decorated with red and blue enamel set with pearl beads; Austro-Hungary, late 19th century; $350–500. ▼

Buckle in white jade embellished with openwork red-glass plaques and two pieces of kidney-shaped green jade; probably China (for export to Europe), 1925–35; $150–250. ▼

Guard rings in white gold set with small square-cut rubies; France, late 19th century; $300–400. ▲

Men's cufflinks set with round cat's-eyes; Europe, late 19th century; $400–500. ▲

Men's cufflinks with textured gold mounts set with rectangular lapis lazuli plaques; England, early 20th century; $300–400. ▲

Victorian belt buckle in steel decorated with cut-steel gems; Germany, late 19th century; $25–35. Cut-steel was a popular 19th-century costume-jewelry material. ▼

Silver coin pendant that conceals a small knife blade, file, and pair of scissors; France, mid-19th century; $150–200. This novel piece may have been intended to be worn on a watch chain. ▲

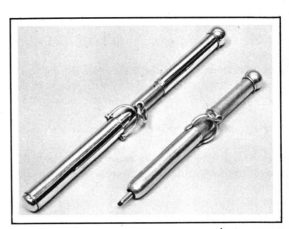

Gold retractable pencils designed to be worn as pendants; England, early 20th century. Left: $300–400. Right: $175–250. The price difference reflects the gold content. ▲

Handbags in gold mesh. Left: Change purse; by Tiffany & Company, France (for the American market), ca. 1930; $500–600. Right: Art Deco purse in white and yellow gold set with two sapphires; Europe, 1920–30; $3,500–5,000. ▲

5

Bronze

Bronze is a sturdy reddish-brown metal composed of approximately eighty-eight parts copper and twelve parts tin. It is relatively lightweight and is malleable enough to be worked by hand or stamped, but it is especially suitable for casting, and the great majority of ware is made in that manner. Bronze was apparently one of the first metals worked by man, and its importance in the development of civilization is reflected in the term Bronze Age applied to the period of prehistory beginning about 3500 B.C. Bronze weapons and utensils have been found in Egyptian tombs and Greek and Roman ruins, and Chinese artisans of the Shang dynasty (1766–1122 B.C.) created remarkable food and wine containers out of bronze.

While often of high quality, these early examples are hard to come by, expensive, and generally of less interest to collectors than later bronze. From the time of the Renaissance on, European craftsmen produced a great variety of bronzeware, including both utensils and sculpture. The metal was especially desirable as a sculptural medium because it could be chemically treated to make it look like ancient bronze or could be weathered to a rich green surface. Well-known Renaissance sculptors such as Verrocchio and Donatello brought the material to a high state of perfection. Like their classical predecessors, these men generally sculpted figures of gods or men, and their creations had a lifelike quality seldom since equalled. In fact, it was not unusual for the forms from which their works were cast to be used for centuries. Models created by the Flemish sculptor Giovanni da Bologna (1524–1608) were serving as a basis for casting at the turn of this century!

Even during the Renaissance bronze served many purposes other than artistic: cooking pots and caldrons in the metal had been known since Roman times, and sets of weights and measures, mortars and pestles, bells, and door fittings were common. At a more sophisticated level, craftsmen of the period produced elaborate candelabra, mirror frames, and small boxes or caskets for storage of precious gems.

Bronze workers continued to make these items during the centuries following the Renaissance, adding to them such things as the elaborately engraved and cast ewers (aquaemanales) used to pour water over guests' hands after each course of a state meal, perfume sprinklers and burners, various drinking vessels, and centerpieces.

Perhaps the most spectacular of the later bronzeware was ormolu, ornamental bronze gilded with ground or powdered gold. Most collectors tend to associate ormolu with furniture fittings—the bright golden handles, escutcheons, and feet found on French furniture of the late seventeenth and early eighteenth centuries—but ormolu appeared as early as the 1660s in France (where most of it was always made), and from the beginning the technique was employed not only in furniture decoration but also in the making of such things as wall sconces, fireplace equipment, inkstands, and the garniture sets of clockstand and two matching vases that decorated so many nineteenth-century mantels.

The earliest ormolu was created by mixing gold dust with an amalgam of mercury, applying this to the bronze, and heating it. The mercury would evaporate, leaving the gold bonded to the metal. The resulting finish was excellent—but at a price. Many gilders died of mercury poisoning. Fortunately, electrolytic gilding was developed during the 1800s, achieving a comparable result with less human suffering.

As other metals gradually replaced bronze in the making of utilitarian items, the medium became more and more the realm of the sculptor. Traditionally, his idiom had been the human figure, and animals, where they appeared, were in subordinate positions, as in the lions bested by Hercules. However, in the mid-nineteenth century a group of sculptors emerged whose major interest was in the accurate and dramatic representation of animal forms. Appropriately known as Les Animaliers, these men took their inspiration primarily from Antoine Louis Barye (1795–1875), whose skills were so universally recognized that many regarded him as the last great bronzer in the Renaissance tradition.

Les Animaliers specialized in single animals, groups of animals, and birds, as was the case with François Pompon, and their pieces were usually of no great size. This, combined with the introduction during the 1800s of industrial foundries which could produce many copies in several sizes from a single original model, led to wide circulation of the work of these French sculptors. Indeed, it may be said that it was at this time that bronzework became accessible for the first time to a large audience. This trend continued throughout the late nineteenth and into the twentieth century.

Factory-produced castings in heroic poses by obscure artists vied for favor with sophisticated and flowing forms in the Art Nouveau manner, and by 1890 it was common to find a standing ashtray supported by a Greek goddess or a bonbon tray the perimeter of which was defined by the flowing tresses of a Mucha-style beauty.

These European influences were felt in the United States, where bronze production had been limited before the mid-1800s. With increasing wealth and abundant tin from the new Missouri deposits, American manufacturers turned to bronze. Most of their early work represented slavish copies of Continental types, but by 1900 Tiffany and other sophisticated manufacturers had begun to create their own version of the Art Nouveau.

While American and European forms followed a more or less consistent development even to the extent of a stylistic progression not unlike that found in the areas of furniture and silver, such was not the case with bronze objects made in other parts of the world. Bronzework was limited in area; not all peoples in all localities learned the art. In Africa, for instance, despite an abundance of raw materials, bronze casting was done only along the north coast and in two areas of the south.

In what is now Morocco and Algeria Islamic craftsmen whose art came from the Near East produced a variety of utilitarian objects, such as door knockers (in the form of a hand grasping a ball), lamps, animal bells, pipes, and water vessels. The style and the floral and geometric decoration of these pieces made it clear that they were inspired by examples imported from Persia and Egypt.

In Nigeria and Ghana there are artifacts of bronze the origin of which is less easily determined but which are among the most collectible of all objects in this medium. In 1897 a British expeditionary force conquered Bini in the kingdom of Benin in what is now Nigeria and discovered hundreds of extremely sophisticated bronze heads, animal figures and scenic plaques. Initially it was believed that the knowledge of bronze casting had been brought to the area by fifteenth-century Portuguese traders, but the discovery in the nearby city of Ife of similar pieces dating to the thirteenth century (before the arrival of the Portuguese) has led to the conclusion that people in the area probably learned their skills centuries ago from wandering Arabs.

In what is now Ghana, the Ashanti people employed small bronze figures as weights in the measurement of gold dust, their most treasured possession. The Ashanti figures, which were produced by a lost wax technique, are generally less than six inches tall, humanoid in form, and certainly less sophisticated than those of Benin and Ife. Nevertheless, they have a certain folk charm that has long endeared them to collectors, and, fortunately, they were made in large quantities until late in the nineteenth century. Most collectors can afford to own an Ashanti bronze.

Bronzework was practiced at an early date in the Near East. In fact, some experts believe that the art first developed there. By the eighth century Islamic workers were turning out such things as ewers and other drinking or eating vessels, often in the forms of various animals, as well as the trays that became in the nineteenth century a staple of the tourist trade. Five hundred years later they had developed complex engraving techniques and were decorating their trays and other utensils with Islamic script and various traditional motifs inlaid in gold or silver or polychrome enamel. Near Eastern bronze was imported by Italian traders, and there is no doubt that Islamic decorative techniques played an important role in the early development of the European craft.

In the Far East the dominant role, as in so many areas of culture, was played by the Chinese. Chinese tradition records the discovery of bronze in the third millennium B.C., and long before the Christian Era Chinese craftsmen had learned to make extremely refined and abstract vessels. These were intended primarily for ritual purposes, including burials (the reason why so many examples have survived), and contemporary records make it clear that only the wealthy could afford to own a tripod-footed wine warmer or a ring-footed food server.

Authorities have been able to trace the development of these vessels from the Shang dynasty through the Han (202 B.C.-A.D. 220), and the number of existing specimens has led to widespread reproduction, some of which goes back hundreds of years, for Chinese collectors have long coveted such pieces. Authentic early bronzes of this quality are rarely seen on the market

and when available bring astronomical prices.

During the period of the Six Dynasties (A.D. 220–589) which followed the Han many Chinese adopted Buddhism; as a result the bronzeworkers began to produce religious statues rather than their traditional forms with the exception of the circular mirrors that had appeared in the preceding period.

Through the following centuries Chinese craftsmen turned out Buddhist statues and ikons, reproductions of Shang-Han ritual vessels, and various utilitarian items, such as cooking pots, horse bits, weapons, and money chests. During the eighteenth and nineteenth centuries they added to these items teapots, tea canisters, storage boxes and candleholders, all of which found a ready market in the West. Unlike earlier pieces intended for purely local consumption, these were often embellished with detailed engraving and enamelwork.

Though late starters by Chinese standards—their first important work dates "only" from the fifth century—Japanese bronze casters have also made an important mark on the antiques world. At first they concentrated on religious figures, including such remarkable achievements as the Buddhas at Kamakura and Nara, which are the world's largest bronze objects, but by the sixteenth century they were turning out many objects that are now eagerly sought by collectors. Among these are two types of bronze mirrors, oval tsuba-sword guards punch-decorated and inlaid in gold or silver, and teapots for use in the tea ceremony. During the nineteenth century various large urns, vases, and statues of no particular style but with a certain charm were added to these items. These were intended for the tourist trade.

Also of interest to the collector are Indian bronzes. The first great eastern religious figures were produced by artisans of the Gupta dynasty (A.D. 320–544), and the standard figural forms created during that period not only have been more or less adhered to until the present day but also had a major influence on figural sculpture in China, Japan, and the rest of Asia. Nearly all the early work is now gone, and it is difficult even to obtain pre-nineteenth-century examples. But many smaller religious figures made during the past century and a half are available to collectors.

Indian craftsmen also produced many interesting pieces of utilitarian bronze, including such oddments as betel-nut cutters, locks in the form of animals, animal bells, and, of course, the ubiquitous water pipe, a late-seventeenth-century form with worldwide popularity. Even today bronze is a major Indian export item.

Although the natives of North America were not familiar with bronze, the discovery of bronze implements in Peru and Argentina indicates at least a limited usage by the pre-Columbian population of the Southern Hemisphere. Once the Spanish and Portuguese colonized the area, they utilized the abundant copper and tin deposits in the production of traditional European forms, chiefly religious objects such as crosses, candlesticks, and other altar regalia. Such pieces are relatively uncommon and of little interest to most collectors.

While figural bronzes of any age or quality always command high prices, the abundance of interesting bronze implements and decorative objects from Asia, Europe, Africa, and North America allows the would-be collector a far wider field for exploration than is the case in many other areas. Much can be purchased reasonably, and great variety can be achieved even in a collection put together for a modest sum.

Figure of a woman in bronze; Egypt, 19th dynasty; $175–250. Despite their antiquity, Egyptian bronzes can often be obtained quite reasonably.
▶

Head of a leopard in bronze; by Benin, Nigeria, late 19th century; $1,200–1,600. Some of the world's finest bronzes were produced from the 13th through the 19th centuries in what is now Nigeria. ▼

▲ *Anklet in cast bronze; by Ashanti, Ghana, late 19th century; $175–250. Often the more jewelry an African woman wore the higher her status.*

Figural gold weights in bronze; by Ashanti, Ghana, late 19th century. Left: Mother and children; $75–100. Right: Mythological figures; $60–90.
▶

98

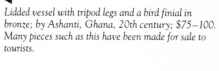

◄
Lidded vessel with tripod legs and a bird finial in bronze; by Ashanti, Ghana, 20th century; $75–100. Many pieces such as this have been made for sale to tourists.

Figure of the deity Parvati on a lotus-leaf base in bronze; Thailand, 19th century; $250–350. ▼

▲ *Figure of a Buddhist deity in gilt bronze; southeast Asia (possibly Cambodia), late 19th–early 20th century; $150–175.*

Jar in bronze with embossed representations of dragons and a scalloped edge; China, 20th century; $30–40. This is typical of the inexpensive export wares.►

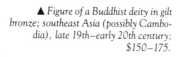

▲ *Figure of a bird with a fish in its mouth in cast bronze; by Bobo, Upper Volta area, early 20th century; $275–375.*

Vase in bronze in the baluster form with elongated neck decorated with applied figures of dragons and fish; China, late 19th century; $250–325. ▶

Tripod-form vessel in bronze with incised decoration; China, 20th century; $5–8. This is a popular form. ▼

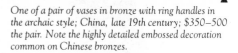

One of a pair of vases in bronze with ring handles in the archaic style; China, late 19th century; $350–500 the pair. Note the highly detailed embossed decoration common on Chinese bronzes.

Incense burner in bronze in the form of a sage astride a water buffalo; China, early 20th century; $90–120.

Vase in bronze in archaic form with a band of cloisonné about its middle; China, late 19th century; $200–275. Most Chinese bronze vessels are copies or near copies of much earlier examples.

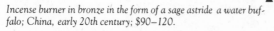

Ovoid vase in bronze with incised scene of village and bridge; Japan, late 19th–early 20th century; $275–350. This piece has been converted to a lamp.

Charcoal burner in bronze with a basin with elephant-head handles on a pierced-bronze stand mounted on turned, ebonized wood base; Japan, 19th century; $600–750.

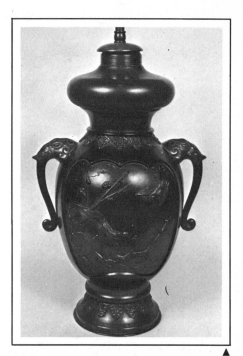

Lidded tripod-form vessel in bronze with a finial in the form of a Foo dog and cloisonné design at its middle; China, late 19th century; $250–350.

Elaborately embossed vase in bronze with tripod feet decorated with a village and mountain scene in relief; Japan, early 20th century; $225–275. Japanese bronzes are often embellished with genre scenes.

Vase in bronze with elephant-head handles and an embossed scene of birds and blossoms in high relief; Japan, 19th century; $200–275. This piece has been fitted out as a lamp, which diminishes its value.

Genre figure in bronze of a peasant farmer leaning on his hoe; Japan, early 20th century; $150–200. This is a companion piece to the preceding example. ▼

▶ *Figure of a peasant woman in bronze; Japan, early 20th century; $135–175. Simple genre figures like this have great appeal for the Japanese sculptor.*

Art Nouveau bust of Lucrece in bronze; by Villanis, France, late 19th century; $900–1,200. French sculptors dominated the field during the 19th century and favored classical themes. ▲

Figure of the goddess Diana with drawn bow in bronze; signed by Falquiere with foundry mark, France, late 19th century; $700–850. ▲

Figure of Bacchus in dore or gilded bronze on a shaped marble base; Europe, 19th century; $650–825. ▼

▶
Figure of Victory with laurel wreath in bronze on Victorian pedestal; Europe, late 19th century; $450–600. Bronzes such as this were once popular mantel decorations.

▶
Figure of a discus thrower in bronze; with foundry mark, Italy, 20th century; $500–650. Sculptor's signature and foundry marks increase the value of bronzes.

◀
Sculpture of a tiger attacking an elk in bronze; by Antoine Louis Barye, Paris, France, late 19th century; $1,500–2,000. This figure bears the foundry mark and signature of Barye (1796–1875), a sculptor who excelled in animal forms.

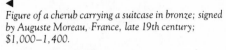

Figure of a cherub carrying a suitcase in bronze; signed by Auguste Moreau, France, late 19th century; $1,000–1,400.

Figure of a cherub leaning on a bow in bronze; signed by Auguste Moreau, France, late 19th century; $1,500–1,800. ▼

Sculpture of a child riding a St. Bernard dog in bronze; by Gaudet, France, late 19th–early 20th century; $1,400–1,800. The Victorians loved whimsical and touching pieces like this.

Figure of a seated cupid in bronze; France, late 19th century; $250–325. As the symbol of love, Cupid appears often in Victorian painting and sculpture.
◄

Figure of a semi-clad female archer in bronze on a rouge marble base; Paris, 19th century; $150–200. This is another typical French production piece.

Figure of a woman in bronze on a green marble pedestal; Europe, 19th century; $150–200. Nudes such as this were made in substantial numbers for sale to the rising middle class. ▼

Figure of an archer in bronze with green patina; mounted on a black marble base; signed by J. F. Pland, France, early 20th century; $350–500.

◄

Figure of a male nude; Austria, late 19th–early 20th century; $175–250. Possibly intended to represent a runner at the finish of a race.

▲

Hunting group in bronze of greyhound retrieving a small animal; Paris, France, late 19th century; $500–600. This piece bears a foundry mark.

105

Figural group in bronze of a man attempting to restrain a pair of chariot horses; signed by F. Gornik, Austria; late 19th century; $1,500–1,800. A large and well-modeled piece.

Figure of Venus in bronze; signed by Ron Sausage, probably United States, 20th century, $100–150. This is an example of the continuing classical tradition.

Classical figure of a wounded warrior in bronze on a rouge marble base; Europe, early 20th century; $500–700. The prototype for this piece appeared as early as the 3rd century B.C.

Figure of a polo player in bronze; Europe, 20th century; $250–325. This piece was modeled after a figure by A. Guiet.

▲
Figural group in bronze of two sailors handling a ship's tiller on a black marble base; signed by Kelety with foundry mark, France, 20th century; $800–1,000.

Figure in bronze of a boy smoking a cigarette; Europe (possibly France), early 20th century; $900–1,200.
▼

▶
Figure in bronze of a Grecian woman modeled after a classical original; with foundry mark from Paris, France, mid-19th century; $350–500.

Bust of a boy in top hat and bow tie in bronze; France, early 20th century; $375–475. A popular piece might be copied many times over a period of years. This is a copy of a Jean Antoine Houdon piece.
▼

Figure of Cupid in bronze with outstretched wings; signed by Auguste Moreau, France, late 19th century; $1,300–1,700.

Figure of André Versale in bronze; by E. Picault, France, late 19th century; $450–600. Bronzes of important public and historical figures were popular signs of culture in the Victorian home. ▲

◄

Bronzes; Holland, 20th century. Left: Boy with cape; $75–100. Right: Dinner bell in the form of a woman; $60–90. These are good examples of novelty pieces.

Figure in bronze of a man attempting to control a horse; England, early 20th century; $225–300. An example of "action" sculpture in the classical mode. ▼

Art Nouveau bust of Sappho in bronze; signed by Villanis, France, late 19th–early 20th century; $1,000–1,300. ►

Figure in bronze of an American Indian; by H.A. MacNeil, with foundry mark of Roman Bronze Works, New York, N.Y.; $12,000–16,000. The Indian has been a popular subject with American sculptors for a long time. ▼

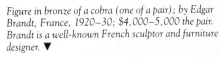

Art Deco figure in bronze of a young girl holding a bird; signed by Henry Arnold, with foundry mark of Paris, France, 19th century; $2,000–2,500.

Figure in bronze of a cobra (one of a pair); by Edgar Brandt, France, 1920–30; $4,000–5,000 the pair. Brandt is a well-known French sculptor and furniture designer. ▼

Vase in gilded bronze; by Gustave-Joseph Cheret, with foundry mark of Paris, France, ca. 1882; $3,500–4,300. This French bronze has been wired as a lamp base. ▼

Bust in bronze of an American Indian holding a peace pipe mounted on an ebonized wood plinth; signed by Boulton, United States or England, 20th century; $200–300. ◀

◄ Art Nouveau bust in
bronze of a young
woman with copper and
brass flower on breast;
Europe, late 19th–early
20th century;
$150–200.

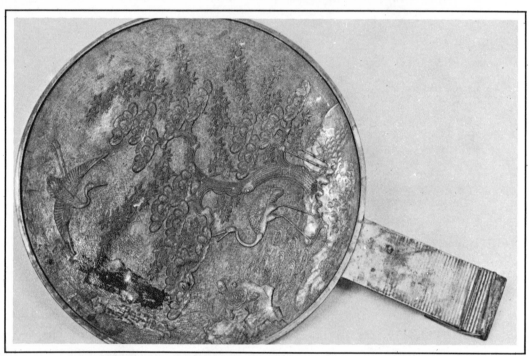

Mirror in bronze decorated with
scene of cranes in a woodland set-
ting; Japan, late Edo period
(1603–1868), ca. 1750;
$175–250 with original black-
lacquer carrying box. ►

110

Art Nouveau figure of the dancer Loie Fuller in bronze in butterfly
costume; by Frances Renaud, France, ca. 1901; $850–1,250.
Fuller was a major Paris cabaret star at the turn of the century. ▲

Figure of a kneeling woman in bronze; by Paul Manship, United
States, ca. 1924; $4,500–6,000. Like most pieces by recognized
sculptors, this one commands a substantial price. ▲

Seven-light candelabrum in bronze with scrolling arms and supports in the form of human figures; German, mid-19th century; $220–280. ▶

Art Nouveau planter in bronze with relief decoration of girl's face; signed by Rolande, France, early 20th century; $550–700. ▼

Openwork lantern in bronze; China, early 20th century; $75–100. ▲

◀

Visiting-card tray in bronze decorated with embossing of a woman's head; United States, late 19th–early 20th century; $90–130.

111

Art Nouveau planter in bronze embellished with two nude female figures; signed by Villanis, France, late 19th century; $1,300–1,700. ▲

◄

Elaborate planter in bronze, cloisonné and white marble with lion's-head bale handles and dore bronze mounts; France, late 19th century; $350–450.

112

Door knocker in bronze in the form of an eagle; United States, 20th century; $30–40. Though in an earlier style, this is a popular 20th-century reproduction. ▲

Neoclassical charcoal burner in bronze on a white marble base; Europe, late 19th century; $75–95. Vessels like this were often used as parts of mantel garnitures or as incense burners. ▲

Art Deco bookends in bronze featuring two mounted Greek warriors and the caption "Homer's Illiad"; England, 1925–35; $150–200.

Five-light candelabrum in bronze (one of a pair) with scrolling arms, a flame finial, and a white marble base; Europe, late 19th century; $900–1,200 the pair.

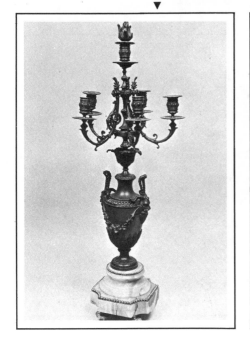

Empire style garniture candleholders in bronze (from a suite that includes a mantel clock) with gilded mounts and marble bases; France, mid-19th century; $450–650 the suite.

Empire style comport or centerpiece in bronze with figural handles, stem, and center medallion; France, mid-19th century; $90–110.

Louis XV figural candlestick in ormolu and bronze with scrolling base (one of a pair); France, mid-19th century; $800–1,000 the pair.

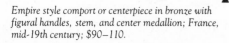

113

Empire style comport in bronze with dore bronze scrolling handles and mounts mounted on a plinth base; France, mid-19th century; $450–600. ▼

Letter opener in bronze featuring a female figure in a flowing robe; Belgium, early 20th century; $65–90. ▼

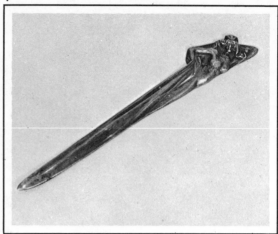

Rococo fire screen in gilt bronze and mesh; Europe, 20th century; $150–200. This is an example of the ever-popular rococo reproductions. ▼

Rococo andirons in gilt bronze on iron bases; France, early 20th century; $90–130 the pair. ▲

Ashtray in bronze and green onyx; Europe, 20th century; $60–80. Bronze is often combined with various semiprecious stones. ▲

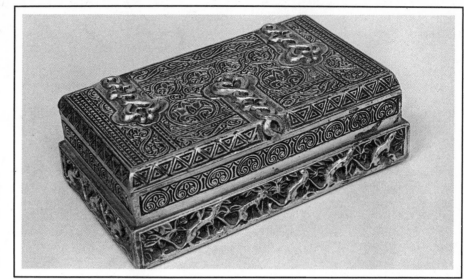

Jewelry box with lid in gilt bronze in the Venetian pattern; marked by Tiffany Studios, New York, N.Y., early 20th century; $150–200.

Neoclassical andirons in bronze and iron; Europe, early 20th century; $120–160 the pair.

Vase in bronze with repoussé decoration; Belgium, early 20th century; $200–275. This piece is in a transitional Art Nouveau–Art Deco style.

Andirons in bronze and marble representing chicks hatching from eggs; France, early 20th century; $200–275 the pair.

Handled caldron in bronze; Morocco, early 20th century; $100–150. Though seldom seen today, bronze utensils were once common in many societies.

6

Metalwares and Weapons

Though they lack the glamor and inherent value of gold and silver, the base metals—pewter, copper, brass, iron, and tin—have played a vital role in man's history. Some have served as substitutes for the precious metals in coinage and manufacture, others have served as a medium for the manufacture of weapons, and yet others have served as the material for many basic household objects.

Perhaps the most prestigious member of this group is pewter, for it has traditionally served as a substitute for silver; it has, in fact, been referred to as poor man's silver. Because of this function, European pewter, since at least the sixteenth century, has mirrored the styles of the more precious metal and has adopted its hallmarks.

No one knows when the discovery was made that alloying tin with lead or other metals created a relatively soft, silvery material, the low melting point of which made it an ideal medium for both casting and working with a hammer. The Chinese were producing pewter as early as the Chou and Han periods (1122 B.C.–A.D. 220), and the Romans were making a similar substance in the third century B.C.

This early pewter consisted of approximately 80 percent tin and 20 percent lead, a combination that resulted in a metal that was so soft it was easily damaged and which darkened so much as it aged that it was commonly referred to as black pewter. These drawbacks were dealt with by the introduction of other alloying materials, such as brass, copper, or zinc, which produced a harder pewter that was not only more durable but that also could take a high, silverlike polish. In the late eighteenth century British craftsmen developed "hard" pewter, or Britannia metal, an alloy of tin, antimony, and copper, which was not only safer than pewter (it contained no lead) but also harder and more attractive. Today's "pewter" is in most cases really Britannia.

Pewter has been made in many areas, with manufacturing centers in the British Isles, Europe, the Middle and Far East, and North America. European production was focused on England for many years because the tin deposits at Cornwall were the major source of raw material until deposits were found in Saxony. As a result of this natural advantage, English pewter smiths controlled the world market to such an extent that Continental manufacturers resorted to such subterfuges as marking their wares "English Tin" or applying false English hallmarks to them.

Nevertheless, high-quality European pewter exists. The Germans made magnificent oversize flagons and tankards (some of which were over three feet tall) of such artistic quality that they were called noble pewter; the Dutch were producing tankards as early as the fourteenth century and are famous for their ornate "town hall" tankards, vessels from which important dignitaries drank when departing on official business. Much more common than these examples, however, are platters, plates, spoons, candleholders, inkwells, salts, and teapots.

Although these objects were made in great quantity, especially during the seventeenth and eighteenth centuries, only a

relatively small percent of the ware has survived. This is due to several factors. Because it is fragile, pewter is easily damaged, and damaged pieces were often either cast aside, or, in most cases, remelted and reused. Since pewter styles followed the styles set by silver, pewter pieces eventually went out of style and, having no inherent value, were melted down and reworked. Finally, since it is about 80 percent tin, pewter could serve as rifle balls.

As is the case with most antiques, the more decorative pieces of pewter tend to be the most sought after, and fine decoration is relatively uncommon in this field. Since the metal is relatively soft it is not feasible to employ repoussé or chasing, and decoration is limited to engraving, application of separately cast elements, and the punching out of designs on flat pieces. The basic methods of manufacture are similar to those employed in silvermaking. Most early objects were cast, either in one piece or in several that were then soldered together, or were hammered into shape over a wooden form or mold. After the introduction of the harder Britannia, spinning, as utilized in silver and brass manufacture, became commonplace.

Most available pewter is European in origin, but some examples were made in North America, particularly during the nineteenth century. This area presents problems for the collector because the faking of American marks on European pieces is not uncommon. The relatively little Asiatic pewter available is usually Chinese, Japanese, or Indian and may be inlaid with brass, copper, glass, enamel, or semiprecious gems.

The history of copper is much more prosaic than that of pewter, though its period of use is certainly much longer. Copper was being mined long before the Christian Era, and it was serving as the major component of Chinese bronzes during the Shang dynasty (1766–1122 B.C.). One of the hardest and also one of the lightest of elements, copper is well suited to a variety of household and industrial uses, from weathervanes to pots and pans, lighting devices, tools, and even jelly molds.

Most copper objects are made by hammering a form into shape over a wooden mold. Copper can also be cast, but this is relatively uncommon. Most European copper is left undecorated or is embellished with hammered patterns; Eastern examples are frequently more elaborate. Artisans in the Near East perfected the technique of damascene work, in which thin strips of gold and silver were inlaid in a copper body. This art was also practiced in China and Japan.

As is the case with the majority of its metalwork, American copper looks like and is easily confused with European examples. One category, however, is distinctive—the weathervane. Weathervanes have been made in Europe for hundreds of years. Iron was employed in their manufacture in Spain, and copper was used in England and much of northern Europe. The most desirable American specimens are made of copper hammered into shape over a mold.

Brass, an alloy composed of two parts copper to one part zinc, is both heavier and more durable than copper. Moreover, its rich goldlike color allows it to be substituted for gold, especially in furniture decoration and the making of candlesticks. In fact, brass examples have traditionally followed the styles set in gold and silver.

Despite these obvious virtues, relatively little brass was made in Europe until the late eighteenth century, a situation that was the result of production difficulties. Brass was made by melting together pieces of copper and chunks of impure zinc ore, a process that was slow and yielded only small amounts of alloy. However, in 1781 an Englishman, James Emerson, discovered a method of fusing the elements directly and in large quantities.

Brass had traditionally been cast, but by the late 1700s it was possible to stamp it into shape on great milling machines and to spin it, as was being done with silver and pewter. In fact, during the nineteenth century spinning became the customary way of manufacturing larger brass vessels, both in England and in the United States. A variety of pots, kettles, and the like are available, and all bear on their bottoms or interiors the concentric marks left by the spinning process.

Collectible European brass covers a wide area, from the choice engraved tobacco boxes made in Holland to the punch-decorated bed and foot warmers of Spain and Portugal to the cast candlesticks, hammered trivets, and elaborate andirons that were made in England. Though examples of early Asian brass are available, chiefly braziers and tinderboxes, the most common items are the Indian and Chinese pieces that were made for export to the West during the late nineteenth and early twentieth centuries. These include Chinese ashtrays, cigarette cases, and pillboxes, which may be enameled or inlaid with glass or semiprecious stones; and cast, beaten, or spun work from India. There is a great profusion of the Indian items, and they are decorated in a variety of ways—through engraving, by application of enamels, or by inlay in the Chinese manner.

Less attractive than the previously discussed metals, perhaps, but certainly more important, is iron. The relative abundance of this metal, the ease with which it can be separated from its ore-bearing components, and the many objects into which it can be shaped have made iron the metal upon which civilization is in large part founded. Its use goes back at least three thousand years and characterizes those civilizations that have dominated the epochs in which they existed.

There are two kinds of ironware, both of which have been utilized by manufacturers for hundreds of years. The first, and no doubt the older, is wrought iron, in which the metal has been refined under heat and pressure to remove nearly all the carbon originally contained in the ore. Wrought iron is malleable—it can be shaped by hand with the use of various blacksmith's tools—but it is also extremely tough and elastic and can take great shocks without breaking. Quite different in its properties is cast iron. Containing up to 4 percent carbon, this metal melts readily and flows well, making it particularly suitable for casting. However, although cast iron is hard, it is also brittle, and lacks the durability of the wrought metal.

Wrought iron can be worked by a skillful smith into a variety of attractive forms, and in no area of the world have the required techniques been brought to such a high state as in Spain. The steel sword blades made in Toledo are famous throughout the western world, and Spanish ironwork, whether in the form of simple spoons and door knockers or the more elaborate weathervanes and the complex house screens known as *rejas*, is considered highly collectible.

Because of the complexities involved in its manufacture, less cast iron is known than wrought iron. The Germans cast embossed firebacks which were used to protect fireplace bricks, as well as entire cook stoves and even grave markers. The English produced a variety of items, including smoothing irons and cooking pots, and manufacturers in the United States excelled during the late nineteenth century in the production of cast-iron toys. All these items were made in basically the same way. A wooden form was carved and set in a bed of wet sand, creating an impression of the object to be cast. The wooden form was removed from the sand, and the impression was filled with molten metal.

Tinware is closely related to iron. Tin, of course, is not really tin at all but, rather, thin sheets of iron coated with rust-resistant molten tin. Little early tin has survived, but those pieces that have come down to us show by their structure that they were hammered out from blocks of iron—a slow and expensive process. The development in the eighteenth century of rolling mills allowed for production of quantities of very thin sheet iron, and most collectible tinware dates from this period.

The majority of tin objects rely on the tin coating alone for their rust resistance, but some examples were also japanned—that is, they were covered with a layer of black, tarlike asphaltum. This covering affords protection and also provides a base for decorative painting. Often elaborately embellished with stylized flowers, figures, and geometric devices, toleware, as these items are called, is very popular among collectors, especially in the United States, where native examples in good condition may bring more than one thousand dollars each.

Because it was so light and inexpensive to produce, tin comes in many different forms. In fact it largely replaced pottery and glass in many areas of housewares during the nineteenth century. Baking and cooking utensils can be found, as well as lighting devices such as the Spanish pole lamps known as *faroles;* tole bathtubs; coffeepots; and jardinaires. With certain exceptions the ware remains relatively inexpensive and is an ideal point of departure for the novice collector. It should be noted, however, that tin making was primarily a Western, industrial process, and few pieces of any age can be found from other areas of the world.

Since they are made of various metals, weapons—both guns and edged weapons such as swords—make up an important part of metalware collectibles. Edged weapons, a category that includes a wide variety of knives, swords, spears, and the like, provide an interesting, if lethal, area. Knives, especially those from the Near East and from Southeast Asia, come in fascinating shapes and are frequently decorated with everything from mother-of-pearl to gold inlay. Swords, particularly the wonderful examples made in Japan, are very popular and bring high prices.

Handguns and rifles attract a large group of enthusiasts who do not hesitate to pay thousands of dollars for a rare example or for a gun made for presentation. American examples associated with the Old West bring some of the highest prices, but early European examples are also in demand. Rifles are also collected, and some of the most spectacular are the jewel- and precious-metals-incrusted specimens from North Africa.

A high degree of expertise is required in the area of weapons collecting, for there are many reproductions and made-up examples on the market. Also, before entering this field one should check local laws concerning the ownership and storage of dangerous weapons. Remember, some of the guns and all of the edged weapons still "work"!

Spoons in pewter. Left: England, late 17th century; $30–40. Right: Two Continental examples, 19th century; $12–16 each. Once common, pewter spoons are relatively rare today. ▲

Fat lamp in pewter; Germany, early 19th century; $235–275. Lamps similar to this were made from the Near East to North America.

Stein in embossed pewter; Germany, late 19th–early 20th century; $175–225. Though better known for their ceramic steins, German manufacturers have produced a variety of pewter versions, too. ▼

Plate in pewter with London mark; London, England, early 19th century; $135–165. Large serving plates such as this are often called chargers. ▲

Unmarked baluster-shaped measures in pewter; United States or England, 1840–60; $70–95 each. Made throughout the Western world, measures came sets that were frequent marked for capacity. ◀

Bulbous storage vessel in brass; Near East, late 16th–early 17th century; $85–115. Though often of considerable age, Islamic brass is generally ignored and undervalued in the West. ▼

▼
Brass; Near East. Left: Miniature bowl; Seljuk, 12th–13th century; $50–60. Right: Handled pot with incised decoration; 19th century; $35–55.

Art Nouveau oval centerpiece in pewter; Denmark, early 20th century; $200–275. This piece is typical of better quality collectible pewter. ▼

Bowl in brass; China, 1890–1910; $40–55. Beginning during the late 1800s, the Chinese produced large quantities of brass for export to the West. ▲

119

*Candlesticks in brass;
Europe, 19th century.
Front: Pair of baluster-
form sticks; $125–145
the pair. Rear: Taller ba-
luster-form candleholder;
$80–95.* ▼

*Pipe in brass; Cameroon, late 19th century; $100–135. African
artisans produced a variety of brass objects from pipes to eating
bowls and ritual figures.* ▼

*Chamber candlestick in brass fitted for use as a camphene lamp;
Germany, 1840–65; $195–245. It was not unusual for candle-
sticks to be converted to camphene or whale-oil burners during the
1800s.* ▼

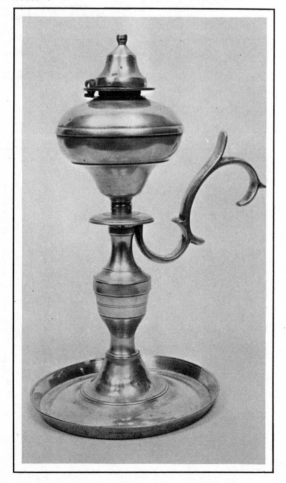

*Candlesticks in brass. Left: Pair of beehive sticks; England 19th
century; $165–235 the pair. Right: Capstan-style holder; Hol-
land, late 18th century; $185–245.*

Lighting equipment in brass; United States, early to mid-19th century. Left: Chamber candlestick; $30–35. Center: Snuffer tray; $20–25. Right: Pair of candlesnuffers; $55–70. ◀

◀ *Rare candlestick in brass in the form of tobacco leaves with built-in cigar cutter; by Tiffany Studios, United States, early 20th century; $800–1,100. Like all Tiffany products, this unusual piece commands a premium.*

Bed warmer in brass with punch decoration; Portugal, 1835–60; $125–150. Filled with hot coals, bed warmers served to allay the discomfort of a cold bedroom. ▼

◀ *Triple-spout fat lamp in brass; Eastern Europe, early 19th century; $175–250. Even after 1900 lamps such as this were in use in Eastern Europe and the Near East.*

121

Mortar and pestle; Germany, 19th century; $75–90. The mortar was used for grinding everything from medicinal herbs to foodstuffs. ▶

Victorian andiron in brass (1 of a pair); England, 1870–85; $165–235 the pair. Though factory made, Victorian fireplace implements have a definite charm. ▼

Watering pail in brass; France, late 19th–early 20th century; $75–90. Elaborate implements such as this reflect the Victorian interest in gardening and nature. ▼

Trivet in brass; England or Holland, early 19th century; $100–145. Trivets come in a variety of sizes and are highly collectible. This one is decorated with a punchwork sunburst motif. ▲

Coal scuttle in wood with brass binding; England, late 19th century; $225–275. ▶

Ewer or water jar in copper with incised floral decoration; Near East, 19th century; $90–115. Elaborate and detailed decoration is common in metalwork from this area. ▼

Bookstand in stamped brass; England, early 20th century; $120–145. This piece shows traces of the Art Nouveau. ▲

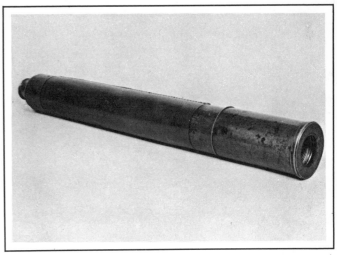

Day-and-night telescope in brass covered partly with leather; England, 19th century; $150–200. Most telescopes bear a manufacturer's mark. ▲

Military belt buckle in brass; United States, 19th century; $45–60. Brass buckles and buttons are popular collectibles, especially if they have a military history. ◀

Pitcher in copper with wrought handle and hammered decoration; Near East, early 19th century; $65–80. This crude piece was probably made by a tribal artisan.

Dish in copper with Islamic decoration; Near East, late 18th century; $125–150. ▲

▲ Cooking pot in copper with elaborately curled handle; France, mid-19th century; $250–300. Every European kitchen had dozens of copper pots during the 1800s, and they remain equally popular today.

Cooking and eating plate in copper with wrought-iron handle; Spain, 1780–1800; ▲ $145–175. Hammering marks may be clearly seen on the bottom of this piece.

Plate in copper; China, 1890–1910; $35–45. Simple pieces like this were made for export, especially to Southeast Asia.

◀ Egg broiler in copper and wrought iron; France, 19th century; $115–145. An egg was placed in each depression and cooked by holding the broiler over an open fire.

Teakettle in copper with dovetailed construction and glass handle; England, 1830–60; $275–325. The form of this pot is particularly appealing. ▼

Bed warmer in copper decorated with punch work and engraving; Spain, early 19th century; $225–275. As with most bed warmers, the handle of this piece is wooden. ▲

▶ Coal scuttle in copper; England, late 19th century; $250–300. Pieces such as this are eagerly sought by decorators, though most collectors of copper have little interest in them.

▶ Serving pitcher in copper and brass in the Arts and Crafts style; England, 1890–1900; $250–325.

Detail of weathervane; United States, 1870–90; $900–1,200. The head is of cast ▲ iron and the body is of copper hammered into shape over a form.

▲ Tray in silver on copper in the Oriental manner; by Gorham, Providence, R.I., late 19th–early 20th century; $150–200.

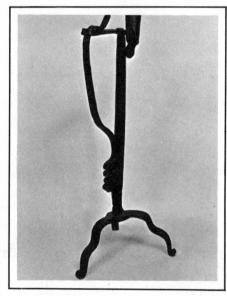

Candle- or rushlight holder in wrought iron; Europe, late 18th–early 19th century; $350–400. Combination holders like this were made for hundreds of years with little change in form. ▶

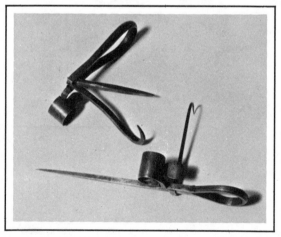

Miner's candleholders, or "sticking Tommies," in wrought iron; ▲ England, mid-19th century; $30–40 each. These lighting devices could be hung from a hook or driven into the wall.

126

Stove kettle in cast iron; Europe, late 19th century; ▲
$35–45. Pieces like this were turned out by foundries
throughout western Europe and North America.

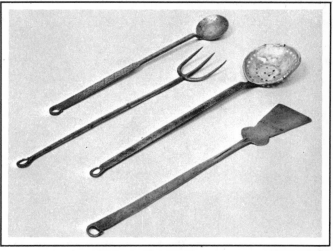

Cooking utensils in wrought iron; Spain, 19th century. ▲
Strainer in brass and iron; $75–90. Other pieces are
$25–40 each.

◄
Branding irons in wrought iron; Texas, U.S., late
19th century; $25–35 each. Now novelties, these
irons once served to mark the cattle of the great western herds.

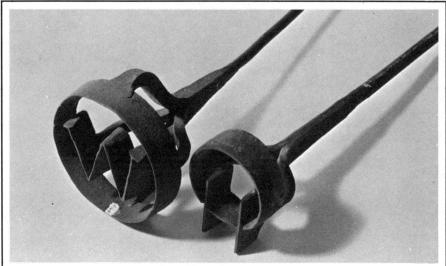

Cast iron; United States, mid- to late 19th century. ▲
Left: Shovel; $25–30. Right: Pot; $20–25.

◄
Above: Skillens in iron;
Europe, late 19th cen-
tury; $45–60 each. Be-
low: Scale in brass and
iron; England, mid-19th
century; $20–25.

127

Coffee grinder in cast iron with lithographed decoration; ▲
United States, late 19th–early 20th century; $225–275.
Coffee beans were sold during the 1800s, and every store
and most homes had a grinder.

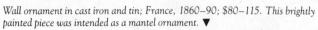

Wall ornament in cast iron and tin; France, 1860–90; $80–115. This brightly
painted piece was intended as a mantel ornament. ▼

Bread tray in painted tin, or toleware; Pennsylvania, U.S., 1830–50; $175–225. ▲

Watering can in painted
tin, or toleware; France,
1880–1910; $65–90.
Brightly decorated
tinware was extremely
popular in central Eu-
rope and parts of North
America during the
1800s. ▶

Tinware; United States, mid-19th century. Above: Milk pan; $35–40. Below: Dipper; $75–90. This dipper was made by a Shaker craftsman. ▼

Cookie cutters in tin; United States, 19th century; $15–25 each. Cookie cutters can be found in shapes ranging from dogs to eagles, fish, and various domestic fowl. ▼

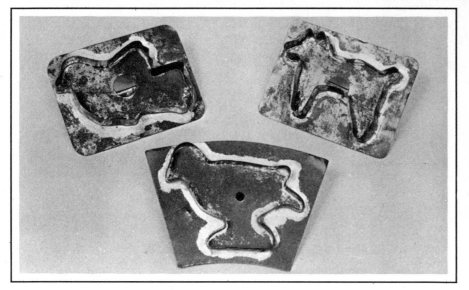

Muffin mold in tin; Holland, early 20th century; $50–60. Tin was used for many different kitchen utensils. ▼

Patented coffeepot in tin; ▲ Massachusetts, U.S., 1865–80; $50–65. Factory-made tinware is still relatively underpriced.

129

Military hatbox in tin
with conical top and
brass nameplate; Eng-
land, early 19th century;
$75–90. Parade hats
were kept in these
containers. ▶

Foot warmer in tin and wood; Europe, mid-19th century; $90–120.
Charcoal-filled foot warmers were commonly used in unheated
churches and on long carriage journeys. ▼

Kerosene store lamp in tin and glass; United States,
mid-19th century; $90–120. This hanging lamp has
an unusual form. ▼

Kerosene lamps in tin; United States and England, 19th
century; $20–40 each. The introduction of kerosene in
the 1870s led to a wide variety of metal lighting devices. ▶

Souvenir piece in pot metal and porcelain; France, 1890–1900; $40–55. The plaques depict various European sights and historical spots. ▼

Candy molds in lead; Germany, early 20th century; $25–35 each. Attractive and easy to display, candy molds are a popular collectible. ▲

Child's cup in pot metal; England, late 19th century; $15–20. Various alloys of lead, called "pot metal," have long been used for everything from toys to serving dishes. ▼

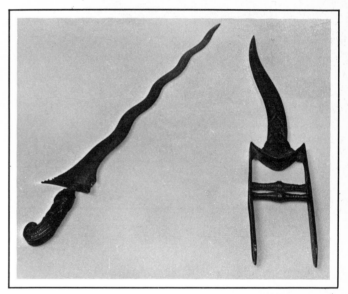

Weapons in iron and metal. Left: Kris with carved wooden grip; Indonesia, mid-19th century; $75–90. Right: Kutar, or stabbing dagger; India, early 19th century; $150–200. ▲

Left: *Short stabbing sword in iron; India, early 19th century; $200–250.* Right: *Bifurcated spearhead in iron; Indo-Persia, early 19th century; $275–350.*

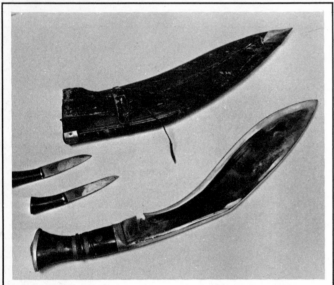

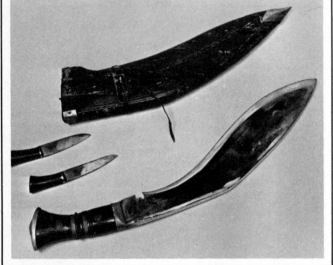

Short sword in steel with wood and lacquer handle; Japan, late 18th century; $400–500. Japanese swords are renowned for the quality of their steel and workmanship.

Kukri, or Gurkha knife, with two smaller knives, wooden handles, and leather scabbard; Nepal, early 20th century. $140–190.

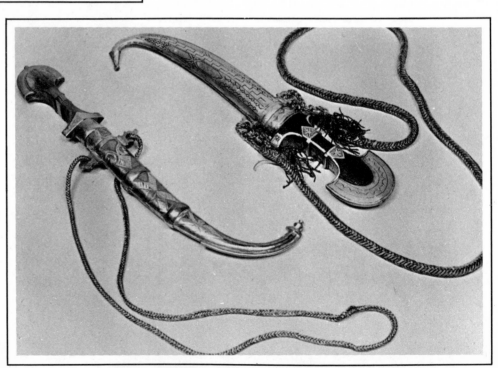

Jambiya knives; North Africa, 1900–10; $200-250 each. Left: With brass and steel handle. Right: With ebony and steel handle.

Powder horn in metal and elaborately carved staghorn; Europe, 18th century; $500–600. Powder horns were frequently decorated with carved scenes, maps, and owners' names. ▶

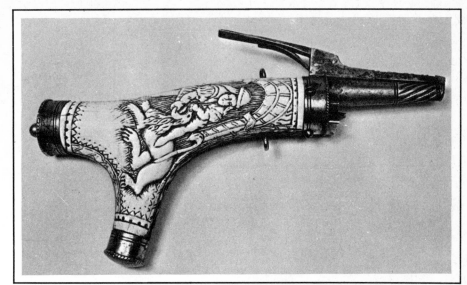

Casque, or helmet, in iron; Germany, mid-17th century; $400–500. This helmet was originally lined in leather for greater comfort and protection. ▼

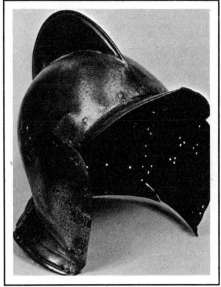

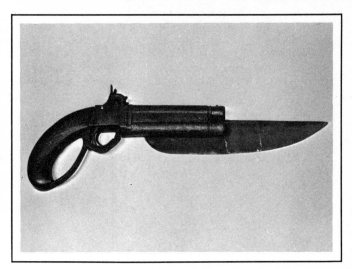

◀
Rare combination percussion-cap pistol with cutlass; Belgium, early 18th century; $600–800. Such weapons were impractical and are uncommon.

One of a brace of flintlock holster pistols inlaid with gold arabesques; by Francisco Antonnio Garzia, Madrid, Spain, 1789; $1,800–2,300 the pair. Matching sets of this vintage are rare. ▼

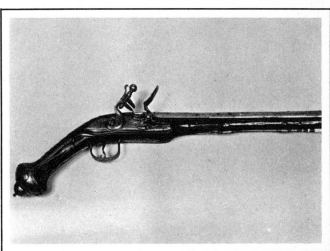

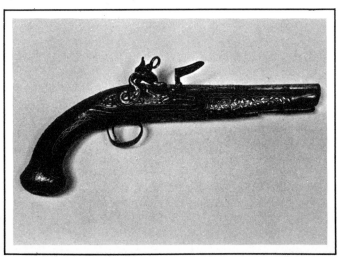

▲
Flintlock pistol in iron with silver inlaid walnut stock and engraved lock; Eastern Europe, late 18th century; $150–200.

Salon breech-loading pistol in walnut and steel with engraved trigger-guard strap and chased butt cap; France, early 19th century; $200–250. The artistry lavished on many early weapons did little to conceal their lethal intent. ▶

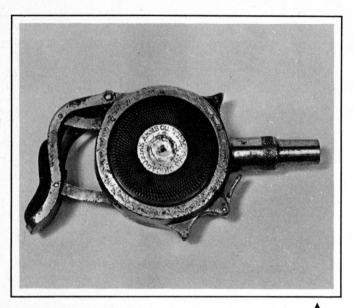

Palm pistol; by Chicago Firearms Company, Chicago, Ill., 19th century; $400–500. This hand-size .32-caliber device was another sneaky weapon. ▲

Boot pistols in engraved steel; by Spies, London, England, late 18th–early 19th century; $500–650 the pair. Concealed in a boot, these .48-caliber, single-shot percussion-cap weapons were a favorite of professional gamblers and others who skirted the law. ▼

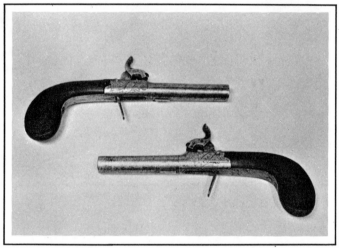

Pin-fire revolver with proofmarks of Liege; Belgium, 1880–1900; $150–200. Note the unusual, unguarded trigger and the grips of gutta-percha, a composition material that replaced wood and bone in less-expensive weapons.

Single-shot, percussion-cap, .41-caliber pistol with brass trigger guard and engraved silver mounts; by T. Gibon, St. Louis, Mo., 1830–50; $2,000–2,500. A rare and attractive example. ▼

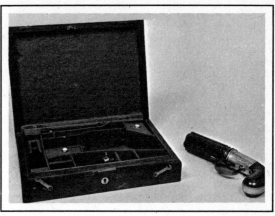

Pepperbox pistol; by Charles Jones, London, England, early 19th century; $4,000–5,000. This choice example comes with its original case and powder flask, always a plus with serious collectors.

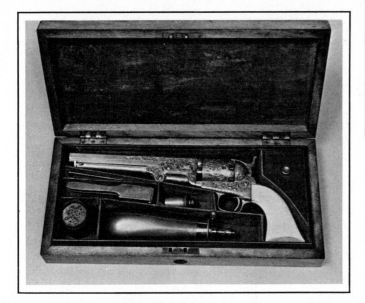

Cased and engraved Colt Navy Model '51 revolver with London proofmarks; by Colt's Manufacturing Company, Hartford, Conn., 1860–70; $1,500–2,000. This pistol is a presentation piece (to a member of the Georgia Volunteers) and therefore brings a premium price.

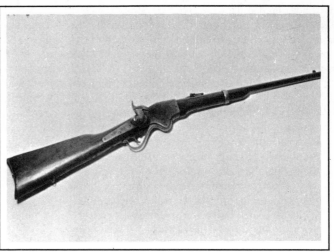

.48-caliber rifle; by J. Henry & Son, United States, 19th century; $600–750. Weapons like this served every purpose, from Indian fighting to buffalo hunting, in the American West.

Detail of stock and lock mechanism of a jzeail with iron barrel and snaphance mechanism, richly engraved and set with silver and coral; North Africa, early 19th century; $700–850.

Flintlock blunderbuss with brass barrel and folding bayonet and marks of the Irish Constabulary; Ireland, late 18th–early 19th century; $1,500–1,800.

7

Pottery and Porcelain

The excavation of pottery shards at almost every archaeological site testifies to the near universality of the potter's art. Indeed, there are few areas of the world that cannot boast of some type of ceramic, even if it is nothing more than a few sun-baked bowls or plates. This situation is a reflection of both the availability of suitable clay and the relative simplicity of the craft.

Potting clay can be found almost everywhere on the earth's surface, and even a child can shape a crude dish or, using the ancient coil method, create a container. In most societies, such basic methods were soon replaced with more sophisticated techniques, which involved the use of various ovens or kilns for firing the objects and many different sorts of clay. The most frequently used of these potter's earths is the common gray or brown clay, which fires to a shade of red and is called redware. Red-fired clays have been used throughout Europe and Asia as well as by the American Indians. They are easy to find, easy to work, and can be fired at a low heat. They are also quite fragile, and they will leak unless they are sealed with a glaze.

The most common glaze is composed of ground lead mixed with clay and water. Applied to a piece of pottery prior to firing, this mixture bakes to a glasslike surface that is both attractive and leak-proof. Moreover, the addition of various mineral substances, such as copper and iron oxide, can create a variety of attractive surface colors. Lead glazes are poisonous, however, and that fact led to their general discontinuance during the 1800s.

Roman potters used red earthenware sealed with lead glazes, as did many Europeans, including the craftsmen who brought their trade to North America during the seventeenth century. But redware is not the only type of earthenware. Yellow-firing clays can be found in England and various parts of the United States, and these were employed extensively during the nineteenth century in the making of both mochaware, an attractive, yellow-bodied pottery decorated with bands or with seaweedlike patterns in blue or green, and Rockingham ware. The latter, known incorrectly in the United States as Bennington ware, has a tortoiseshell-like appearance, which is achieved by sponging the yellow surface with brown slip.

There is also white-bodied earthenware. Various forms are known, including the relatively soft pearlware that was manufactured in large quantities by such British makers as Wedgwood and by the numerous kilns located at Leeds. Such cream-colored wares were also made in France and Germany. Harder-bodied ceramics include the so-called ironstone china, which served as a base for the Staffordshire mantel figures as well as for durable tablewares produced in both England and the United States.

An even more durable ceramic is stoneware, the clay for which can be found in a few areas of Europe and North America. This blue or gray earth fires to a body hue ranging from gray to red brown and has the hardness, though not the tensile strength, of steel. The Chinese knew stoneware at an early date—by the time

of the Sung dynasty (A. D. 960–1279) they were producing great quantities of it. In Europe the potters of the German Rhineland were making gray stoneware vessels during the sixteenth century, and German steins and mugs remain among the most sought-after examples of stoneware.

All the pottery materials discussed thus far can be found in a natural state. Porcelain, perhaps the most important and certainly the most costly to produce of all ceramic bodies, is not a true clay but rather a mixture of ingredients. There are two distinct types of porcelain, or "china": hard paste and soft paste. Hard paste is composed of kaolin, or china clay, mixed in proper quantity with petuntse, an aluminum silicate. When fired at a very high temperature, this combination will produce a white, glasslike and more or less translucent ceramic of great beauty.

Hard-paste, or "true," porcelain has been made in China since at least the ninth century, and some sources claim that its manufacture antedates the Christian Era. Regardless of when the manufacture began, the Oriental craftsmen guarded their formula well, and it was not until 1708 that a German chemist, Johann Friedrich Böttger, succeeded in arriving at a workable formula for producing the precious ware.

China, the home of true porcelain, is of great importance in the study of all ceramics, for some of the finest pottery ever produced came from its kilns. The Chinese were making red and black earthenware as early as 3000 B.C., and they perfected white earthenware during the Shang-Chou period (1776–256 B.C.). Such pottery is only of academic interest to the collector, but later wares are available and are highly collectible.

The ceramic most commonly perceived as "Chinese" is celadon, a blue, green, or gray earthenware that is customarily bathed in a dense, lardlike glaze, which gives it somewhat the appearance of jade. Celadon was developed at least as early as the Sung dynasty, and it is still made today. Most available pieces date to within the past three hundred years.

Important as Chinese pottery may be, however, it is that nation's porcelain that draws greatest collector interest, and most of the available examples were made during the Ch'ing dynasty (1644–1912), when Chinese potters were making wares specifically for export. Unlike earlier pieces, which were usually undecorated or adorned with shaped and incised devices reminiscent of Chinese metalwares, export ceramics bore a variety of decorations. In the field of porcelain there were two types of decoration: underglaze and overglaze.

Underglaze is achieved by painting a pattern directly on the ceramic surface, dipping the piece in a glaze solution, and then firing it. This assures that the decoration will be protected by the glass-hard glaze, but it limits the available hues to blue and red because only these colors can stand the high temperature at which porcelain must be baked. Overglaze decoration consists of first baking the glazed pot and then applying enamel colors and reheating it at a lower temperature to set the hues. Overglaze decoration allows for a veritable rainbow of colors.

Chinese export porcelain employs both types of decoration. Underglaze examples include the richly blue Canton and Nanking ware, with its characteristic Chinese houses, bridges, trees, and figures. Although some collectors claim they can distinguish between those pieces made in Canton and those made in Nanking on the basis of their decorative structure, with particular reference to the composition of the border (Canton is said to have a "rain and cloud" border, while Nanking is distinguished by the so-called spearhead border), leading authorities see little difference between the wares.

Chinese overglaze porcelain can be readily classified according to color and pattern. In the ever-popular *famille rose* porcelain, floral patterns are set against a traditional rose-pink background; a yellow ground identifies *famille jaune*; a green one is associated with *famille verte*; and black gives *famille noire*.

Japanese ceramics are closely related to those of China. Though its potters did not begin to work with porcelain until the 1500s, Japan soon distinguished itself in the field. At present, the most popular of Japan's translucent wares are Imari, a brilliantly hued ware characterized by brocaded borders surrounding a floral center; Kakiemon; and Kutani, a rich green-glazed ceramic still made today. The Japanese also made many types of earthen- and stoneware; these are generally preferred by Japanese collectors.

The earliest European pottery appears to have been redware, which was usually glazed in lead. However, the technique of glazing this ware with an opaque white glaze produced from tin oxide proved far more durable. The method probably began in ninth-century Mesopotamia, from whence it was carried by Muslim warriors and traders. It appeared in Spain during the thirteenth century and was already popular in Italy a century later.

In Italy, the ware was called majolica, reflecting the popular belief that it had been discovered on the island of Majorca off the Spanish coast. Italian majolica is characterized by simple patterns in blue, green, yellow, or purple glaze against a universal white ground. These bright colors were immediately popular among people accustomed to the more somber-colored earthenwares then available. Though Italian production diminished with time, Spanish majolica manufacture continued unabated, and collectors in the field treasure examples from such important centers as Talavera and Seville.

From Italy the art spread to France, where the product was called faience, from Faenza, Italy, an early center of production, and where overglaze decoration, such as that employed in porcelain, became popular. But it was in Holland, during the seventeenth and eighteenth centuries, that majolica-making reached its height. Though they made a great deal of polychrome ware, the Dutch distinguished themselves by the manufacture of sophisticated blue-on-white pottery, which came to be called delft, named after the city that was the center of its production. Previous European potters had relied primarily on design concepts originated during the Renaissance—the Dutch craftsmen looked to China and to the blue-and-white porcelain that was just then beginning to reach Europe from that prolific source. Employing Oriental motifs and the new color combination, the Dutch manufacturers dominated the European pottery trade for two hundred years. Like the Spanish and Italians, they made decorative plaques, platters and dishes, tiles, and household dishware; but they also produced giant vases and cisterns and a variety of commemorative pieces.

The eventual decline in majolica production throughout Europe was largely precipitated by the introduction of high-quality earthenware and porcelain. The latter was first made on the Continent in the late 1600s, but the industry did not get a firm footing until Böttger's discovery of hard paste was followed in 1710 by the establishment of the Meissen porcelain works. Despite changes in ownership, wars, and internal upheavals, Meissen has survived until the present time, and its skillfully modeled china figures and elaborately decorated tablewares have gained a place in the heart of every collector.

Neither the secret of porcelain manufacture nor the facilities to make it could long remain in the hands of a single factory owner or even within the bounds of a single nation. Workmen were lured away, formulas were stolen, and within a century the knowledge of china making was widespread. A factory opened at Vienna in 1717, and in 1763 the Royal Factory was established at Berlin. In the meantime, the French had not been idle. They had had a soft-paste manufactory at Chantilly since 1725, and in 1738 they had established a factory at Vincennes. In 1756 this was moved to Sèvres, where it became the greatest of all French potteries. The addition of the Limoges works at the end of the eighteenth century assured France of a prominant place in the world porcelain market.

Italy, too, had some early shops, including those at Venice, the first two of which opened in 1720, Doccia and Capodimonte. The delicate china figures made at Capodimonte are among the most sought after and the highest priced of all Continental porcelain. England, primarily because of the lack of royal patronage that supported most European factories, was late in the field. The first successful porcelain manufactory was that erected at Chelsea in 1745. It was followed by concerns at Bow, Lowestoft, Bristol, and Worcester. However, the competition of high-quality low-priced goods from the Continent seriously limited the growth of the English factories. A similar situation existed in the United States, where china-making was not profitably pursued until after the mid-nineteenth century.

If the English trailed their European counterparts in the manufacture of porcelain, they more than made up for it through their triumphs in the field of fine earthenwares. Employing sophisticated molding techniques and the finest clays, British workmen flooded world markets with inexpensive, high-quality industrial wares. By the 1780s, their various cream-colored wares were being decorated by transfer printing from engraved copper plates, offering a wide variety of attractive patterns both Oriental and Western in concept. And, of course, Josiah Wedgwood invented his extremely fine-bodied stoneware, which became known as jasper ware and is today synonymous with the name Wedgwood.

It was in England that the so-called art pottery movement arose at the end of the nineteenth century, with highly trained and individualistic studio potters turning out new, one-of-a-kind designs in a reaction to the assembly-line production of the great factories. The art pottery movement spread to the United States and flowered there, with such firms as Rookwood, Weller, and Grueby producing a variety of sophisticated ceramics.

Ceramics have been collected for decades, and enthusiasm remains at a high level. Good buys can still be made in the areas of industrial earthenware and art pottery, but good-quality porcelain is at a premium, a fact that has led to faking of pottery marks and even whole pieces. Collectors in this field must exert great caution in their purchases.

Plates in blue-on-white porcelain; China, Ming dynasty (1368–1644); $100–120 each. Dishware such as this was made for use in China, not for export. ▶

Mugs in blue-on-white porcelain; China, ca. 1820. Left: Canton design; $500–550. Center: Nanking with spearhead border; $400–450. Right: Canton with rare dragon-form handle; $600–650. These pieces are made in the European form and were intended for export. ▼

Charger in blue-on-white porcelain; China, ca. 1820; $600–675. The so-called rain-and-cloud border identifies this as a piece of Canton porcelain. ▶

◀
Export porcelain in blue and white; China, 1830–40. Left: Canton shrimp plate; $625–675. Center and right: 3-piece oval Canton butter tub; $675–750.

Fitzhugh pattern meat platter and strainer in Nanking porcelain; China, ca. 1790; $1,200–1,350. Rare pieces of china such as this bring a high price on today's market. ▼

Reticulated bowl and underplate in famille rose porcelain; China, 1830–40; $500–575. The presence of figures in yellow, blue, and orange set off from the pink background in medallion-shaped reserves marks this as a piece of rose mandarin. ▲

Export porcelain in a pattern intended for the Persian market; China, 1790–1800. Left: Cup with matching saucer; $150–175. Center: Teapot; $350–400. Right: Creamer: $200–275. ▼

Cut-corner bowl in green and off-white porcelain; China, ca. 1790; $950–1,050. The monogram C on this piece indicates it was once part of a set. ▲

◄

Tea service in famille rose porcelain; China, 1830–40. Left: Teacups; $30–35 each. Center: Saucer; $40–50. Right: Teapot; $250–290. The medallions in these pieces are filled with flowers and birds, so the pieces are called rose medallion.

Vases in variation of
famille rose known as
rose mandarin; China,
1870–90; $450–550
the pair.
◀

Planter in rose mandarin pattern; China, 1850–60; $500–575. ▲

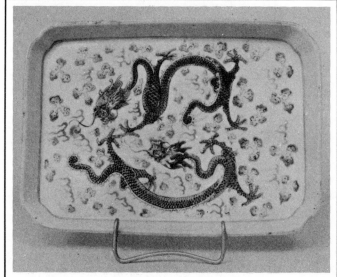

Plate in rose medallion; China, 1840–60; $55–65. Pieces of this
period were often lavishly decorated to cover up defects in the pottery
body. ▼

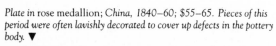

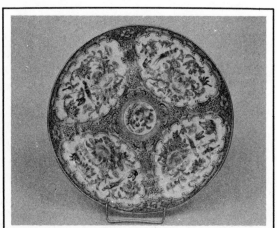

Platter in famille verte;
China, 1840–50;
$195–225. ▲

140

Set of stacking trays or boxes in porcelain in blue, yellow, green, and pink; China, 1900–10; $45–55 the set. Pieces like this were exported in large numbers at the turn of the century.

Vase in porcelain in blue and white; China, ca. 1900; $200–250. Large vases such as this made popular umbrella and cane holders in Victorian homes.

▲ Fitzhugh pattern teapot in porcelain; China, 1810–20; $325–375. The unusual crab-form finial and the twist handle make this a desirable example.

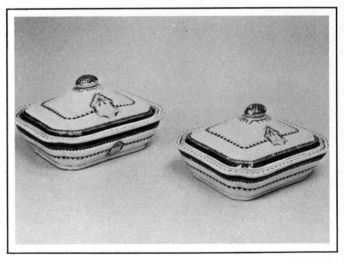

Pair of covered serving dishes in porcelain; China, ▲ 1800–10; $700–850 the pair. These pieces, which were made for the American market, are decorated in blue and gold and bear the monogram of the owner for whom they were made.

◄ Imari porcelain; Japan. Left: Gourd vase; ca. 1890; $130–140. Center: Dish; 1840–50; $100–110. Right: Two handleless cups; 1870–90; $30–40 each. Strong red, white, and blue colors characterize Imari, one of the finest Japanese porcelains.

141

Double-gourd vase in Imari porcelain; Japan, 1880–1900; $400–450. This red, white, and blue piece is in a traditional Oriental form. ▼

Dish in porcelain in white, blue, and gold; Meissen, Germany, 1870–80; ▲ *$90–130. Established in 1710, the Meissen works is the oldest in Europe, and its wares are prime collector's items.*

Plates in Dresden china in pink, green, white, and gold; Germany, 1920–30; $50–60 each. German potteries exported large quantities of such practical and inexpensive china. ▼

▲ *Kakiemon style vases in porcelain in iron red, white, green, and black; Japan, 1890–1900; $150–200 the pair. Kakiemon ware was made at Arita, Japan, as early as 1650.*

Potschappel garniture vases in porcelain; Germany, 1860–80; $350–450 the pair. Detailed, hand-shaped decoration such as this took hours of work and years of training. ◄

Porcelain; by Sèvres, France, early 20th century. Left: Plate; $70–90. Right: Tazza; $140–180. Both pieces are decorated in pink, green, and yellow on a white ground. ▼

Covered urn in porcelain mounted in bronze; by Sèvres, France, ca. 1900; $1,200–1,400. Sèvres is, from the collector's point of view, the leading French pottery. Its bronze-mounted wares are particularly popular. ◄

Pair of vases; by Sèvres, France, 1860–75; $2,000–2,400. The hand-painted scenes in blue, brown, green, red, and black and the elaborate gilding make these pieces works of ceramic art. ▼

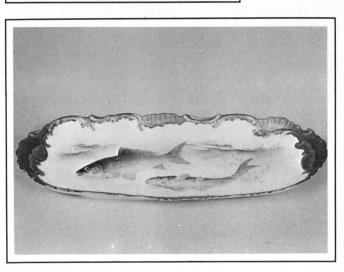

Fish platter in porcelain; by Limoges, France, 1900–10; $110–140. Some of the ▲ finest pottery painting has been done at Limoges.

143

Jewelry box in porcelain with scene taken from a painting by Watteau; by Sèvres, France, 1890–1910; $350–425. The skillfully executed painting is in pink, tan, and brown, and the background is plum highlighted with gilding. ▼

Vase in porcelain; Paris, France, 1860–80; $275–350. This bronze-mounted piece has been fitted out as a lamp, something that usually hurts an example's value.
◄

Miniature sheep and a poodle in porcelain; France, 1850–60; $30–40 each. Even the 19th century had its fakes. These pieces were made by the Paris firm of Samson et Cie in imitation of popular English mantel figures such as those produced at Chelsea. Such pieces were often given false Chelsea potters' marks. ▲

Flower-encrusted garniture vase in porcelain in pink, green, blue, and white; France, late 19th century; $150–200.
►

Plate in porcelain in blue, gray, green, pink, and black; Vienna, Austria, 1880–90; $400–500. This piece is decorated with a representation of a meeting between Alexander and Cleopatra. ▲

▲

Watch holder in porcelain; by Springer, Austria, 1870–75; $175–200. The form and bright colors of this blue, green, brown, and yellow piece are reminiscent of English Staffordshire.

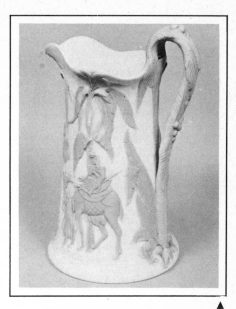

▲

Pitcher in Parian porcelain; by Samuel Alcock, England, 1860–65; $250–300.

▲

Plate in green celadon with overglaze decoration in yellow, blue, and black; 1810–20; $90–100. Celadon is the pottery most closely associated with China and is one of the world's loveliest earthenwares.

Figurines in polychrome porcelain; Russia, 1880–90. Left; From St. Petersburg; $500–600. Right: By Gardner, Moscow; $350–425. ▶

Serving bowl in majolica decorated in green, yellow, blue, and brown slip; Talavera, Spain, 1780–90; $450–550. The characteristic opaque white background resulting from the tin glaze is especially suitable to slip decoration.

◀

"Empire" cup in porcelain in tan, brown, black, and pink with extensive gilding; Russia, late 19th century; $100–125. ▶

Delftware bowl in blue, yellow, green, and red on white; Holland, 1770–90; $375–450. ▶

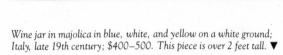

Delftware tile in blue on white; Holland, 1820–50; $75–90. Though they made a great deal of polychrome majolica, the Dutch pioneered the development of blue-and-white ware that, appropriately, came to be called delft, for a city in Holland where the trade was carried on. ▼

Wine jar in majolica in blue, white, and yellow on a white ground; Italy, late 19th century; $400–500. This piece is over 2 feet tall. ▼

Plates in majolica, or fiance, in brown and yellow on white; by Moustiers, France. Left: 1750–75; $300–350. Right: Ca. 1790; $225–270. Moustiers was an early center for the production of tin-glaze ware.

Figurine of a woman and child in majolica; Italy, 1820–30; $150–180. The Italians were among the first Europeans to make tin-glazed figures, and their work is generally on a high order. ▶

Hand-painted majolica in traditional patterns in blue and white; Spain, early 20th century. Left: Plate; $70–90. Right: Serving dish; $55–65.

Pitcher in black and white earthenware with transfer decoration; Leeds, England, ca. 1824; $650–750. Commemorating the visit of Lafayette to the United States in 1824, this piece is typical of those made for export ▼

Delftware covered jar in blue on white; Holland, early 20th century; $150–190. ◀

Delftware charger in blue on white; Holland, 1790–1800; $475–550. The decoration of early Dutch majolica is similar to that done in southern Europe. ▼

▶ *Teapot in white earthenware in blue on white; Leeds, England, 1795–1815; $350–400. Leeds was a major British pottery-making center. This piece is in the so-called Castleford shape.*

Tea caddy in white earthenware decorated with relief figures in blue, yellow, and green; England, 1780–1800; $300–350. Since many such pieces were made by the potter Felix Pratt of Staffordshire, they are often referred to as prattware.

◀ *Prattware in white earthenware with green and yellow decoration; England, 1780–1810. Left: Sugar; $275–325. Right: Teapot with lid; $300–350.*

147

Mantel ornament in white earthenware hand painted in red, green, and yellow; Staffordshire, England, 1850–70; $65–80. At one time nearly every middle-class English home was adorned with figures such as this. ▶

Spatterware in blue; England. Left: Vegetable bowl; ca. 1870; $125–150. Right: Vase; 1880–90; $130–145. Spatter was applied with a sponge or cloth to a white earthenware body. ▼

Rare Gaudy Welsh sugar, creamer, and teapot in white earthenware glazed in red, yellow, green, pink, and mulberry; England, 1800–10; $1,500–1,650 the set. ▼

Toby pitchers in polychrome earthenware; England, 1840–60; $185–215 each. ▲

Mochaware; England, 1850–70. Left; Bowl banded in blue, gray, tan, and white; $275–300. Center: Mug in green, blue, white, and brown; $350–400. Right: Teapot in green and tan agateware; $475–550. Mocha like Gaudy Welsh and Gaudy Dutch was bright, inexpensive ware for the working-class family. ▼

Jardiniere in jasper ware with lion's-head handles; by Wedgwood pottery, England, 1840–60; $275–350. Though he made many different kinds of pottery, Josiah Wedgwood is best known for his fine-grained stoneware that he called jasper ware. ▼

Cup and saucer in creamware; by Wedgwood pottery, England, 1800–10; $90–140. Black transfer decoration was used on this piece. Wedgwood perfected cream-color ware in the 1760s and called it queen's ware.
◄

Tureen with platter and ladle decorated with black transfer decoration; by T. Mayer, Staffordshire, England, 1840–50; $800–900. During the 19th century, the English mastered the art of transferring colored decoration from printing plates to white earthenware. ►

◄
Tureen and cover in ironstone with vine-pattern decoration; by Anthony Shaw, Burslem, England, 1820–40; $200–275. Ladle in coin silver; England, ca. 1850; $140–175. Durable and attractive, ironstone was a staple of every English and American household throughout the past century.

149

Plates in white earthenware with blue transfer decoration; Clews, Staffordshire, England, 1820–40. Right: "The Valentine"; $240–280. Left: Dr. Syntex painting a portrait; $250–300. ▶

Prattware cream jug with pewter top and figures in pink on black ground; England, 1850–60; $250–300. ▼

Children's pottery with transfer decoration; Staffordshire, England, 1880–90. Left: "Crossing the brook" in brown on white; $75–85. Center: Alphabet plate "playing at lovers" in black on white; $90–110. Right: Cup with child and elephant in blue on white; $85–100. ▶

Flow blue ironstone; Staffordshire, England. Left: Plate; by James Edwards, 1870–90; $100–125. Right: Sauce boat; 1840–50; $140–155. ▼

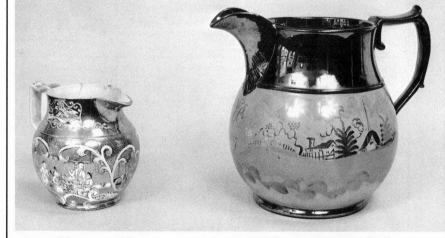

Decorated white earthenware glazed in metallic oxides; England. Left: Cream pitcher in silver resist with oriental design; ca. 1810; $375–450. Right: Pitcher in copper luster with blue glaze; dated 1817; $450–550. Silver copper, gold, and platinum have been employed to create luster effects. ▲

Cream pitcher in red earthenware with tan and yellow slip glaze; Segovia, Spain, early 20th century; $30–35. Common brick clay was used to make utilitarian pottery in most areas of the world. ▼

Tobacco humidor in Rockingham glaze in brown on yellow earthenware; by United States Pottery, Bennington, Vt., ca. 1849; $250–300. ▶

Rockingham ware; United States, 1850–70. Left: Creamer; attributed to Bennington; $225–245. Right: Uncle Sam bank; $125–150. ▶

◀
Glazed redware; United States. Left: Pie plate; Pennsylvania, 1870–80; $60–75. Right: Whiskey or water flask in black on red sponged decoration; Connecticut, 1830–40; $175–225.

Common yellowware; United States, 1880–1910. Left: Pitcher; $40–50. Center: Pie plate; $35–40. Right: Rolling pin; $75–90. Yellowware was the basic American kitchen ware in the late 19th and early 20th centuries. ▶

151

Jug in stoneware dipped in ocher and salt glazed; United States, late 18th–early 19th century; $275–325. Stoneware making was a highly perfected art in England and Germany; American potters made more simple objects. ▼

Crock in stoneware with blue slip decoration; United States, 1863–79; $150–180. Decorated in freehand, salt-glazed stoneware made in the eastern United States during the second half of the 19th century often had an appealing folk quality. ▼

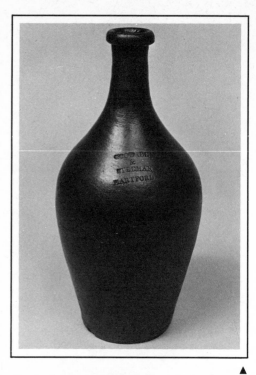

Rare bottle in stoneware salt glazed and slip dipped; Hartford, Conn., 1822–25; $300–375. ▲

Mug in lathe-turned machine-decorated stoneware; United States, ca. 1896; ▲ $135–175. Only at the very end of the last century did American stoneware begin to resemble the more sophisticated German product.

◄
Jugs in stoneware salt glazed and dipped in ocher; United States, 1800–30. Left to right: $50–65; $200–250; $70–85.

152

Vase in scratch-decorated stoneware in blue on white; Taiwan, early 20th century; $75–90.
▶

Bowl in earthenware in black on white; American Indian, 1300–1400; $270–330. As was the case with some other primitive groups, American Indian potters preferred geometric designs. ▲

▲

Art pottery vase in turquoise and purple; by Charles Catteau, France, 1930–40; $120–145. The art pottery movement in the late 19th and early 20th centuries led to a rejuvenation in the field of European and American ceramics.

◀
Bowls; American Indian, 1920–40. Left: Santa Clara pueblo; $70–95. Right: Acoma pueblo; $150–175.

Art pottery vase in green and brown with gilded applied decoration; by Amphora Pottery, Austria, 1920–36; $300–350. ▲

Art pottery vase; by Charles Catteau, France, 1930–40; $90–120. ▲

Art pottery vase; by Jean Luce, France, 1920–30; $130–155. ▶

▶
Two-handled vase with applied decoration in beige, blue, and tan; by Amphora Pottery, Austria, 1925–35; $350–425.

154

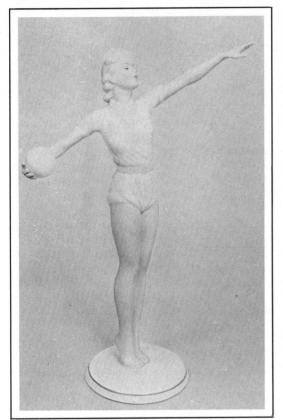

Art Deco figure of a volley-ball player in porcelain; by K. Steiner, Schaubach factory, Germany, 1930–40; $275–350. ▼

Art pottery mug in brown and blue on tan ground; by George Ohr, Biloxi, Miss., 1900–10; $90–120. Like many of Ohr's other pieces, this one incorporated a bit of humor — a ceramic snake in the bottom of the mug.
◄

Art pottery bowl in blue mat glaze; by Rookwood Pottery, Cincinnati, Ohio, ca. 1932; $80–85. ▼

Tankard in brown and mustard glaze with painted representation of a bird on a branch; by Rookwood Pottery, Cincinnati, Ohio, 1897; $1,000–1,200.

Art pottery vase in green and blue; by Weller Pottery, Zanesville, Ohio, 1910–25; $150–200. Like Rookwood, Weller was an important name in art pottery.

Art pottery covered box in tan and blue glazed stoneware; by Denbac Pottery, 1915–30; $200–300.

155

8

Glass

Glassmaking is one of man's most ancient arts—it originated in the Near East more than two thousand years ago. Given the complexity of the craft it is surprising that it reached a high level of development at a relatively early date. The first efforts, of course, were relatively crude. Egyptian glassmakers made their vessels by wrapping strips of molten glass (called metal in the trade) around a damp sand form. The result was plain and generally unattractive. However, by 300 B.C. the Syrians had developed the blowpipe, a hollow metal tube through which air could be forced to expand a glob, or "gather," of hot glass much as a child blows a gum bubble. Then, in the first century A. D., Roman craftsmen began to employ stone or metal molds in the form of the objects to be made. These molds were filled with glass forced in by blowing through a blowpipe and were then opened to remove the finished vessel.

As a consequence of these various techniques a substantial quantity of glass was made in Egypt, the Near East, and the eastern provinces of the Roman Empire (most so-called Roman glass was actually made in areas other than Italy). Numerous examples, such as drinking vessels and unguent bottles, have been uncovered in archaeological research, and these are certainly collectible though they are of less interest than later glass.

These pieces were created in stable, well-organized societies. Indeed, the difficulties inherent in glassmaking make it unlikely that a primitive culture could obtain successful production. Glass is a compound of silica, which is found in sand, and an alkali, typically potash or lime. Heated together to a high temperature, they melt and combine in a viscous mass that while hot can be shaped and expanded much like taffy candy. However, obtaining the right materials in the proper proportions is difficult, and the craft requires skilled workmen and large furnaces. Therefore, early glassmaking was seriously affected by the fall of the Western Roman Empire and the collapse of the Egyptian and Syrian dynasties.

Some production of glass did continue, however. Roman glass had been introduced into what is now Germany as far back as the first century A.D., and during Europe's Dark Ages tiny forest furnaces turned out dark-green glass vessels known as waldglas. Beakers and other drinking glasses were made, and a sufficient quantity was exported that fragments of such ware have shown up from the British Isles to Spain.

Although the Black Forest manufactory was important, especially since it laid the groundwork for the more important Bohemian glass industry, the major European glassmaking center was Venice. As early as the fifth century, fleeing Roman artisans had begun to make glass on the site of what was to become the great trading city of Venice. By the thirteenth century glass factories had become so numerous that glassworkers were granted guild status, and at approximately the same time the dangerous furnaces were confined to the island of Murano.

There is no question that Venetian glass is the foundation stone of all European glassmaking, but the craft there owed much to Eastern experience. Despite internal upheavals, Syrian glassmakers remained active throughout Europe's Dark Ages. In the ninth century they discovered that the addition of manganese to a glass batch would remove mineral impurities in the silica. Then, in the thirteenth century, they developed enameling and gilding, decorative techniques whereby metallic coloring agents or liquid gold were applied to the surface of glass vessels. In fact, mosque lamps embellished in this manner were sold throughout the Islamic world.

With their active eastern trade, Venetian glass manufacturers were among the first to learn of these innovations, and by the middle of the fifteenth century they were supreme. Employing manganese and the finest raw materials, they produced a clear glass—the first crystal—which could be cut and engraved: decorative techniques employed by the Romans and rediscovered by the Syrians. The Venetians also developed enameling to a high state of perfection with their best examples having an almost jewellike quality.

The men of Murano were more than mere copyists. They brought to perfection the ancient art of millefiore in which thin rods of multicolored glass are fused and then cut to produce a patterned cross section, and produced latticinio, which consists of woven threads of clear and milk glass. Another Venetian first was aventurine glass, achieved by trapping copper or brass filings between two layers of hot glass.

As their trade expanded the island glassmakers sought to protect their monopoly by imposing harsh penalties on workers who tried to carry secrets of the trade to other areas. Indeed, death was not an uncommon penalty for such transgressions. But the lure of profit proved stronger than the threats, and throughout the sixteenth century craftsmen from the Venetian factories made their way to northern Europe. Many went to Germany, where the already existing waldglas furnaces offered ready employment. By 1650 German manufacturers were utilizing the technique of enameling, specializing in large armorial pieces known as alderglases. These drinking vessels usually bore a gilded and enameled coat of arms or heraldic device. By the eighteenth century the making of enameled glassware was common throughout central Europe, and the so-called Bohemian glass provided a bit of color on shelves throughout the western world.

Germanic craftsmen also developed a fine clear-crystal glass that proved extremely suitable for cutting and engraving. The former technique involves the employment of a lathe equipped with numerous iron cutting wheels with which grooves are cut into the glass. The facets thus created reflect light like a diamond. Engraving involves the cutting of shallow surface designs either through the use of much smaller copper wheels or a diamond-pointed stylus that is gently tapped to create a background of tiny dots, a technique known as stippling.

Glassmakers at the German cities of Kassel and Potsdam

created some remarkable pieces of cut and engraved glass, but they were soon rivaled by artisans in Belgium and, particularly, the Netherlands. In the sixteenth and seventeenth centuries, the Dutch developed engraving to a high art, making a variety of beakers, pitchers, and other vessels whose surfaces were covered with floral and animal images in a distinctly calligraphic style.

The English industry was slower to develop, receiving its major impetus from the discoveries of George Ravenscroft (1618–1681), who found that the addition of burnt flint to a glass batch resulted in a clear and brilliant metal, which came to be called flint glass. Though too soft for engraving, flint was most suitable for cutting, and English cut glass soon came to have a worldwide reputation. British manufacturers also have turned out a variety of glass related to Venetian types, including good-quality, opaque milk glass, marbled slag glass, which looks like stone, and both threaded and enameled glassware.

English glass developments affected areas within its sphere of influence, such as Ireland, where the well-known Waterford crystal was made, and the United States. Early American glass was limited in quantity, and with the exception of the works operated at Philadelphia by Caspar Wistar (active ca. 1739–1780) and at New Breman, Maryland, by John Frederick Amelung in the 1780s, there were no major manufactories until the nineteenth century. However, once started, the Americans made major contributions to the field, not the least of which was pressed glass. European manufacturers had long puzzled over the problem of producing an inexpensive version of cut glass, which was always in demand but which cost so much to produce that few people could afford to buy it.

In 1828 two groups of American glassworkers, one headed by Bakewell & Company of Pittsburgh, the other by Deming Jarves of Massachusetts, developed machinery that could press molten glass into patterned shapes. At first these devices could produce only simple, flat items, such as jar tops and cup plates, but by the 1840s, factories in the United States were producing nearly every form known to the glassmaker. Better yet, this ware looked like cut glass. Close examination revealed that the edge of the faceted patterns on the glass surface lacked the sharpness of cut glass, but to the casual observer there was no great difference, and pressed glass cost a fraction of what cut glass cost.

The invention of glass-pressing machines marked the beginning of mechanization in the glass industry. As glass manufacturers throughout Europe gradually adopted the new machinery, the necessity for hand-blowing and shaping glass ended.

American pressed glass is found in over a thousand different patterns, and this lacy glass, as it is often called, offers a major field for collectors. There is also a substantial quantity of European ware in this mode, though Continental collectors tend to prefer hand-formed and decorated examples.

Engraved glass was also duplicated. At an early date European decorators discovered that etching was a good substitute for the more time-consuming and expensive method. A piece of glass would be coated with wax and the intended design scratched through this wax into the glass. Hydrofluoric acid applied to the piece would eat away the exposed area, creating a decorative pattern similar to engraving, and the wax-covered areas would not be affected.

The introduction of mechanization and labor-saving devices did not put a complete end to the glassworker's art. In Venice and many other areas of Europe skilled workers still labored over their creations, from the delicate lamp-work figures (so-called because the glass from which they were made was reheated

over a spirit lamp) produced in France to the filigree glass jewelry of Murano. Moreover, in the late nineteenth century the reaction to the mechanization that was becoming rampant in Europe led to the development of renewed interest in handmade glass.

Called art glass, the new product was at first made in small studio glassworks not unlike the potteries that at the same time were beginning to produce art pottery. Art glass was produced in limited quantities, was intended more to be looked at than to be used, and, unlike most commercial glass, was customarily marked or signed by its maker. Though the new wares were manufactured in various areas of Europe, France was the cradle of the art. The most important makers there, Daum, Galle, and Lalique, turned out pieces that even in their time were regarded as of museum quality and are today among the hottest items on the market.

The Daum brothers, Antonin and August, built their factory at Nancy in the 1890s and specialized in exotic shapes produced from ground-glass paste, pâté de verre. Similar pieces were made by their collaborator, Amalric Walter. Even more innovative was Emile Galle, a major figure in the Art Nouveau world. Galle, who also designed furniture, was active as early as 1897, producing cameo cut glass as well as pieces made with dripped enamel decoration and pieces of multicolored glass. Lalique began his career making ornamental glass in the Art Nouveau manner. In 1911 he obtained a contract to make perfume bottles for Coty, the great French perfumer, and from there he went on to create a large number of exotic pieces in clear crystal.

The French manufacturers were not without competition. In England the firm of Webb & Sons of Stourbridge made excellent cameo glass (a ware in which the glassworker cuts through one layer of glass to reach another of a contrasting color) as well as the yellow-pink Burmese glass. In Austria the Lotz works specialized in an iridescent glass, whose appearance was not unlike that of ancient glass that has lain long buried in the earth.

Perhaps the greatest of all art-glass producers was an American. From the middle of the nineteenth century factories in the United States had made steady advances not only in the production of inexpensive glass, an area where they led the world, but also in the field of art glass. American designers created colored glasses, such as Amberina and Agata, and even fathered the legend of Mary Gregory, the little old lady who painted children on blue glass and spawned a thousand imitators. But all these achievements were cast into the shade by the exploits of Louis Comfort Tiffany (1848–1933), the son of the noted silver maker and himself a gifted artist and glass designer. Tiffany started out with stained glass, with which he achieved notable effects, and then developed an iridescent glass with a metallic luster, which came to be known as favrile.

In contrast to all this activity in Europe and North America, very little glass was made in most other parts of the world, and very few pieces of antique glass can be found. The Chinese knew of the substance as early as the period of the Three Kingdoms (A.D. 220–265), but for fourteen hundred years they saw it only as an inexpensive substitute for jade or gemstones. It was not until the opening of a glass factory in Peking in 1680 that the Chinese began to manufacture glass vessels in any quantity. Today it is possible to find many types of Peking glass beads as well as high-quality milk glass and some extraordinary carved and enameled snuff bottles. The Japanese made glass beads to imitate pearls, and Philippine craftsmen turned out high-quality lampwork figures. Beyond these, one will find very little collectible glass that dates to before the twentieth century.

◄ Iridescent Roman glass bottles; Italy, A.D. 200–300; $65–80 each. Thanks to excavations, early Roman glass of this quality is surprisingly easy to obtain.

Mosque lamp in etched green glass with glass beaded chain and brass hook; Near East, late 18th–early 19th century; $550–700. Mosque lamps were a major product of the Islamic glassworks. ▶

Sugar bowl in mold-blown cobalt-blue glass; New Jersey, U.S., early 19th century; $200–250. Because artificial color for glass was costly, relatively few early pieces are anything other than the natural aqua, amber, or light-green shades. ▼

◄ Dish in blue glass; Near East, A.D. 600–700; $90–110. Islamic glass-makers along the eastern shore of the Mediterranean were active at an early date, and they provided much glass for Europe as well as for home consumption.

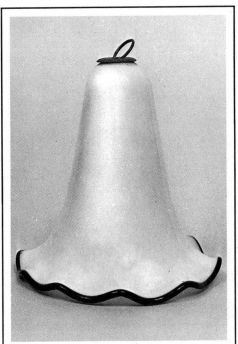

Bohemian glass tobacco
humidor; Germany,
1850–70; $70–85. This
piece is in the off-white
color known as vaseline
glass and is hand deco-
rated in bright enamels, a
common Bohemian
technique. ◄

Vase in enamel-decorated milk glass with peach-blow interior; Germany, late 19th
century; $85–110. Brightly decorated ware such as this was made in Germany and
sold throughout the Western world. ▼

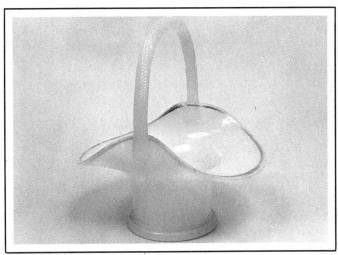

Whimsy in blown milk glass with a cobalt-blue edging;
England, mid-19th century; $60–75. Bell-shaped
pieces such as this could be ornamental or could serve
as food covers or even candle extinguishers.

Flower basket in free-blown clam-broth glass highlighted by gold striping; England, ▲
late 19th century; $90–105. Clam broth is a popular shade of off-white.

Bohemian vase in milk
glass with enamel decora-
tion; Czechoslovakia,
late 19th–early 20th cen-
tury; $85–115. ▶

Milk-glass eggs in a woven-wire basket; United States,
late 19th century. Eggs; $8–12 each. Basket;
$30–35. False eggs were once used to encourage hens
to lay. ▲

Toothpick holder in pressed milk glass; United States,
mid-19th century; $60–70. A wide variety of milk-
glass objects was used to decorate the Victorian table.
▼

Serving bowl in pressed custard glass; National Glass ▲
Company, United States, early 20th century;
$90–120.

Fairy lamp in fluted yellow and opaque white glass; Venice, Italy, 1865–75; $225–250. ▶

Bud vase in vaseline glass in the hobnail pattern; probably by New England Glass Company, United States, late 19th century; $110–125. ▶

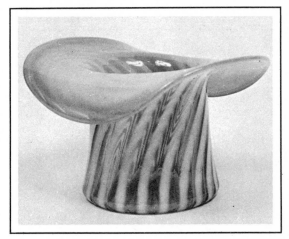

Whimsy in pink-and-white milk glass; England or United States, ▲ *19th century; $110–125. Once thought to have been items made for the use of the glassblowers, whimsies are now known to have been production items.*

Vases in threaded white on orange and green glass; Venice, Italy, 1910–20; ▲ *$165–200 the pair. Venetian craftsmen have long been known for their elaborate wares.*

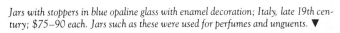

Jars with stoppers in blue opaline glass with enamel decoration; Italy, late 19th century; $75–90 each. Jars such as these were used for perfumes and unguents. ▼

Decanters in clear and green cut overlay glass; Italy, early 20th century; $300–400 the pair.

Bohemian candlesticks in cut and engraved overlay glass in clear and amber; Austria, late 19th century; $125–160 the pair.
▼

◄ Wineglasses in blown glass with threaded stems, decorative prunt work, and engraving; Germany, 19th century; $300–350 the set of 6. These pale-green wineglasses reflect a long tradition of sophisticated German glassmaking.

► Wineglasses in clear blown and molded glass; England, late 19th-early 20th century; $200–250 the set of 6.

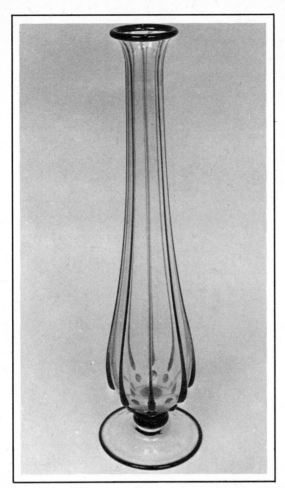

Vase in clear and amber Art Verrier marquetrie-sur-verre glass; France, early 20th century; $165–200. French craftsmen were among the leaders in the art-glass field. ◄

Bohemian ruby glass. Decanter in cut and etched glass; late 19th century; $50–65. Goblets in etched glass; 20th century; $30–35 the pair. ▼

▲ Glass goblets in Vedar enamel; France, ca. 1930; $125–155 the pair. The detailed work on these pieces is of excellent quality.

Goblet in free-blown clear, ruby, and pale-green glass; by Durand, United States, 20th century; $150–175. ◄

Ewer in cranberry glass with silver overlay; France, late 19th century; $150–190. The pierced silver overlay is in a foliate design. ◄

Powder jar and underplate in tortoiseshell glass; Europe, 20th century; $30–40. This glass closely imitates popular but hard-to-obtain natural tortoiseshell. ▲

Tazza and two footed sherberts in ruby glass (from a set of 83 pieces); Czechoslovakia, early 20th century; $450–600 the set. All these pieces are hand blown. ▲

Cocktail set in ruby glass flashed in silver; Europe, 1930–40; $155–180. The Art Deco styling of these pieces is typical of the era. ►

Bud vase in clear crystal overlaid in brass with enamel jewels; Germany, 1920–30; $80–100. This lovely piece is in the Art Deco style. ▶

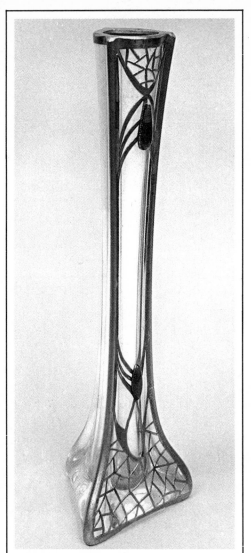

Scroll flask or whiskey bottle in aqua glass; United States, 1825–35; $70–90. Attractive pieces such as this are popular collectors' items. ▼

▲

Mold-formed historical flasks in dark amber glass; United States, 1830–45. Left: Cornucopia; $55–65. Right: Double eagle; $85–115.

Art Nouveau vase in green slag glass with brass overlay; England, 1880–1900; $75–90. The design reflects the more rectilinear English interpretation of Art Nouveau.

◀

▲ *Whiskey flask in light amber glass marked "Lowell Railroad"; United States, 1820–30; $150–180. Called historical flasks, pieces such as this were made in a wide variety.*

Biscuit jar in cut crystal in hobstar and vessica pattern; England or Ireland, late 19th century; $175–215. Though known for centuries, the art of glass cutting reached its zenith during the 1800s. ▼

◄Cut glass; Europe. Left: Pitcher; 20th century; $30–45. Right: Vase, late 19th century; $100–135. The difference in price reflects the fact that the pitcher is of a much later date.

Whiskey bottles in the calabash form; United States, Left: Sheaf of wheat in aqua; $90–110. Right: Hunter/fisher in dark amber; $150–180. ▲

Large punch bowl on stand in cut glass in hobstar and fan pattern; England, late 19th–early 20th century; $325–375. ►

Shallow cut-glass bowl of extremely heavy crystal; Holland, 1880–1900; $90–125. The latticework on the interior of this piece is unusual. ▲

Cruet in cut glass with acorn-form stopper; Europe, late 19th century; $85–105. This delicately cut piece was probably part of a set. ◄

Art Deco cut and enameled glass; France, 1930–40. Left: Ashtray; $75–90. Right: Decanter; $125–145. Both pieces show a bold contrast of black enamel against clear crystal. ▲

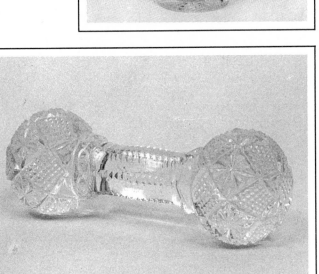

Knife rest in cut glass; Ireland, 1870–85; $30–40. Smaller pieces of cut glass such as this are interesting and inexpensive. ▲

Inkwell in cut glass and brass; England, 20th century; $65–75. Pieces such as this were produced in quantity at the turn of the century. ▶

Pressed glass; United States, 1880–1900. Left: Salt and pepper shakers in yellow-green with Britannia metal tops; $75–90 the pair. Right: Bell in blue glass; ▲ $65–80.

167

Spooner in pressed glass in the diamond-point pattern; Europe, early 20th century; $60–75 ▶

Perfume bottle in gold-washed pressed glass; England, 1865–75; $70–85. This large and elaborate bottle bears an English registry mark. ▼

Comport in pressed glass in graduated and indented thumb-print pattern; Europe late 19th century; $200–250. ▶

◀ Punch bowl and cups (from a set of 8) in pressed glass in the pinwheel-and-fan pattern; by Heisey Manufacturing Company, United States, 20th century; $90–120 the set. Heisey glass is considered highly collectible.

Inkwell in pressed glass; England or Europe, late 19th century; $45–55. Inkwells appeared in many forms during the 1800s. ▶

Decanter and liqueur glasses in iridescent glass; by Louis Comfort Tiffany, United States, early 20th century; $575–700 the set. All Tiffany glass brings high prices. ▼

Cruet set in pressed and molded glass in an electroplated silver stand; United States, 1875–90; $165–200. Every Victorian table had a cruet set. ◀

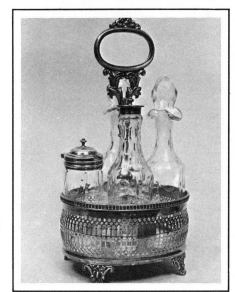

Vase in iridescent blue glass; by Louis Comfort Tiffany, United States, early 20th century; $375–450. Iridescent glass, known as favrile, was Tiffany's most famous creation. ▼

▲ *Candleholders in iridescent glass; by Nash, United States, 1930; $300–400 the pair. Nash succeeded Tiffany and produced ware similar to Tiffany's.*

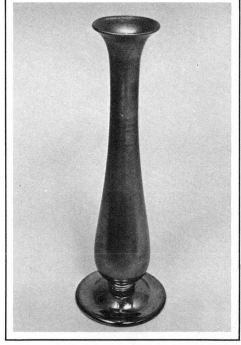

Shades for electric lights in iridescent gold glass; by Quezal, United States, 1901–20; $200–250 the set of 3. ▼

Vase in opalescent glass with handles fashioned in the form of two ▲ rams; by René Lalique, France, 1920–24; $1,200–1,500.

Vase in opalescent glass with design of parrots on a leafy background; by René Lalique, France, ca. 1922; $550–700. Lalique was one of the foremost designers of ▼ French art glass, and his works bring high prices today.

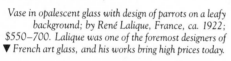

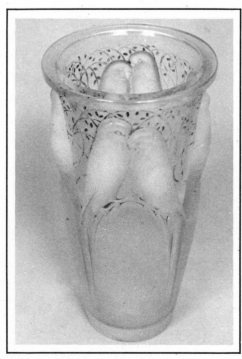

Vase in iridescent pink, green, and blue glass; by Durand Art Glass Company, ▲ United States, 1925–30; $175–235.

170

Bowl in amber glass in the gros scarabees pattern; by
René Lalique, France, 1920–22; $5,000–7,000.
The body of this rare piece is decorated with representations of large beetles, and the details are accented
through the use of white patinated enamel.
◄

Bowl in blue, green, and peach pâté-de-verre glass; by G. Argy-Rousseau, France,
early 20th century; $3,200–3,800. The brilliant hues of pâté-de-verre glass are
achieved by allowing a mixture of crushed glass and metallic colors to harden in a
▼ mold.

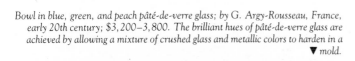

Covered box in pâté-de-verre glass; by G. Argy-Rousseau, France, ▲
early 20th century; $1,500–1,800. The colors in this piece are vio-
let, green, and pink.

Bowl in green and brown
frosted pâté-de-verre
glass; by Decorchemont,
France, early 20th cen-
tury; $1,000–1,200.
►

Ewer in enameled and polished cameo glass; by Daum, Nancy, France, early 20th century; $900–1,200. Cameo glass is produced by cutting through glass of one color to ▼ another layer of glass in a contrasting hue.

Art Deco vase in crystal with etched form of a nude female archer; by Orrefors, Sweden, 20th century; $175–250.

Goblet-form vase in etched green glass; by Daum, Nancy, France, early 20th century; $300–400. Though best known for their cameo glass, the Daum brothers worked in numerous styles. ▼

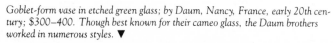

Bud vase in amber glass; by Sabino, France, 1925–35; $300–400. This Art Deco ▲ piece is, like much art glass, marked with the name of its manufacturer.

Urn-shaped vase in
blown glass in shades of
green and rose mottled
with amber; by Charles
Schneider, Germany,
early 20th century;
$175–250.
◄

Vase in rose and amber glass blown into a bronze mount;
by Charles Schneider, Germany, early 20th century;
$85–125. ▼

Octagonal vase in etched
crystal; by Moser, Ger-
many, mid-20th century;
$225–275. A good ex-
ample of later art glass.
▶

Overlay glass; by Emile Galle, France, late 19th century. Left: Handled vase in
peach, lavender, and green; $900–1,200. Right: Vase in open, petal form in pink
and purple; $650–800.

173

Paperweights; 20th century. Left: In pink and white with lilies on a white ground; by Degenhart, France; $75–100. Right: Murano swirl in orange-pink on blue; Venice, Italy; $80–110.

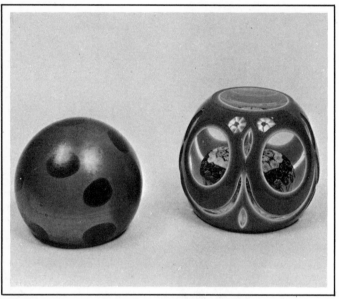

Vase in purple glass streaked with yellow, embellished with figures of women in classical garb playing musical instruments; by Georges De Feure, France, early 20th century; $150–175.

▲ Paperweights; 20th century. Left: In spotted green on amber; by Louis Comfort Tiffany, United States, early 20th century; $100–125. Right: Bohemian double-overlay basket in millefiore and royal blue; $125–150.

▶ Left: Paperweight in millefiore glass; by Clichy, France; $450–500. Center: Paperweight inkwell with stopper in green, white, blue, and mauve; by Whitefriars, England, late 19th century; $550–650. Right: Paperweight in millefiore glass; by Baccarat, France, dated 1968; $175–200.

*Camphene lamps in clam broth and milk glass with brass fittings; United States,
19th century; $300–400 the pair.* ▼

Fairy lamp in milk glass; Europe, late 19th century; ▲
*$150–165. Small lamps like this were used in bedrooms
and nurseries.*

▲
*Sulphide paperweights; France. Left: With bust of Louis Kossuth, Hungarian pa-
triot; by Clichy, 19th century; $450–500. Right: With head of Adlai Stevenson;
by Baccarat, 1960s; $125–150.*

Lamp with pot-metal base and puffy-form shade in reverse painting; by Pairpoint Manufacturing Company, United States, early 20th century; $250–350. ▶

Kerosene lamp in mold-formed teal-blue glass; by Baccarat, France, late 19th century; ▼ $135–150.

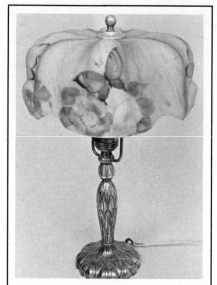

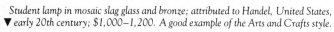
Student lamp in mosaic slag glass and bronze; attributed to Handel, United States, ▼ early 20th century; $1,000–1,200. A good example of the Arts and Crafts style.

Student lamp in bronze with damascene glass shade; by Louis Comfort Tiffany, ▲ United States, late 19th–early 20th century; $2,000–2,500. Tiffany lamps of all sorts are popular and expensive collectibles.

Opposite: Snuff bottle in reverse-painted glass with ivory top; China, late 19th century; $100–135. Chinese artisans made snuff bottles from a great many materials.

A Gallery of World Antiques

Opposite: Cat in faience; marked "E. Galle Nancy," France, 1905–10; $850–1,000. Galle's importance as a designer adds value to even a simple piece of redware. Left: Doll in stuffed cloth and leather with painted face and woven serape; Mexico, 20th century; $60–80. This doll is in the form of a charro, or Mexican cowboy. Bottom left: Doll with bisque head and kid body dressed in greatcoat and leather boots; Germany, late 19th–early 20th century; $500–600.

Top left: Miniature desk clock in gold and gold-color metal; by Van Cleff & Arpels, France, early 20th century; $800–1,000. Top right: Cartel clock in lacquer and mother-of-pearl with gilded frame; France, 19th century; $350–450. Above: Mantel clock in bronze, marble, and glass; France, late 19th century; $850–1,250. Right: Mantel clock in gilded blue pottery with ivory face; Europe, late 19th century; $350–450 (clock is part of a garniture set and price is for clock and two matching urn-form garnitures). Opposite: Mantel clock with green slag-glass case, copper trellis-work overlay, and enamel dial; by Tiffany Studios, United States, ca. 1900; $1,800–2,200.

Opposite: *Figure in gilt bronze of the deity Avalokatesvara; Tibet, 18th century; $450–600.* Top: *Doorstop in cast iron in the form of a bulldog; United States or England, late 19th century; $50–60.* Above: *Large lidded koro in champlevé enamel; Japan, late 19th century; $900–1,200.* Right: *Bear in bronze; by Lieberich, Russia, 19th century; $1,500–2,000.*

Above: Covered urn in polychrome porcelain (one of a pair); by Capodimonte, Italy, mid-19th century; $1,250–1,750 the pair. Above right: Ewer in polychrome porcelain (one of a pair); with artist's mark, Vienna, Austria, 19th century; $1,800–2,500 the pair. Right: Charger in stick spatter polychrome pottery; England, ca. 1870; $625–700. Far right: Covered urn in polychrome decorated porcelain (one of a pair) with gilded mounts; by Limoges, France, 19th century; $1,000–1,300 the pair. Opposite: Miniature urn clock in enamel on metal with gilded bronze fixtures; Switzerland, ca. 1890; $2,000–2,300. A very unusual small clock.

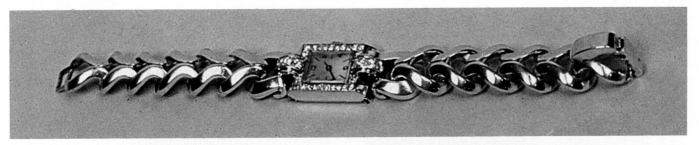

Opposite: Brooch in gold set
with diamonds, rubies, and opals;
France, late 19th–early 20th
century; $2,300–3,000. Top:
Lady's wristwatch in gold set
with diamonds and diamond chips;
France, 20th century; $850–1,100.
Above: Bracelet in jadeite and
gold with elaborate foliate
openwork; Europe, 1880–1900;
$750–1,000. Above right:
Pocketwatch in gold and yellow
metal with enamel dial; by
J. W. Benson, London, England,
1890–1910; $400–500. Right:
Bangle bracelet in gold set
with small rose-cut diamonds
and with clasp in the form of
two bull heads; India, 19th
century; $4,000–5,000.

Opposite: Miniature cupboard in
walnut with glass doors and brass
pulls; England, 19th century;
$400–500. Top left: Sauce boat in
silver with leaf-capped scroll
handle and reeded body; Vienna,
Austria, 19th century; $550–750.
Left: Miniature kerosene lamp in
satin glass; United States, ca.
1900; $150–190. Sometimes called
"fairy lamps," small lights such
as this were used in bedrooms and
nurseries. Above: Vase in overlay
glass; by Emile Galle, Nancy,
France, ca. 1900; $550–700.

Left: Ink pot in pewter; England, 1840–50; $90–120. Like much 19th-century pewter, this piece was turned to shape on a lathe, a process called spinning. Below left: Islamic hanging lamp base in brass with perforated decoration; Near East, 12th–13th century; $250–325. Much brass was produced in the Near East. Below: Tea pot in cast iron with embossed decoration; Japan, mid-19th century; $85–135. Iron pots have long been used in the Japanese tea ceremony. Opposite: Empire style candelabrum (one of a pair) in bronze and ormolu; France, 19th century; $900–1,200 the pair.

Above: Panel (one of a pair) in carved wood; China, 20th century; $90–120 the pair. Right: Embroidery picture of two fighting cocks; China, early 20th century; $175–250. Opposite left: Folk figure of a cock in polychrome carved wood; France, 20th century; $75–100. Opposite right: Rug in woven wool; China, 20th century; $100–150. Chinese rugs are distinctly different, both in color and in pattern, from those woven in the Near East.

193

Opposite: *Side chair (one of a set of four) in walnut inlaid
with satinwood and ivory; Italy, 19th century; $2,500–3,200
the set. Above: Writing desk in ebonized wood inlaid with
ivory; Italy, 19th century; $1,500–2,000. Sophisticated inlay
work is the hallmark of the European cabinetmaker.*

Above: Herez rug in woven wool;
early 20th century; $225–300.
Right: Geometric crazy quilt in
silk and satin; United States, 19th
century; $200–250. Bold forms and
colors are the hallmark of better
American quilts. Opposite:
Lilihan rug in woven wool with
stylized floral pattern; 20th
century; $125–175. Even small
Oriental rugs bring good prices
in today's seller's market.

196

Top: *Jardiniere (one of a pair) in cloisonné; China, 19th century; $750–950 the pair.* Above: *Bookend (one of a pair) in pâté de verre; by Amalric Walter, Nancy, France, 20th century; $1,800–2,200.* Opposite: *Marriage cup in silver; Austria-Hungary, early 20th century; $450–600.*

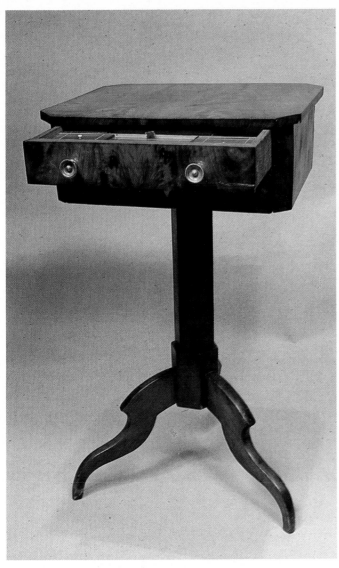

Opposite: *Figure of a Fudo, or celestial guardian, in carved and gilded wood; Japan, late 19th–early 20th century; $600–800. Much Japanese carving is of a religious nature.* Above: *Regency two-drawer stand in walnut; England, 19th century; $450–575. Walnut often served as a substitute for mahogany.* Right: *Figure of a Kuan Yin in carved amber; Japan, late 19th–early 20th century; $145–195. A soft and attractive material, amber is popular with Oriental carvers.*

Right: Bracelet in the form of a belt and buckle in gold, diamond, and enamel; probably United States, 19th century; $650–850. Below right: Jeweled compact in silver gilt with a cover encrusted with emeralds, rubies, and sapphires; probably from France, ca. 1910; $1,000–1,350. Bottom right: Brooch of white and yellow gold with an openwork design centering a large amethyst; England, 19th century; $500–600. Opposite: Gueridon in mahogany; designed by Louis Majorelle, France, ca. 1895; $2,200–2,650. The sinuous lines of this piece are typical of the Art Nouveau.

Top: Face mask in polychrome wood; by Ba Teke, Congo, early 20th century; $125–175. Above: Netsuke figure of two skeletons in carved wood; Japan, 19th century; $125–175. Right: Mask in polychrome carved wood; by Shalish, northwest coast United States, early 20th century; $400–550. Masks made by the coastal tribes are now eagerly sought by collectors of primitive art. Opposite: Pre-Columbian figure in polychrome earthenware of a seated man; by Chinesco, South America, 1300–1500; $350–500. Much high-quality folk pottery has been unearthed in South America.

Top: *Face mask in polychrome wood; by
Ba Teke, Congo, early 20th century;
$125–175.* Above: *Netsuke figure of
two skeletons in carved wood; Japan,
19th century; $125–175.* Right: *Mask
in polychrome carved wood; by Shalish,
northwest coast United States, early
20th century; $400–550. Masks made
by the coastal tribes are now eagerly
sought by collectors of primitive
art.* Opposite: *Pre-Columbian
figure in polychrome earthenware
of a seated man; by Chinesco, South
America, 1300–1500; $350–500. Much
high-quality folk pottery has been
unearthed in South America.*

Opposite: *Embroidered sampler; England, Ireland, or United States, dated 1823; $250–325. Since samplers from the English-speaking world are very similar, it is difficult to attribute them precisely.* Above: *Carved and painted model of a 19th-century sailing ship with properly rigged sails and lines; England or United States, 1900–10; $175–250. Many ship models were made by sailors or shipyard employees.* Left: *Portrait in oil on canvas; United States, 19th century; $600–750. Folk painting provided family records until replaced in the 1850s by photography.*

*Woven embroidery picture of a warship; England,
1840–70; $300–400. Embroidery pictures of ships are
rather uncommon.*

10

Primitive and Folk Art

For a long time now, many collectors have been drawn to certain sculpture and painting that falls outside the Western academic tradition—works by artists who were not concerned with the traditions of perspective, color mixing, and realism that, at least until the twentieth century, were the foundations of European art. The terminology is occasionally in dispute, but this nonacademic art may be divided into two categories: primitive art, which is that done by painters and sculptors working in societies outside the influence of traditional Western and Eastern art centers; and folk art, which is work done by untrained artists who live in but are largely unaffected by the academic art of the developed societies.

Though it appears in many areas of the world, the great centers for primitive art are Africa; Oceania; and the northwest coast of North America, including those areas inhabited by the Inuit, or Eskimo. At an earlier time similar work was done in South America, and pre-Columbian pottery and metal- and stonework are often classified as primitive.

Anyone with the most rudimentary knowledge of the great precolonial cultures of Africa and South America will question the use of the term "primitive" for the art of those cultures, but the above categorization has existed for many years and is generally accepted by collectors.

Primitive artworks differ in significant ways from the art produced in those societies that are generally regarded as more advanced. The craftsmen in an African village or on the island of New Zealand were usually creating religious works, in the sense that their carvings or paintings were designed to placate certain deities to assure a good hunt or a good crop or to be used in rituals associated with the tribal faith. This was a great responsibility in societies in which survival often depended on uncontrollable and unpredictable natural forces. Artists were often, as in parts of Africa, members of a priestly class or, as in New Guinea, held their posts as a hereditary privilege. Regardless of how they came by their posts, these artists were professionals, whose work conformed to certain concepts of form and design traditional in the community and whose continued success depended in large part on the results their efforts produced.

African art is to a great extent concerned with the men's societies, secret groups that played a major role in the life of most tribes. The men's groups traditionally performed sacred dances designed to bring luck in the chase or in war, and these dances required numerous carved and/or painted masks. Made in traditional forms that vary from tribe to tribe, such masks are among the most common and most desirable of all African artifacts. However, African carvers also produced and continue to produce (for the craft is not extinct, though it has diminished in quality) figures of the gods, fertility figures, and various animal forms.

African masks and figures are made from ivory, bone, leather, various basketry materials, or all in combination, but the traditional medium is wood. This may be painted or it may be embellished with various shells, grasses, or even human hair. In all cases, though, the form is basically abstract, for the carver was not seeking an exact rendition of the subject matter. Indeed, since in many cases the subject matter was a god or spirit, such a goal would have been impossible to achieve. What the artist sought was to capture the spirit or essence of the object—those of its essential characteristics (lightness and swiftness in a bird, for example) that would make it immediately recognizable to his audience. This is, of course, similar to the goal of many twentieth-century artists and explains, at least in part, the great interest in African art manifested by some cubist and abstract-expressionist painters.

Folk carving was done throughout most of Black Africa, and some of the finest examples come from the areas that are today Zaire and Mali. The former, once known as the Congo, has produced a variety of carved masks and figures, including the extraordinarily sophisticated ivory face masks done by the Bwame society in the Kinshasa area. Perhaps the best-known of the Mali types is the headdress called a Bambara Chi-Wara, an extremely graceful animal abstraction.

Folk artists in that huge area of sea and islands known as Polynesia have created works of great interest. On the large islands such as New Guinea and New Zealand many different types of wood were available, and carvers created elaborate designs on doorposts, house gables, and canoe prows. Where less material was obtainable the sculptor confined himself to ritual figures, masks, and the embellishment of weapons and household objects. In all cases, the carving was extremely abstract and intricate and was often highlighted by the use of color in flat planes. Among the more popular of these creations are those from the Fiji Islands, the Solomons, and New Guinea, where pieces from the Sepik River area are especially well thought of.

Unlike the situation in Africa, the impulse toward creation has largely expired in Polynesia. Overwhelmed by modern society, from which the vastnesses of the ocean offered them surprisingly little protection, the people of this area have abandoned the old gods and their images altogether or have substituted for them bizarre sects such as the cargo cult with its faith in the white gods who will drop food from airplanes. The crude renditions of planes produced by these believers have little appeal to most Western collectors.

Some of the world's most remarkable primitive painting and carving was the product of the Indian tribes that lived along a thousand-mile stretch of northwestern American coast from Washington to southern Alaska. Blessed by a mild climate and an abundance of fish and game, such tribes as the Salish of Washington and the Nootka and Kwakiutl of Vancouver Island indulged themselves in orgies of ritualistic gift-giving, called potlatches, and in the creation of highly sophisticated art forms.

209

Their best-known works are the gigantic totem poles that stood in front of the homes of wealthy and influential tribesmen and the large carved canoes and house fronts that served to proclaim the power of those who ruled. Similar objects are found among the different tribal groups, and their work is united by a common technique and design style, though subtle differences in approach to the subject matter make it possible for the knowledgeable to distinguish between, for example, a Haida dance mask and one made by a Salish carver.

The work is highly abstract, with representations of sacred or mythological animals, such as the killer whale, wolf, and lightning snake worked into the design. Color, such as the characteristic blue green, red, and black, is very important; experts generally agree that the Northwest Coast tribes were painters before they were carvers. Once metal tools became available through white traders, the tribal carvings grew far larger and more elaborate. It is interesting to note that, unlike most primitive cultures, the coastal tribes seemed to thrive on contact with the West, and were able to employ new tools and new concepts to enhance their own creativity and to foster a trade in tourist-oriented objects that was thriving as early as 1850.

Most examples from this area are representations of deities or characters from extraordinarily complex tribal and family histories. Scenes from these tales were often painted on large cedar boards, a type of mural art rare among primitive peoples. More frequently encountered are totemic animals and deities represented by masks carved to be worn by dancers in performances that may be either religious or intended purely for entertainment.

North of the coastal tribes live the Eskimo, or Inuit, as they now prefer to be called. These people were carving bone, especially ivory, as far back as 400 B.C. While some of the woodland Inuit worked in wood and produced masks not wholly unlike those of the Northwest Coast, the majority used what was available to them—prehistoric and walrus ivory. Objects in this material, particularly the earlier ones, tend to be small, and the most common items are amulets designed to bring luck in hunting and small animal figures employed as pieces in gambling games. Though stylized, Inuit carvings are generally more naturalistic in quality than those of the Indians.

Following the Second World War the traditional ways of living of the Inuit began to change, and with a reduction in the role of the hunter there was less need for amulets and religious effigies (the efficacy of which had already been put in doubt by white missionaries). When restrictions on the taking of game and the use of ivory were imposed in the early 1950s the Inuit turned to stone carving. They had always been excellent carvers, and even before 1900 they had been making engraved cribbage boards and similar items for sale to white traders and tourists.

Lacking ivory, they now began to employ soapstone, jade, and greenstone in the creation of naturalistic but highly sophisticated carvings of men, women, and children. Carefully shaped and polished, these contemporary pieces (few date to before 1948) work very well in today's surroundings, and they are eagerly collected. Modern Inuit sculpture, especially signed pieces, represents an attractive area for the antiques investor.

Folk art, as opposed to primitive art, is a by-product of Western and, to some extent, Eastern civilization. In every highly developed society there have been craftsmen whose job was to create necessary carved and painted objects such as signposts, ships' figureheads, and decorative house carving. In some cases, as with the makers of religious or votive figures for use in churches and family chapels, their role was analogous to that of the primitive deity-carver. Good examples of this kind of artwork are the *santos* figures that can be found in the Spanish-settled areas of North and South America and the simple representations of Amida Buddha common in roadside shrines throughout Japan.

The great majority of folk artists, however, did work of a purely secular nature, and in most cases did not even think of themselves as "artists"—that name was applied to them at a later date by antiquarians and collectors. They were just men and women doing a job. This job might consist of any number of things. In France during the eighteenth century itinerant painters might one day paint a shop or tavern sign or refurbish a barn wall and on the next day do a traditional homecoming portrait for a soldier. In England artists depicted in oil the fat prize cattle that competed for awards at the country fair, and in the United States they set down for posterity the homes of wealthy farmers and the factories of the new industrial barons.

In most cases such paintings had a flat stylized look more on the order of modern advertising or "pop" art than the academic art of the period. In the more charming examples the colors were bold and the relationship of figures reflected the artist's preference or whim rather than reality. Thus a child might tower above a house or a chicken peer down at a man. These naive qualities have a certain appeal to the modern collector, and folk art, both nineteenth century and later, brings a high price.

Like folk painting, folk sculpture grew out of daily tasks. Half-models used in ship design gave birth to fully rigged models of sailing ships. Quaint shop signs, the shapes of which (such as a large shoe or spectacles or a mortar and pestle) were intended to provide information to those who could not read, have become valued as pieces of sculpture and are hung on walls alongside brightly colored game boards, weathervanes, and even fragments of Victorian gingerbread moldings.

As one might expect from their essentially common heritage, the categories of folk art and sculpture are very similar in Europe and North America. In some cases, particularly wood carving, European examples are more elaborately shaped and decorated or more brightly painted (as with Scandinavian wall paintings or eastern European folk toys), but all too often European and North American pieces are so similar that they lead to confusion in the mind of the collector. As an example, the carving and painting of the Germanic settlers of Pennsylvania can easily be confused with that of Germany and parts of central Europe.

It is interesting to note that the collecting of folk art has its largest number of devotees in North America. Despite the abundance of such painting and sculpture in England and on the Continent, it has only been quite recently that dealers and collectors there have begun to acquire it. The same may be said of Japan, which has a long history of folk carving. For hundreds of years religious and secular figures have been carved and sold at temples and during holidays, but it is only within the past decade that anthropologists have begun to study this rich folk heritage and collectors and museums to acquire it. Even today it is possible to acquire excellent examples of folk sculpture in the rural provinces of Japan.

One of the reasons for the booming interest in primitive and folk art is that it speaks directly to the heart and reminds one on a conscious or subconscious level of the hopes, the aspirations, and the essential unity of all mankind. For this reason alone it should have a special place in the collecting world.

Carving of a seated cat on a rectangular wooden base; Egypt, mid-19th century; $150–200. This piece is a copy, one of many made of tomb figures during the 1800s. ▶

Reliquary figure in ▲ carved wood covered with strips of hammered brass and brass wire; by Ba Kota, Congo, late 19th century; $1,000–1,500. Highly stylized figures such as this greatly influenced Western art.

◀

Sarcophagus mask in wood with brown face with black eyes and black-and-white beard; Egypt, 7th century; $800–1,000. Masks such as this are among the oldest folk forms.

Carving in bone of stylized human figures supporting ▲ totemic heads; by Ba Lega, Congo, late 19th century; $300–400. This piece of dark bone has been highly polished.

Divination board decorated with elaborately carved heads and geometric border; by ▲ Yoruba Ifa, Nigeria, early 20th century; $350–400. An interesting and uncommon form.

Dagger in carved and fire-hardened wood decorated with a stylized death mask of clay with inlaid cowrie shells, boar's tusks, and polychrome paint; Sepik River, New Guinea, late 19th century; $220–270. ▶

Staff-form stylized wood carving in pink, yellow, and tan; New Guinea, late 19th–early 20th century; $175–235. Most oceanic carving was done in softwood and had a short life. ▼

▲ Elaborately carved animal form of Bambara Chi-Wara in hardwood with brass earrings; Mali, early 20th century; $300–400. These figures are extremely popular with Western collectors and are reproduced in large numbers.

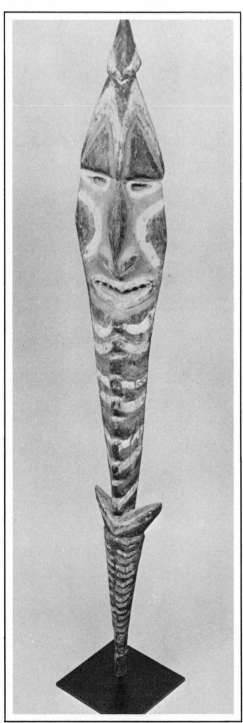

▶

Figure in carved wood with red painted body and black pants; Congo, 20th century; $125–175. This figure reflects the influence of Western forms and concepts on African art.

Pre-Columbian carved stone figure; Central America, 1300–1400; $125–175. Though quite old, much pre-Columbian folk art is reasonably priced. This is due in part to its abundance and in part to the large number of reproductions on the market.

Figural effigy in red ▲ clay; by Colima, Central America, 13th–14th century; $250–350. Vessels incorporating more than one figure are relatively rare.

◀
Carved and painted house mask inlaid with cowrie shells set in clay and decorated with raffia and boar's tusks; Sepik River, New Guinea, late 19th– early 20th century; $300–375. Primitive art from the Pacific is highly prized.

Wood carving with polychrome painting in pink, white, tan, and ▲ black, by Washkuk, Polynesia, early 20th century; $250–300. Most pieces from this area are highly stylized.

Cat effigy vessel in black clay touched with white; ▲ by Tiahuanco, Mexico, 800–1100; $200–300. Many pre-Columbian pieces had a ritual purpose.

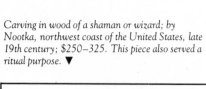

Carving in wood of a shaman or wizard; by
Nootka, northwest coast of the United States, late
19th century; $250–325. This piece also served a
ritual purpose. ▼

► Well-formed spouted vessel in the form
of a man in baked red clay touched
with white; by Chavin, Central
America, 13th–15th century;
$650–800.

► Figure of a man with a ball on his
shoulder, probably a player in a ritual
game, in pink clay; by Jalisco, Mexico,
100 B.C.–A.D. 250; $225–275.

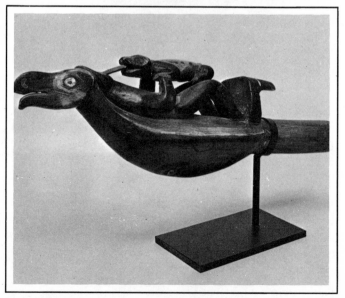

Fish-form ritual vessel of gray clay molded and ▲
decorated with incised patterns; by Chimu, Central
America, 900–1400; $150–200.

Carved and painted wooden rattle in the form of a lizard atop a ▲
supine human figure both borne by a large bird; by Nootka, northwest coast of the United States, late 19th century; $500–650. The
coastal tribes have produced some of the world's most sophisticated
primitive carving.

Carving in greenstone of a parka-clad man dancing; by Eskimo, Canada, mid-20th century; $650–800. Once great bone carvers, the Eskimos have lately turned to stone carving, and their products are in great demand. ▼

Stone carving of a stylized human figure; by Northern Quiche, Guatemala, 400–100 B.C.; $150–200. Many small figures such as this have been found in graves. ▼

Game counters in ivory in the form of seals and a seal head; by Eskimo, Thule culture, United States, 1100–1300; $100–125 each. These pieces were used in a game similar to jacks. ▼

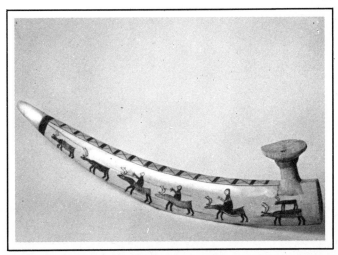

Hunting amulets in carved ivory in the form of foxes; by Eskimo, ▲ Fort Barrow, Alaska, area, late 19th century; $150–180 each.

Pipe in carved and scrimshaw-decorated ivory; by Eskimo, United ▲ States, late 19th century; $1,200–1,600. The Eskimos are among the world's great bone carvers, and their pieces bring high prices.

Group of miniature paintings in oil paint on ivory, including portraits of sultans and sultanas and views of various palaces; India, late 19th century; $1,200–1,600. ▶

Carving in teakwood of a mounted elder bearing a religious image on his back; China, 20th century; $300–400. Though of no great age, this piece is a fine example of sophisticated wood carving. ▶

▲ Tantric painting in watercolor on paper of a demon; India, mid-19th century; $200–300. Rare today, these paintings were once common devotional aids.

▶ Figure of a Buddha in carved and gilded wood in a traveling case; China, late 19th century; $200–275. The lacquered case closes to protect the figure while it is in transit.

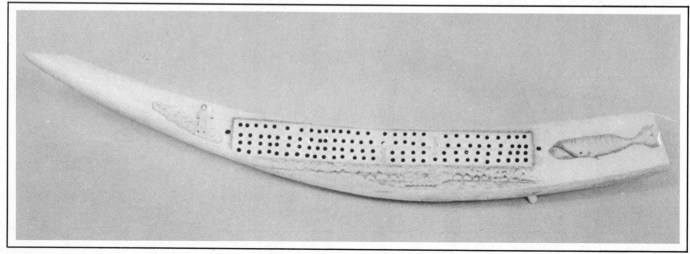

Cribbage board in carved walrus tusk decorated with scrimshaw representations ▲ of a village, a whale, and an Eskimo hunter; by Eskimo, United States, 1910–20; $850–1,100.

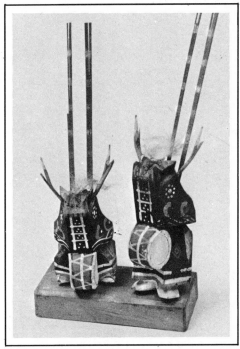

Wall pouch in carved and polychrome wood, corn silk, cloth, and rice straw representing a lion dancer; Japan, early 20th century; $60–75. ▶

Folk figures in carved and polychrome wood; Japan, early ▲ *20th century; $50–70. Small figures such as those were sold for a few pennies at shrines and during street fairs.*

◀

Mask in carved wood for use in a Kabuki play; Japan, early 20th century; $90–120. Carvings of characters from the traditional Kabuki plays are popular Japanese folk objects. Other commonly seen characters are an old man and a young woman.

Figures in carved wood with gilded and polychrome decoration; ▲ *China, 20th century; $125–165 the pair.*

Figures of elders in carved and polychrome wood; China, late 19th ▲ *century; $100–135 each. Note the excellent detail in the piece at the left.*

Santos group in carved and painted wood; South America, early 20th century; $200–250. Santos ("Saints") are placed in churches or home shrines. The carved figures are called bultos, while similar paintings are known as retablos. ▼

Figure of Kwannon in carved ivory; signed by Yoko, Japan, ca. 1900; $200–275. Bosatsu Kwannon is the Japanese deity most closely associated with Buddha. ▼

Bulto in carved and painted wood; ▲ Mexico, late 19th century; $100–125. Most bultos represent saints or members of the holy family.

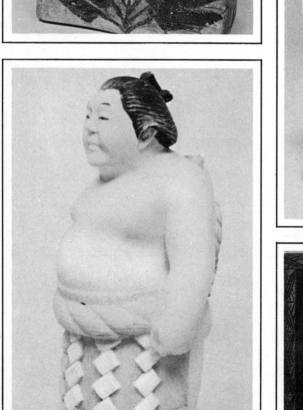

Figure of a sumo wrestler in ceremonial costume; ▲ Japan, early 20th century; $250–325. Sumo masters, who are always large men, engage in a highly stylized form of wrestling.

One of a pair of ivory and lacquerware pictures depict- ▲ ing birds and flowers; Japan, 20th century; $100–125 the pair.

Mule in carved and painted cottonwood, probably a ▲ shop figure; southwestern United States, late 19th century; $900–1,200. Shop signs and figures are popular collectibles.

Representation of a leaping salmon in carved ▲ and painted wood; Canada, 20th century; $120–160. A good example of 20th-century folk art.

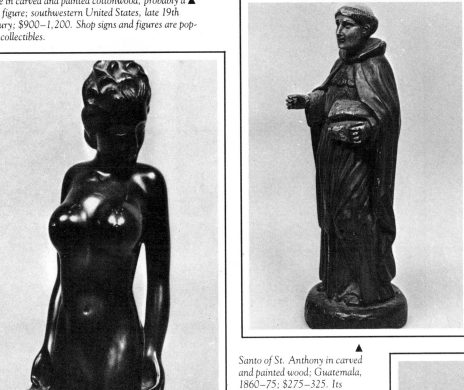

Bulto of Christ in carved and painted wood; Central America, late 19th century; $135–185. Most santos figures were made by professional carvers who earned a living selling the figures to churches and private individuals. ▼

Santo of St. Anthony in carved and painted wood; Guatemala, 1860–75; $275–325. Its greater sophistication marks this piece as the work of a trained sculptor. ▲

◄ Figure of a woman in carved teakwood; Guatemala, mid-20th century; $100–150. This piece is similar to those made in the Philippines for sale to tourists.

Human figure carved from a branch; central Europe, early
20th century; $120–150. ▼

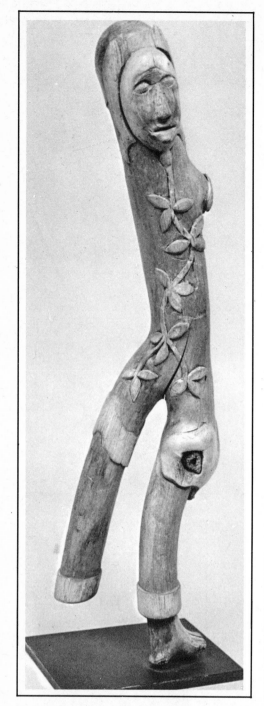

Trade sign in the form of a bear in carved and gilded wood; Canada, mid-19th ▲
century; $2,500–2,800. This fine piece was once in a western Canadian
trading post.

Barber's trade figure in the form of a razor in wood painted black and silver; Europe
or United States, early 20th century; $175–250. These pieces appear frequently on
both sides of the Atlantic. ▼

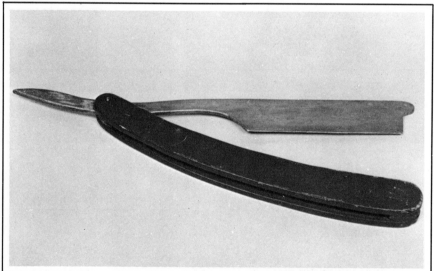

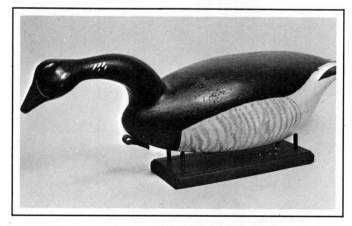

Canada goose decoy in carved and painted wood; New Brunswick, Canada, ▲
20th century; $225–275.

Merganser decoy in carved and painted wood; United States, early 20th century; ▲
$150–200. Decoys are among the most popular and most available of folk carvings.

Swan decoy in carved and painted wood; by Herters, United States, early 20th century; $750–850. Swan decoys are uncommon and much sought after. ▼

Model of Sicilian cart in carved and painted wood and papier-mâché; Italy, early 20th century; $125–175. Festive carts like this are still made in Sicily. ▼

Small head in carved wood with black paint; United States, 19th century; $150–200. This folk carving is probably a representation of George Washington. ◀

Small crudely carved squirrel in wood painted red; United States, early 20th century; $65–80. ▼

Figure of a woman in carved wood with traces of paint; ▲ Italy, 16th–17th century; $650–750. This piece probably decorated a church.

Representation of an ox cart in carved and painted wood; Europe, late 19th–early 20th century; $100–150. A model of a crude plow is in the cart. ▼

Watermelon in carved and painted wood; United States, mid-20th century; $35–40. An interesting example of contemporary folk sculpture. ▼

▲ *Model of a 1930s automobile in tin and wood; United States, early 20th century; $100–125.*

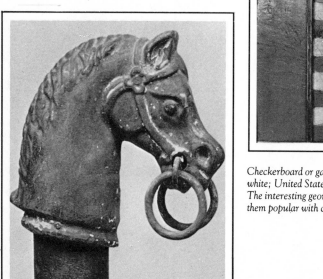

Checkerboard or game board of pine painted green and ▲ *white; United States, early 20th century; $150–200. The interesting geometric form of these boards make them popular with contemporary collectors.*

◀

Detail of horse head in cast iron; United States, late 19th century; $145–175. This head is the finial for a hitching post.

Whirligig or wind toy in carved pine and maple painted red, white, and blue; United States, 20th century; $145–185. Many whirligigs have been made during the past century. ▼

Weathervane in the form of a cow in copper with traces of original gilding; United States, late 19th century; $2,200–2,500. Large and attractive vanes bring high prices. ▼

▲ Miniature weathervane in the form of a plow in wrought iron and sheet iron; United States, 1860–70; $900–1,000.

Whale's tooth decorated with scrimshaw representation of a spouting whale; United States, 20th century; $100–150. The popularity of scrimshaw has led to many later reproductions, such as this one. ▼

Weathervane in the form of a fish in carved and painted wood; Canada, early 20th century; $500–600. The earliest weathervanes were generally hand shaped from wood or wrought iron. ▶

Half-hull architect's model of a sailing ship; by G. Smith, Rye, England, mid-19th century; $200-300. ▼

Large hanging tavern sign in oil paint on wood; England, late 19th century; $1,200–1,700. Trade signs, especially those in good condition, bring substantial prices on today's market. ▼

Folk painting in oil paint on artist's board of a village scene; France, 20th century; ▲ *$125–175. The market for later folk painting like this is developing rapidly and has high investment potential.*

Whale's tooth decorated with scrimshaw likeness of ▲ *Benjamin Franklin, United States, late 19th century; $400–500. Good sailors' scrimshaw brings big prices.*

Folk painting in oil paint on board of a river and city; Italy, late 19th century; ▲ *$175–225. Note the excellent detail.*

◄
Folk painting in oil paint on board of a New England farmhouse with attached barns; United States, late 19th–early 20th century; $900–1,000. Folk painting of this period now brings high prices.

Over-mantel painting of two vases of flowers in oil paint on board; United States, early 19th century; $1,400–1,500. Over-mantel paintings were placed over a fireplace. ▼

Small but appealing seascape in oil paint on tin, featuring a lighthouse and several ▲ ships at sea; Holland, 19th century; $300–400.

Folk painting in oil paint on canvas of balloon in a small village; France, 20th ▲ century; $150–200. Another example of appealing contemporary folk art.

Silhouette of a man in a pillbox hat; England, late 19th century; $75–100. Until the camera became well established, the silhouette was the least expensive likeness available. ▼

Silhouette of a man sitting in an Empire style chair ▲ *with touches of watercolor; England, 1850–60; $200–250. A complex "shade" like this required much more skill than the usual bust.*

Sandpaper painting of a Hudson River scene; United States, late 19th century; $200–275. Sandpaper paintings, which were made with charcoal or chalk on a piece of sandpaper, were a popular Victorian pastime. ▼

Portrait in oil paint on tin, "Abagail Bunk": United States, early ▲ *19th century; $700–900. A small but appealing picture.*

Chalkware grouping of child with animals; Europe or United States, mid-19th century; $225–250. Though of great interest to some American collectors, almost all of these inexpensive figures appear to have been made in Europe, particularly in Italy. ▼

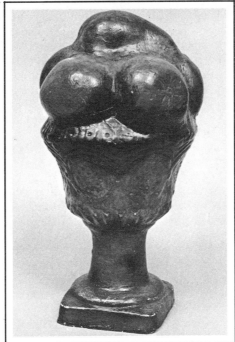

Reverse painting on glass of a still life with ▲ bee and compote of fruit; England or United States, late 19th century; $350–500. An extremely well executed example of a difficult art.

◀

Chalkware representation of a compote of fruit; Europe or United States, mid-19th century; $325–375. Made in molds, these pieces were often copies of ceramic mantel figures such as those produced at Staffordshire.

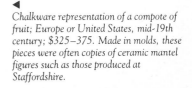

Theorum painting in watercolor on velvet; United States, 1835–50; $700–800. ▲ Theorems were executed with stencils and were once a traditional woman's art.

Still life in oil paint on canvas in the Victorian style; United States, late 19th ▲ century; $400–500.

11

Textiles

Whether in the form of rugs, bed coverings, or clothing, textiles have long been a necessity in every culture. Hand-woven tapestries have been found in Egyptian tombs, embroidery was practiced in India as early as the fourth century B.C., and textile dyeing was common in pre-Columbian South America. The techniques practiced—quilting, batiking, brocading—are as varied as the cultures whence they come.

Perhaps the best-known and most sought after textiles are rugs, particularly the hand-knotted, woven floor coverings, bag faces, and the like manufactured from Turkey to China. Known generally as Oriental rugs and carpets (the term *rug* is applied to pieces six feet by nine feet or less), these textiles have traditionally served, particularly among nomadic herdsmen, not only as floor coverings but as cushions, beds, and wall hangings.

The earliest known Oriental rugs date from the third century B.C., but the extreme sophistication in technique and design evident even at that early period indicates a much longer history. Most examples available to collectors were made during the past century, and even these frequently bring high prices.

To the uninitiated, such textiles may look very much alike, but there are distinct regional types. Probably the best-known types are Persian rugs, such as the Heriz and the Kirman (originally rug names referred to the locality where a certain type was produced or to the ethnic group that made it, but today such nomenclature refers to specific designs regardless of where they were manufactured). Persian weavings are characterized by abstract renditions of floral and animal forms and often remind the viewer of a formal garden.

Turkish rugs are much more abstract and geometric in design than Persian rugs, and their colors are brighter than the mellow pastels associated with Persians. The most common form of Turkish rug is the prayer rug, with its design dominated by the mihrab, or pointed arch panel, in which believers kneel when at prayer. There are single and double prayer rugs and characteristic types include the Oushak, Mudjur, and Ghiordes.

Caucasian rugs have a deep, "wooly" pile and are characterized by bold, primary colors (until the late nineteenth century these colors were produced from natural dyes) and markedly geometric designs. Better-known Caucasian forms are the Kouba, the Kazak, and the Chichi.

Chinese and Turkestan textiles are somewhat less popular with collectors. Although they were exposed to Western rug-making influences, Chinese artisans appear to have begun making such textiles no earlier than the seventeenth century. Their products are a blend of imported design elements and native motifs, resulting nevertheless in extremely sophisticated compositions in pale blues, yellows, and tans.

Lying between Persia and China, the area known as Turkestan has produced rugs that reflect the influences of both major cultures. For example, pieces from Khotan and Samarkand sometimes employ the typical Chinese tendril-and-lotus design with the strong reds and blues seen in Turkish carpets rather than the softer Chinese hues.

Oriental rugs are extremely popular with collectors, and modern, factory-woven examples vie with earlier pieces for the enthusiast's dollar. Since few such textiles were ever signed, and since traditional patterns have been used for hundreds of years, it is frequently difficult to date Oriental rugs. Experts examine the weave (which may be one of two knotted types, the Sehna, or Persian, or the Ghiordes, or Turkish; or of a flat weave known as the Kilim), the material composition, and the dyes used. Novices are advised to rely on a reputable dealer.

Well-to-do Europeans have been buying Oriental rugs since the time of Marco Polo, but it was not until the seventeenth century that a viable rug industry was established on the Continent. Hand-woven floral and pictorial tapestries were being made in France and Belgium as far back as the 1300s, and for several hundred years the cold, dank walls of European castles were brightened by these brilliantly colored textiles. Rug making also arose in France, where King Henry IV established a shop at the Louvre in 1605. Twenty-two years later the master weaver at this shop, Pierre Dupont, became a partner in a new shop, the famous Savonnerie carpet factory. Finely made Savonneries set the standard for European carpet manufacture until the early 1800s, though they were not without rivals, notably the products of Aubusson (established in 1743), Beauvais (established in 1787), and the great English centers at Axminster and Wilton.

The products of these shops were intended for the halls of the very rich. Even during the 1700s few others could afford any sort of floor coverings. Wooden floors were generally painted in bright colors or covered with a linoleumlike material. Even during the nineteenth century, when the introduction of machine-made carpets made it possible for the middle class to cover their floors with imitations of Amxinsters and Savonneries, many people wove their own.

Among the more notable homemade rugs are the hooked ones made in the United States and Canada. With a burlap foundation and made from old rags, shredded and dyed, hooked rugs imitated everything from Oriental and American Indian textiles to quilts. Most popular with contemporary collectors, though, are the pictorial rugs, which may be adorned with anything from a cat or a cow to a whole village scene.

Weaving was employed for the making of textiles other than rugs, carpets, and tapestries. Woven bed covers or coverlets were produced by many European and North American shops during the eighteenth and nineteenth centuries. Initially these pieces were in geometric patterns because the small looms on which they were produced could create only angular patterns. However, in the early 1800s a Frenchman, Joseph Jacquard, invented a loom attachment that made it possible to create elaborate curvilinear designs.

Though they were also made in Europe and the British Isles,

the so-called Jacquard coverlets reached their greatest development in the United States and Canada, where spectacular examples in red and white or blue and white or up to four different colors were adorned with pictorial compositions that included anything from lions and peacocks to railroad trains and the Great Seal of the United States.

Jacquard coverlets were always a commercial venture, and in time they came to be made in large, water-powered factories. But there was another, simpler form of loom weaving done in North America. In the Southwestern states and in Mexico Indians and Spanish-speaking settlers turned out small rugs, saddle blankets, and capes on crude but efficient hand looms. Often called Navajo rugs in honor of the people who produced many of the finest examples, these textiles feature powerful abstract compositions and dynamic primary colors, such as red, black, and blue. Made for sale since the late 1800s, they are still in sufficient demand for the ancient craft to continue today.

Spanish American weavers also produced loomed woolen textiles, including shawls, floor coverings, and blankets. Usually more complex in design than Indian examples, the majority of these pieces were made in the Chimayo valley of New Mexico, the only place where the craft is still practiced.

Not all textiles were created on looms; most, in fact, were not. Embroidery, the ornamenting of cloth with various needlework stitches, has a particularly long and distinguished history. It appeared in India at an early date and was practiced extensively in the Greek islands of the Aegean, where both skirts and bed hangings were covered with formalized floral patterns, often on a red cloth background. In North Africa the patterns, which were frequently embroidered in red or blue silk, were cruder in concept and larger, often consisting of one or two large flowers surrounded by a floral border.

Continental European embroidery is highlighted by samplers and ornamental needlework pictures. The former appeared at an early date (the first written reference is from 1502) and consisted in most cases of a series of letters and numbers embroidered on a linen background along with various pictorial and floral elements. The design of so many samplers is similar that one suspects the existence of forms from which they were copied, a reasonable assumption since they were primarily learning tools through which girls and young women displayed their skill with various stitches as well as their knowledge of the alphabet and numbers. Samplers are found from Spain and Italy to the British Isles and Scandinavia. The earliest ones are long and thin, but later examples may be as large as two by three feet, and by the 1800s the form had stabilized at about fourteen by sixteen inches.

Samplers are especially popular with collectors because so many bear dates and the names of their makers or the places where they were made. It is fortunate that this is the case for the similarity among various national examples often makes it nearly impossible to attribute samplers on any other basis. This problem is especially acute for American collectors, who are prepared to pay substantial sums for samplers made in this country but are frequently bewildered by the similarity of these pieces to those made in the British Isles or even Germany.

Embroidered textiles also appear in South America, where Mexican, Chilean, and Peruvian seamstresses still adorn skirts and blouses with delicate needlework patterns. These are often an interesting blend of native elements and motifs introduced by the Europeans who colonized the area.

Needlework pictures are usually more complex than samplers, and in composition and style they seem related to tapestries. Most of the scenes appear to be based on period paintings or prints and often have a religious or mythological background. Although some are composed entirely of stitchwork, others incorporate watercolor on a paper ground or are built upon a raised wool or cotton surface, a technique known as stumpwork. Examples of American needlework pictures exist, but the great majority are European in origin.

Two other important textile-making techniques are patchwork and quilting. Patchwork, which is essentially the sewing together of various smaller pieces of cloth to make a larger whole, was known in Egypt; quilting is a Chinese innovation by which three layers of material (the center one consists of a loose, soft material like cotton batting) are stitched together to create a single unit. Japanese craftsmen have long been famous for a patchwork brocade consisting of varicolored pieces of woven silk brocade, and quilting was practiced not only in China but also in seventeenth-century France.

It was in the United States that the two techniques were combined in the quilt, a folk textile that now ranks among the most popular of all antiques. The traditional American quilt consists of three layers: a bright patchwork front, an inner lining, and a back, usually of printed textile. All three are stitched together with a running stitch. Collectors look for elaborate stitchwork and for bold, primary colors, with particular preference shown for geometric examples such as the Amish quilts of Pennsylvania, which often resemble abstract paintings. Other quilt types commonly collected include the appliqué, which consists of a front composed of various cut-out pieces stitched onto a solid piece of cloth, and the crazy quilt, a late Victorian type made of silks and satins joined with showy embroidery stitchwork. Although many crazy quilts were made in the British Isles, the other quilt types are found only in North America.

There is no doubt that some of the finest textiles come from the Orient. The Chinese developed the technique of making woven and embossed silken brocades, and the first silk was a revelation when it began arriving in Europe during the fifteenth century. Like the Europeans, the Chinese also made tapestries (known as *Ko ssu*), which were woven from the finest silk threads. While earlier examples were rarely exported, later, heavier pieces became popular tourist items during the late nineteenth and early twentieth centuries.

The batiks that come from Malaya, Indonesia, and India are less sophisticated but extremely interesting. Batiking involves marking a pattern on a piece of cotton or silk cloth with dye-repellent clay or wax; when the piece is dipped in dye the areas so treated stand out in white against the colored background.

Block printing was also practiced in these areas. A simple motif is carved into a block of wood, and the block is then dipped into color and applied to a piece of cloth. Anything from a single swatch to a whole bolt of cotton may be decorated in this manner, and the textiles so embellished have long been popular in Europe as dress fabric and for bed coverings and table clothes.

The various types discussed here represent but a portion of the many textiles available to the collector, which range from fragments of ancient woven cloth to whole bolts of nineteenth-century factory-printed cotton—the introduction of which radically changed the nature of textile manufacture, at least in the Western world. Whatever one's preference, the textile collector has much to choose from, and in many cases acquisition will not prove costly.

Afshar rug with a gold field and a double blue border; early 20th century; $600–750. While originally intended to denote the place of a rug's origin, rug names today indicate a pattern or style. ►

Kirman Persian rug in pastel blue; early 20th century; $350–450. The floral patterns and leafy scrolls characteristic of Persian rugs suggest a formal Near Eastern garden. ▼

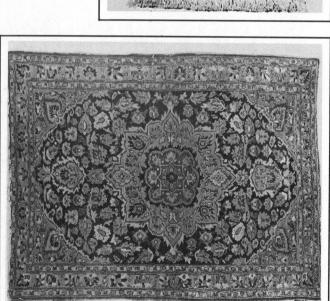

▲ Sarouk Persian rug in blue and rose; late 19th century; $1,650–2,000. This rug exemplifies the highly formal composition favored by the weavers of Persian rugs.

Anatolian rug in silk with a green field and blue border; early 20th century; $850–1,000. Turkish rugs such as this may be embellished with bird or animal forms as well as with the floral motifs found on many Persian rugs. ►

Turkoman flatwoven
torba with yellow trel-
liswork on a red-brown
ground; early 20th cen-
tury; $200–250. Var-
ious tribes in Russian
central Asia weave
bright, geometric rugs
such as this.
◀

Baluchistan rug with a brown field and ivory border; late 19th century; $600–750.
The Baluches are one of the nomadic tribes whose rugs are classified as Turkoman.
▼

Yomud chuval rug in light brown and ivory; 20th century;
$200–275. In light of the high prices being realized for Persian rugs
today, it would appear that Yomuds and other rugs produced by nomadic Turkoman weavers are an excellent investment.
◀

Tekke rug in purple, blue, and pink; late 19th–early 20th century; $800–950. This
is an example by one of the finest groups of nomadic Turkoman weavers.
▶

231

Baluchistan bag face in red and cream on a dark blue field; early 20th century; $600–750. Small and easy to display, bag faces make attractive wall hangings. ◄

Complete Yomud Asmalyk in red and green with a dark brown field; late 19th century; $1,000–1,300. Strong colors and interesting design make this a remark-▼ able textile hanging.

Afshar bag face in ivory and dark blue; early 20th century; $600–750. Afshar ▲ textiles are very similar in form to those from Shiraz.

Shiraz bag face in dark blue and ivory; late 19th century; $500–650. Persian rug-making centers also produced bag faces, and this one is a good example. ►

Kurd Bidjar bag face in a blue ground with a cruciform motif surrounded by stylized animal forms; late 19th century; $550–700. ◀

Shirvan rug with a red field and a design in various ▲ shades of blue; late 19th–early 20th century; $1,200–1,500. Caucasian rugs are extremely colorful and complement modern furnishings.

▲ Shirvan rug in ivory and blue on a red-brown field; late 19th century; $2,750–3,500. Shirvans are one of the various Caucasian rug types—Oriental rugs in bold colors and geometric patterns that originate in the Caucasus area of Russia.

Kurd bag face in ivory and dark blue with a piled skirt and brocaded kilim top; early 20th century; $450–600. Kurd rugs are Persian in classification and come from northern Iran. ▼

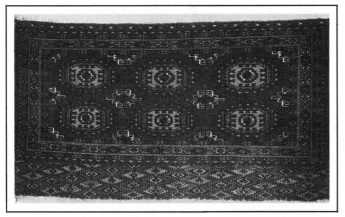

▲ Kazakh rug in blue, ivory, red, and orange; late 19th century; $3,700–4,500.

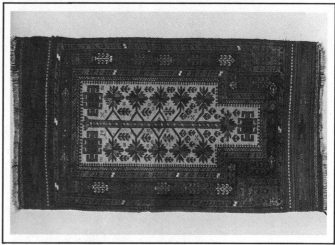

Karashli rug in red, tan, and light blue on a dark blue field with the so-called fork-leaf design and leaf-and-cup border; late 19th century; $3,000–4,000. ◀

Baluchistan prayer rug in blue and tan; early 20th century; $950–1,250. This is an attractive Turkoman rug with the arched panel or Mihrab characteristic of prayer rugs. ▲

▲ *Shirvan rug in ivory, red, and blue with a wide border or stepped design and tartan striped guards; late 19th century; $2,500–3,000.*

◀
Meles prayer rug in green, ivory, and aubergine on a red field; late 19th century; $5,000–6,500. Meles rugs are included among those rugs classified as Turkish, and prayer rugs are the most typical Turkish form.

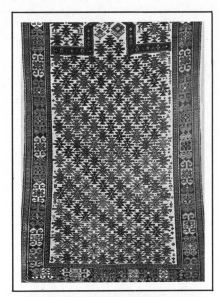

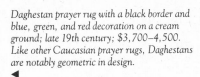

Daghestan prayer rug with a black border and blue, green, and red decoration on a cream ground; late 19th century; $3,700–4,500. Like other Caucasian prayer rugs, Daghestans are notably geometric in design. ◀

Caucasian prayer rug in ivory, blue, and red on a predominantly ▲ brown ground; late 19th century; $2,700–3,500.

Baluchistan prayer rug in tan with stylized leaves and rosettes and kilim skirts; early 20th century; $1,000–1,300. ▼

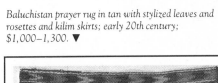

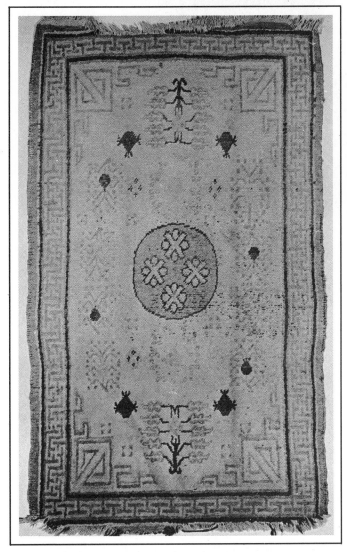

▲ Smarakand rug in tan and ivory with central medallion and key fret border; early 20th century; $400–550. Since Samarkand lay on the trade route between China and the Near East, its rugs often blend Chinese and Near Eastern motifs.

Mat in the traditional light-blue and white with Shou center medallion and cloud borders; China, early 20th century; $200–275. In both color and design Chinese rugs are distinctly different from other Oriental rugs. ▶

Circular rug in pale blue, cream, and apricot with peony vine decoration; China, early 20th century; $650–800. ▼

▲ Rectangular mat in pale blue and white with circular medallion and narrow thunder border; China, early 20th century; $375–500.

Hooked rug in woolen floral pattern in red, green, gray, and brown; United States, late 19th century; $150–200. Relatively easy to make and a fine way to recycle old material, hooked rugs have been a popular American product for over a hundred years. ▶

236

Hooked rug in geometric patchwork pattern of blue and gray; United States, early 20th century; $150–165. Rugs such as this were often copied from quilt ▼ patterns.

Hooked rug in red, gray, and blue; United States, early 20th century; $125–175. ▲ Rugs such as this reflect familiarity with Near Eastern carpets.

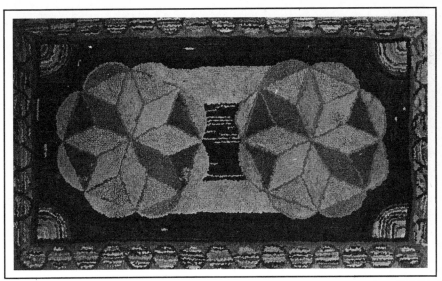

Hooked rug in geometric design in red, blue, ▲ gray, and black; United States, late 19th century; $225–250. Geometric hooked rugs are popular with contemporary collectors because they complement modern furniture.

◄

Hooked seat cover with geometric design in red, white, and blue; United States, early 20th century; $70–90. Circular hooked seat covers are common, but square or rectangular ones are not.

Machine-woven tapestry in gold, red, white, brown, and black; Belgium, 20th century; $85–115. The introduction of machine weaving during the 1800s made it possible for everyone to afford tapestries. ▼

Hooked rug depicting a black horse on a green and pink ground; United States, 1930–40; $175–200. Collectors are drawn to animal-related rugs. ▼

Rug in pale blue, tan, and gold; Aubusson, France, late 19th century; $400–550. Aubusson has been one of the world's great rug-making centers for centuries, especially for tapestry woven rugs. ▶

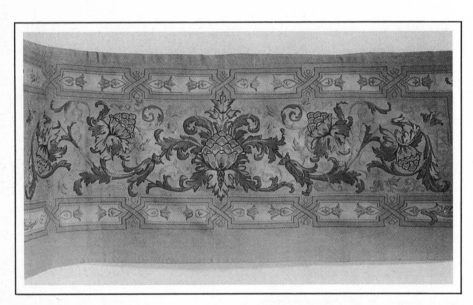

Detail of a woven tapestry panel in blue, red, gold, ▲ and green; Aubusson, France, late 19th–early 20th century; $350–450.

Pictorial hooked rug; Nova Scotia, Canada, 1920–30; $90–110. Though recent, this interesting pictorial rug is a desirable collector's item. Its colors are pink, yellow, gray, and white. ▶

238

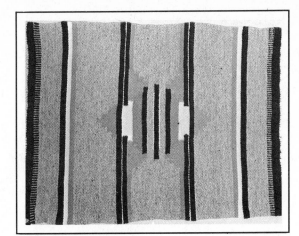

Woven mat in gray, green, red, and white; by Navajo Indian, United States, 20th century; $120–160. The Indian weavers of the American southwest are among the world's most creative craftsmen. ◄

Woven pillowcase in pink, white, and green; by Navajo Indian, United States, 20th century; $70–95. As the prices of large Navajo rugs have climbed steadily, smaller examples such as this have become good investments. ▼

Bag in woven hemp in tan and brown; by American Indians, northwest coast of ▲ the United States, late 19th century; $250–325.

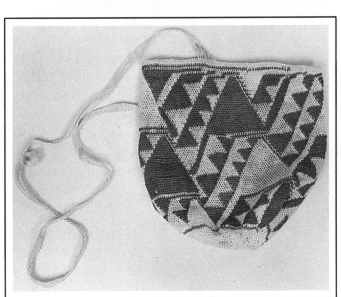

Machine-woven tapestry wall hanging in cream, brown, red, ▲ gold, blue, green, and black; Italy, late 19th century; $200–275.

Woven blanket in red, white, and black; by Navajo Indian, ▲ United States, 20th century; $100–130. Smaller pieces such as this were usually made for sale to tourists.

Fragment of textile with multihued birds on a yellow ground; Chancay, Peru, 1200–1400; $200–275. ◀

Woven and brocaded shawl; Spanish-American, ▲ southwest United States, early 20th century; $190–270. This piece reflects skills brought to the New World by Spanish colonists.

◀
Fragment of a woven textile with white birds on a brown ground; Peru, 1100–1400; $300–450. Some of the world's earliest textiles have been discovered at South American archaeological sites.

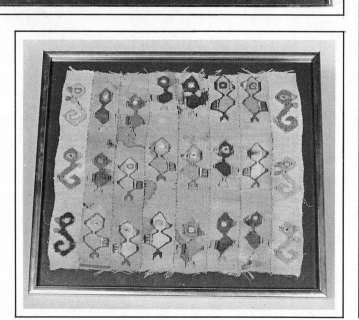

Fragment of textile with bands of woven cloth in pink, yellow, red, and brown ▲ sewn together; Chancay, Peru, 1200–1400; $450–550. Most pre-Columbian textiles are embellished with abstract geometric designs such as those seen here.

Woven wool blanket in red, green, brown, and ▲ black; Spanish-American, southwwest United States, 20th century; $350–500.

Beaded bag in trade cloth with backing decorated in multicolored seed beads in floral motifs; by Woodlands Indians, United States, early 20th century; $200–250.
▶

Child's vest in trade cloth embellished with multicolored seed beads and metallic beads; by Sioux, United States, early 20th century; $500–650. ▼

Loin cloth in beadwork and cloth in purple, orange, and red, decorated with cowrie shells; by Zulu, Africa, late 19th century; $175-225. The use of beads to decorate textiles was popular in various primitive societies. ▼

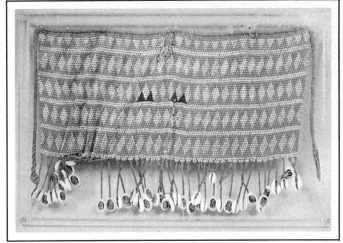

Child's embroidered dress in the Mola fashion; Mexico, 20th century; $45–60. Interesting examples such as this are still made in some rural areas of Central and South America. ▼

Child's dress in red trade cloth decorated with cowrie shells and ▲ pieces of metal; by Plains Indians, United States, late 19th century; $400–500.

241

Embroidered needlework sampler; England, dated 1840; $245–300. Other things being equal, older samplers bring higher prices. ▼

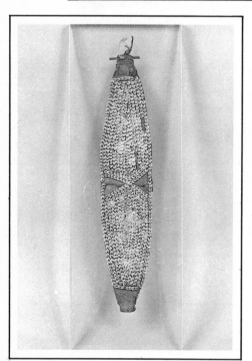

Needlepoint fans with turned ivory handles; Spain, late 19th century; $150–250 the pair. Needlework was regarded as a necessary skill for a woman in 19th century Europe, and many interesting examples from the period exist today.

Belt in red and blue cloth embellished with shells; from ▲ the Ramu River area, New Guinea, late 19th century; $175–250.

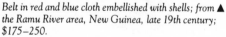

Detail of needlepoint pole screen with mahogany base and brass shaft; England, mid-19th century; $450–550. Pole screens served to protect people from the direct heat of an open fire. ◄

Embroidered needlework picture in carved and gilded frame; France, late 19th century; $135–185. Many hours would be spent in creating a textile of this sort. ▶

Picture in embroidery and stump- ▲ *work of St. Peter; France or Italy, early 19th century; $235–315. Needlework with a religious theme seldom brings high prices.*

Embroidery panel in blue, gold, red, and green; China, mid-19th century; $120–160. The Chinese have produced some of the world's most sophisticated and delicate needlework. ◀

Embroidered family birth record; England, 1845–50; $175–250. Needlework ▲ *birth records are less common than samplers and are usually of a somewhat later date.*

243

Detail of embroidered design on a robe in gold on ▲ *dark-red silk; China, early 20th century; $200–275. With the increasing interest in all things Chinese, prices of embroideries are bound to rise.*

Quilted jacket in silk brocade in gold trimmed with black velvet; China, 20th century; $125–165. ▶

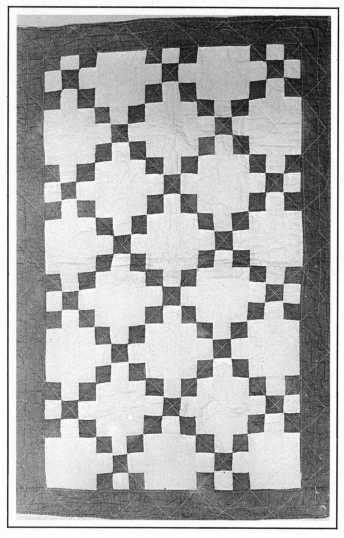

Pieced crib quilt in blue and white Irish chain pattern; United States, early 20th ▲ century; $135–165. A unique American creation, quilts are now collected in Japan and throughout northern Europe.

◀ Ladies' handbag in silk brocade and lacquerware; Japan, early 20th century; $100–150. Japanese brocades are of extremely high quality.

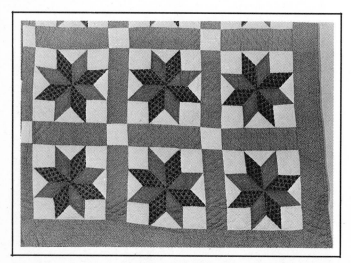

Pieced quilt in the LeMoyne star pattern in pink, white, and gray; United States, ▲ late 19th century; $500–550. Variations of the star pattern are very popular with collectors.

Detail of embroidery at the edge of a shawl; Kashmir, ▲ India, late 19th–early 20th century; $200–275. Imported into England by the thousands, these shawls were a Victorian rage.

Pieced quilt in the feathered star pattern with sawtooth border in blue and white cotton; United States, late 19th century; $650–750.

Pieced quilt in the steeplechase pattern in pale blue and white; ▲ United States, early 20th century; $450–550. This geometric design is more complex than most American quilts.

Appliqué album quilt; United States, dated 1912; $3,500–4,000. ▲ Rare, one-of-a-kind presentation pieces, album quilts are extremely desirable.

◄

Pieced quilt in the grandmother's garden pattern in blue and white cotton; United States, 1900–20; $400–500. Quilt collectors often prefer quilts in blue and white.

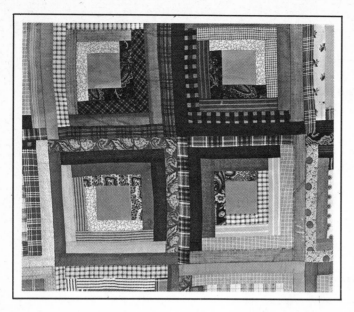

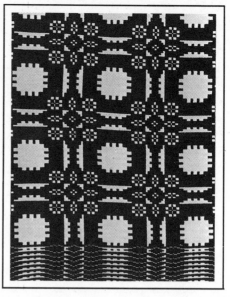

◄ Detail of a woven coverlet in a reversible blue and white geometric design; United States, 1830–50; $265–325. Woven at home or by itinerant weavers, heavy coverlets were common on American beds throughout the last century.

▲ Detail of a pieced quilt in the log cabin pattern in red, blue, brown, white, and black, including various suiting and dress materials; United States, early 20th century; $250–300. Though common, log cabin quilts may be quite attractive.

Detail of an appliqué quilt in the oak leaf pattern in red and white material with cut-out corners for a four-poster bed; United States, 1850–60; $550–650. ▶

246

Pieced quilt in the lightening pattern in red and blue figured ▲ fabric; United States, late 19th century; $650–750.

Detail of crazy quilt in silk and satin; England, late 19th ▲ century; $150–200. Made of pieces of scrap materials stitched together with fancy chain stitches, crazy quilts were the only American examples to appeal to the British.

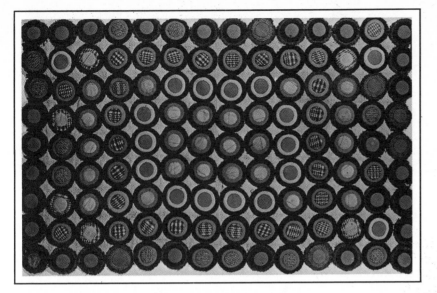

Penny rug in red and
blue velvet on a burlap
base; United States,
late 19th century;
$135–165. These
"rugs" were actually
table or furniture
coverings.

Detail of a fringed geometric coverlet in the snowflake pattern in red, white, blue
and tan; United States, 1860–75; $325–385. ▼

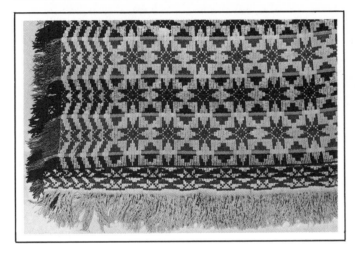

Detail of border and center of a Jacquard coverlet in blue and white; ▲
United States, dated 1841; $425–525. Most coverlets are made of
wool and cotton and have no more than two colors.

Detail of a Jacquard coverlet in red, white, and blue; Pennsylvania, U.S., dated ▲
1845; $350–450. Many coverlets are signed and dated—a real plus for the
collector.

Border detail of Jacquard coverlet in red and green with overall floral pattern; ▲
United States, late 19th century; $350–450.

247

12

Timepieces and Scientific Instruments

The ability to determine the time of day, whether through use of an hourglass, a sundial, or some sort of mechanical timepiece, is an essential underpinning of every civilized society. All the great historical civilizations, from South America to China to Egypt and Rome, had some form of timekeeping, but it was a long time before accurate clocks and watches were developed.

The first mechanical clocks appeared in Europe during the thirteenth century. These crude, weight-driven timepieces were placed in towers in larger communities where they served to alert clock keepers, who announced the hour by striking a bell. It was not until well into the fifteenth century that these tower clocks were provided with dials and hands so that passersby might read the hour, but once such useful timepieces became available they spurred a variety of related activities. Wealthy landowners and merchants, unwilling to settle for a look at the town clock, began to demand their own timepieces, and by the 1550s smaller, "chamber" clocks began to appear. The first of these were driven by a series of weights, just like their larger cousins, and their size and bulk made them difficult to move about. They were soon supplemented by spring-driven examples.

With the availability of smaller, spring-powered timepieces and the development of other improvements leading to more accurate timekeeping, watchmakers began to assume an independent role. Before this they had functioned as wandering novelty makers, dependent on royal favor and lacking even a guild of their own (until 1543 German clockmakers were part of the locksmiths' guild). They started to set up shops, especially in Nuremberg, and to experiment with portable timekeepers. Out of these efforts came the first true watches, drum-shaped timepieces with engraved brass cases that were worn around the neck.

Watches proved immediately popular, not only for practical purposes but also because they became objects of personal adornment—a form of jewelry. Before this could be achieved, however, it was necessary to make watches considerably smaller than the sixteenth-century examples. And more accurate, for some early watches were of such dubious veracity that they were equipped with built-in sundials so that they could be set frequently (at least on sunny days)!

Both German and French clockmakers set out to resolve the problem of form, and before 1600 spherical watchcases had begun to appear. These were followed by circular, oval, and even octagonal examples. Worn about the neck or on the vest, these timepieces became the focal point of a man's dress, especially when embellished with such luxurious additions as chains, fobs, and bars. For those who preferred a bit of novelty there were the so-called form watches, whose cases assumed shapes quite unrelated to their function, such as birds, books, flowers, and even human skulls.

By the beginning of the seventeenth century watchmaking was closely related to the jeweler's art, and cases were of richly engraved gold or silver or were carved from semiprecious materials such as agate, quartz, and garnet. And, especially in France, finely enameled watchcases began to appear, many of them adorned with detailed historical or mythological figures. Swiss artisans in the Geneva area soon followed the French lead, establishing a tradition of Swiss supremacy in this field that remains unbroken to the present day.

The decorative embellishments evident in the field of watchmaking were not lost on clockmakers, and it was not long before the plain iron clock was replaced by ones of very different form and appearance. Among these were the tabernacle clocks, the blocky bodies of which were surmounted by cast-brass figures; and the long-popular table clocks, spring-driven timepieces that were often equipped with alarms and came in a variety of forms. There were also crucifix clocks, a particular product of the Augsburg, Germany, area; and bracket clocks, the name of which originally referred to a timepiece that had a bracket for wall mounting but eventually came to indicate a wood-cased shelf or table clock.

More than just the form of the clock was changing. Innovations such as the pendulum and the balance spring made timepieces more accurate, and the constant demand for portability led to a steady decrease in size. In the late seventeenth and early eighteenth centuries the center for most of this innovative clockmaking was England, where the renowned craftsman Thomas Tompion (1638–1713) laid the groundwork for mass production in a field that had theretofore been highly individualistic.

The major mechanical refinements had been made before the end of the 1600s, and the following century was devoted more to changing fashions in clockcases and dials than to substantive improvements in the works. There was always a tendency for clocks to reflect architectural forms, and this trend became even more pronounced during the rococo and neoclassical periods, with identical moldings, cornices, and decorative embellishments gracing clocks and highboys or commodes. This was particularly noticeable in the long case clocks, whose development had followed close upon that of the pendulum. The great height of these clocks, as much as seven feet, lent itself to cabinetwork, and, especially in England, they became household furnishings, with cases painted or japanned, depending on the current decorative taste.

French clocks were usually smaller but more elaborate than their English counterparts. Table, shelf, and musical clocks were veneered in tortoiseshell, lacquered and mounted in ormolu, or gilt bronze; forms included lush scrolling in the rococo manner and decorative clocks mounted atop bronze elephants, bulls, or lions. Enameling was still popular, and by the 1700s white-enamel dials had become preferred because of their greater visibility, and enamel decoration for watchcases and even clockcases was widespread, especially on the Continent. Such embellishment was, however, limited to smaller table or shelf clocks.

The eighteenth century saw a few important technical advances. Among the most critical was the employment of jewels in the manufacture of pivot bearings as a means of reducing the serious problem of abrasive wear among clock parts. Other innovations included the creation of watch springs that were not affected by changes in temperature and marine timepieces that could maintain accurate time despite the unstable conditions prevalent at sea.

Thanks to these and other discoveries English clock- and watchmakers maintained a preeminent position throughout the first half of the eighteenth century. However, despite the high regard in which British timepieces were held (even to the extent of counterfeiting English marks on Continental products to insure greater salability), clockmakers in other areas were not idle. A Frenchman, A. L. Breguet (1747–1823), building on previous discoveries by his countrymen, introduced a thinner and more elegant pocketwatch at the end of the century—and produced the first reliable and inexpensive version of such a timepiece.

Soon after 1800 Swiss artisans took the same road and began to introduce a form of mechanization to their craft, including the manufacture by machine of standardized watch parts. However, the Swiss also maintained high standards in the creation of expensive "fashion" watches, a field in which their dominance has continued.

The French in general and Breguet in particular made advances in other areas. Responding to the need for clocks for travelers—a need that had been served in a very inadequate manner by large watches—Breguet invented the glass-and-brass carriage clock. These timepieces proved extremely popular, particularly when combined with calendar devices, and by the end of the eighteenth century French manufacturers were expanding to serve an enormous export market.

The watch market continued to grow through the nineteenth century. More and more people could afford to own watches, and clock manufacturers continued to find ways to cut costs. In Switzerland this involved the integration of the industry until it became, in effect, a single company. In the United States, a latecomer to the ranks of clock and watch producers, it took a different form. Americans had been making clocks on a semifactory basis since the turn of the century, and by the 1850s they had become a major factor in the low- to medium-price range.

American makers such as the Seth Thomas Clock Company (established in 1813) and the New Haven Clock Company gained a reputation for high-quality, durable, and inexpensive wall, shelf, and ships' clocks that enabled them to export such large quantities of timepieces to England and Europe during the second half of the last century that even today many American clock collectors look to those areas for choice acquisitions.

In 1880 the Waterbury Clock Company, an American firm located in Connecticut, turned out a nonjeweled pocketwatch that could be retailed at only $3.75. This low price reflected the use of mass-production techniques based on interchangeable parts and a willingness on the part of the manufacturer to sell in quantity at a relatively low per-unit profit.

The Waterbury watch proved an immediate hit not only in the United States but in England and on the Continent as well. As foreign orders poured in, other American firms joined the trend toward less-costly timepieces, with the crowning achievement being the marketing in 1893 of Robert H. Ingersoll's dollar watch—"the watch that made the dollar famous."

U.S. producers dominated the production of inexpensive watches for several decades, but the Swiss were not far behind, and in the twentieth century they began introducing timepieces that were both inexpensive and of better quality than the American imports.

The late nineteenth and twentieth centuries saw innovations in areas other than production techniques. As women began to leave home and enter business and the professions the watch, which had previously been designed primarily for men, had to be redesigned. At first manufacturers tried to adapt the pocketwatch by attaching it to a piece of jewelry and creating the pendant, or fob watch, a smaller timepiece that could be pinned to the blouse or skirt. This was only a partial solution, however, and in any case men's tastes were changing, too. Fewer and fewer men found the gold pocketwatch and chain a mark of status and distinction. It was clumsy and awkward to use. Soon after the First World War the wristwatch appeared. Though men's and women's models were distinguished by differences in size and design, both were much smaller than the pocketwatch.

Wristwatches soon dominated the field except in specialized areas such as athletic stopwatches and watches used in scientific work, where the larger timepieces were still preferable. Pocketwatches were still made, of course, especially for sale by fine retailers, such as Cartier and Tiffany.

There were also substantial changes in the field of clockmaking. During the late nineteenth century American and German manufacturers had pioneered in the marketing of cheap, tin- or pot-metal-plated alarm clocks, gaudy marble-mounted shelf clocks for parlor display, and the oak clocks that once dominated every schoolroom and public office. With the advent of electricity it became practical to electrify these timepieces, and by the 1920s large numbers of relatively inexpensive electric clocks were on the market.

Many of these new timekeepers were in a distinct and revolutionary style, Art Deco, which featured industrial materials such as chrome, plastic, and blue glass in place of the traditional materials like marble, silver, shagreen, and enamel. Art Deco clocks and watches (for these also exist in some numbers) are now a popular collectors' item, as are the comic watches, such as those featuring Mickey Mouse, which were all the rage in the 1930s.

Watch and clock collecting is confined primarily to these twentieth-century types and to the watches, both fine and common, made during the nineteenth century. Clocks are sought, too, though usually in the smaller shelf or table sizes, for few collectors can afford either the space or the money to own the larger timepieces. Relatively few pre-1800 examples are available, and since these also command very substantial sums, they are seldom seen in the average collection.

Unlike timepieces, scientific instruments do not have a long history as collectibles. This is due in part to their relative scarcity, in part to the fact that few people are familiar with them. Nevertheless, it is possible to amass an interesting group of such objects. Best known and of the most general interest are such items as microscopes, sextants, and sundials.

One should keep in mind that almost any early (pre-1940) scientific instruments can serve as the basis for an interesting collection. Category collecting is particularly appropriate. For example, doctors and dentists acquire the tools of their trade and chemists the objects with which their predecessors worked. In fact, every such area of human endeavor offers the potential for an interesting and educational collection: and, fortunately, in most cases these pieces remain relatively inexpensive.

Baroque style mantel clock in gilded bronze (part of a 3-piece garniture set that includes a pair of five-light candelabra with Sèvres porcelain panels); France, late 19th century; $1,500–2,000 the set.

Empire style clock in gilded bronze; Ledure bronze works, France, late 19th century; $550–700. Ornate mantel clocks were popular with Victorians in all Western countries.

Empire style figural mantel clock in dore bronze; Paris, France, ca. 1815; $1,700–2,200. An excellent example of an early figural clock. ▼

Empire style mantel clock in dore bronze with enamel face and fluted column flanked by figures of Grecian girl and cupids; France, ca. 1820; $400–500.

Miniature table clock in silver with cherub of carved ivory and dial in enamel and gold; Austria, late 19th century; ▼ *$1,000–1,400.*

◄ *Table clock in silver and enamel with inset pearls and semiprecious stones; Switzerland, 1875–1900; $1,500–1,900. Made for the Turkish market with dial in Turkish characters.*

Egyptian Revival style standish ▲ *with clock and two inkwells in bronze and marble; United States, late 19th century; $450–600.*

▲ *Shelf clock in mahogany veneer with reverse-painted glass panel; by E. N. Welch, Forestville, Conn., 1856–64; $400–550.*

◄ *Mantel clock in cast and ebonized metal and brass with patriotic and military motifs including an eagle; United States, mid-19th century; $150–200.*

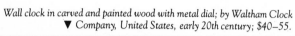
Wall clock in carved and painted wood with metal dial; by Waltham Clock ▼ *Company, United States, early 20th century; $40–55.*

▲ *Table clock in silver with enameled decoration; France, late 19th century; $1,300–1,800.*

Mantel clock in porcelain in the form of a tall case ▲ *clock with hand-painted floral decoration; Dresden, Germany, late 19th century; $300–400.*

Miniature mantel clock in silver and orange enamel; Europe, late 19th–early 20th ▲ *century; $500–650. Miniature clocks have long been popular collector's items.*

◀
Urn-shaped clock in sitra
and enamel on a hard-
stone base; France, late
19th–early 20th cen-
tury; $2,200–2,700.
These unusual timepieces
bring high prices.

◀
Miniature desk or table clocks; Switzerland. Left: In
silver case and enamel in red, blue, and purple; by Ze-
nith, 20th century; $700–850. Right: In silver and
blue enamel; by Eterna, ca. 1900; $300–375.

Table clock in gilt metal and enamel; Germany,
ca. 1910; $500–600. Art Deco timepieces such as
this are increasing in value.
▶

Miniature table clock in enamel and silver with multi- ▲
colored scenes of classical figures and putti; Austria,
late 19th century; $2,200–2,700.

Art Deco chiming clock in the Chinese manner; by Tiffany & Company, New York, N.Y., early 20th century; $3,500–4,500. This clock has a Swiss movement, carved jade finial, enameled decoration, and rose quartz feet. ▼

"Six Hirondelles" boudoir clock in frosted glass; signed by R. Lalique, France, ca. 1922; $650–800.
▼

Table or mantel clock; France, 1930–40; $90–120. This glass-and-chrome timepiece is typical of inexpensive Art Deco clocks.

Carriage clock in brass and glass with enamel dial; ▲ England, late 19th century; $250–350. Carriage clocks are extremely popular collectibles.

Carriage clock in brass and glass with enamel dial and visible works; ▲ France, ca. 1900; $450–550. French carriage clocks are generally regarded as the best examples.

Art Moderne mantel clock with humidity gauge, barometer, and thermometer in original case; Switzerland, early 20th century; $200–300. ▶

Folding travel clock in silver and enamel; made in Europe for the American market, 20th century; $350–425. ▼

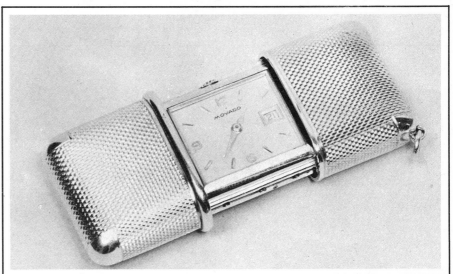

Travel clock in gold with date indicator; by Movado, Switzerland, 20th century; ▲ *$2,000–2,500. Pushing the two ends of the case together closes the clock compartment.*

Travel clock; by Flato, United States, ca. 1933; $2,000–2,500. ▲ *This view of the clock shows the white-enamel face and the winding dial. A rare form.*

Travel clock in the form of letter with silver and enamel case; by Flato, United ▲ *States, ca. 1933; $2,000–2,500. The case is inscribed with a Long Island, N.Y., address.*

◄ *Unusual pedestal clock in enamel and silver on marble base; by Tiffany & Company, New York, N.Y., 1915–30; $500–600.*

Gold-filled pocketwatch; by Elgin Watch ▲ Company, United States, ca. 1920; $75–100. For those who could not afford a gold watch American makers produced well-made but inexpensive substitutes.

Art Deco pocketwatch with platinum face and ▲ numerals set with tiny diamonds; by Tiffany & Company, New York, N.Y., early 20th century; $2,500–3,000.

Art Deco pocketwatch, the VeriThin; by Gruen, ▲ United States, early 20th century; $200–300. A plain but efficient timepiece.

Pocketwatch in gold, the Centre Seconds Chrono- ▲ graph; by G. Taylor, England, ca. 1879; $1,000– 1,500. Unlike most pocketwatches, this one is wound with a key.

Pocketwatch; by Chronometre Mitzpa, Switzerland, ▲ 1920–30; $450–600. This gold watch is typical of the Swiss types that eventually dominated the international market.

▲
Pocketwatch with chain;
Switzerland, early 20th
century; $900–1,200.
With original case.

Pocketwatch in platinum case with gold digits and a black-suede ribbon embellished
with diamond set borders; by Baume & Mercier, Geneva, Switzerland, early 20th
century; $2,500–3,000. ▼

Pocketwatch in gold; by Waltham, United States, late 19th–early 20th century;
$300–400. ▼

Lady's pocketwatch in gold with enamel face and engraved initials; Switzerland, ▲
ca. 1910; $250–325. Women's timepieces are smaller in size than those made
for men.

Case of a lady's pocket-watch; Switzerland, ca. 1900; $2,000–2,500. The back of this timepiece is elaborately decorated with polychrome enamel cherub and floral pattern on a black ground.

Lady's pocketwatch in enamel and gold set with tiny rose-cut dia- ▲ monds; by David I. Magnin, Geneva, Switzerland, ca. 1860; $3,500–4,200. The cover design of this hunting-case watch is in the popular Egyptian manner.

Face of lady's pocketwatch; Switzerland, ca. 1900; $2,000–2,500. ▲ The face of the preceding watch. Dial is of yellow metal with delicate embossing, and the numerals are in black.

Lady's pocketwatch in gold with ▶ hunting case and chain; by Elgin, United States, late 19th–early 20th century; $800–950. The cover protects the watch face from damage.

▶ Lady's pocketwatch in gold with hunting case engraved in a pictorial and foliate design; United States, ca. 1900; $550–650.

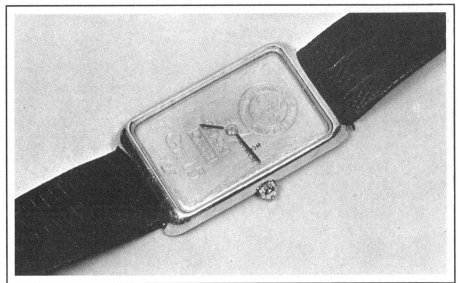

◀ Wristwatch with 24-carat-gold face ingot; by Corum, Switzerland, 20th century; $2,000–2,800. Of no great age, but a distinct novelty.

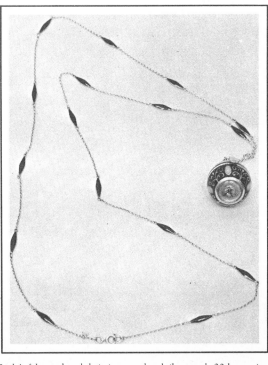

Lady's fob watch and brooch combination in diamond and ▲ gold with the brooch set in pearls and diamonds; Switzerland, ca. 1900; $4,500–6,000.

Lady's fob watch and chain in enamel and silver; early 20th cen- ▲ tury; $400–500. Prior to popularization of the wristwatch, most women wore brooch or chain-hung watches.

Wristwatch in gold with
black-suede band and
textured face; by Van
Cleef & Arpels, France,
early 20th century;
$800–1,000.

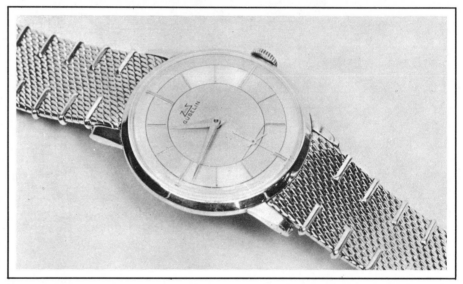

Round wristwatch in gold with white and gold flexible mesh band; by Gubelin, ▲
Switzerland, early 20th century; $2,000–2,750.

Art Deco wristwatch in white gold with alligator band; ▲
by Cartier, Paris, France, early 20th century;
$1,500–2,000.

Lady's watch set in a cuff bracelet in gold set with a small cabochon sapphire; by
Udall and Ballow, Switzerland, 20th century; $650–800. As might be expected,
women's wristwatches are more elaborate than men's. ▼

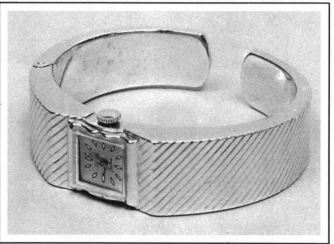

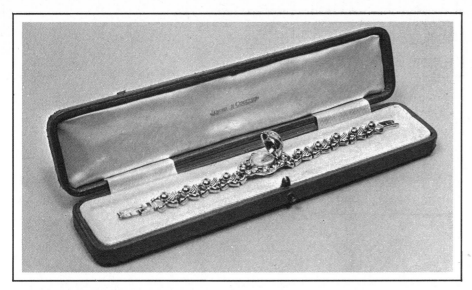

◀
Lady's wristwatch in gold and ruby with lid over the face set with small rubies and diamonds and gold bracelet embellished with rubies; by Jaeger-Le-Coutre, France, early 20th century; $1,200–1,600.

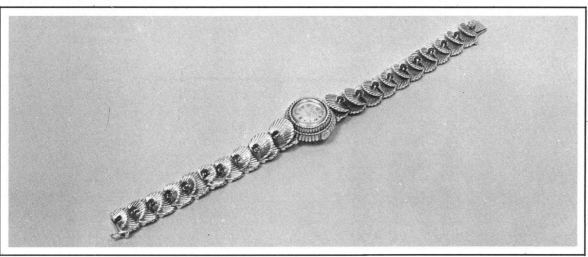

▲ *Lady's wristwatch in gold with flexible gold bracelet set with round sapphires; by Van Cleef & Arpels, France, early 20th century; $900–1,200.*

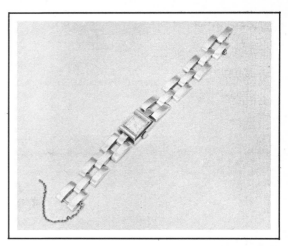

Lady's wristwatch in gold with massive gold-linked bracelet and ▲ guard chain; by Blycine, Switzerland, early 20th century; $400–500.

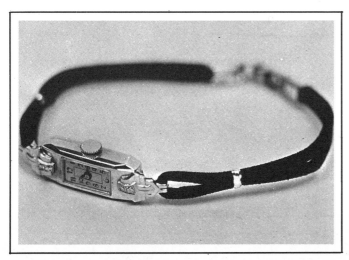

Lady's wristwatch in gold and white gold with diamond set shoulders; Europe, ▲ 1910–20; $275–350. A common form of early 20th-century timepiece.

◄ Lady's wristwatch in gold set with numerous small diamonds; by Nicole, France, early 20th century; $650–900. Early ladies' wristwatches looked like 19th century brooches.

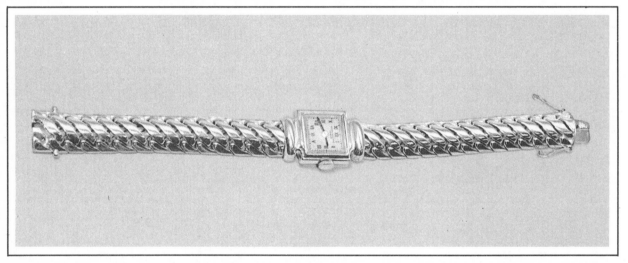

▲ Lady's wristwatch in gold with gold-link bracelet; by Patek Philippe, and Company, Geneva, Switzerland, early 20th century; $1,500–2,000. The manufacturer's reputation has much to do with the value of collectible watches.

Lady's wristwatch in platinum set with small diamonds and rubies; by Tiffany & Company, New York, N.Y., early 20th ▼ century; $1,500–2,000.

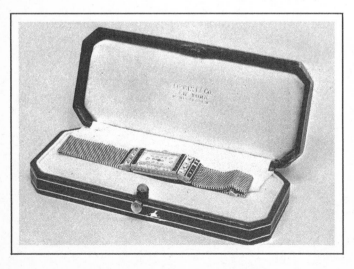

Lady's wristwatch in gold set with two rows of diamonds; by Brondax, Switzerland, ▲ early 20th century; $200–300.

Lady's wristwatch in 18-carat gold with flexible mesh bracelet; by Ebel, Switzerland, early 20th century; $850–1,000. ▼

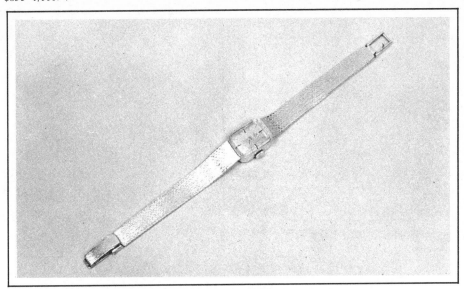

Stopwatch in chrome case; by North and Sons, ▲
London, England, early 20th century; $75–125.
Stopwatches have a limited collector following.

Stopwatch in chrome case with enamel dial; Switzerland, early 20th century; ▲
$200–275. Known as a mikrograph, this stopwatch was designed to measure 1/100
of a second.

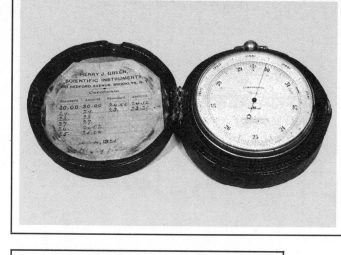

Altimeter with 1925 testing certificate; by Tycos, London, England, early 20th century; $90–130. Instruments such as this are just beginning to attract collector attention. ▶

▲ Chronometer watch with chrome case, enamel face, and outer case of silver; by Patek, Phillippe and Company, Geneva, Switzerland, 1920–22; $1,500–2,200. The high price placed on this piece reflects its use on the first dirigible crossing of the Polar Sea in 1926.

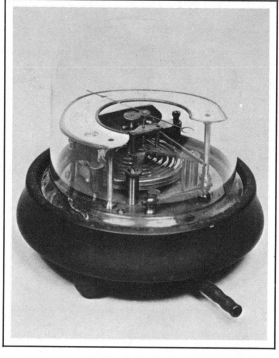

Demonstration model aneroid barometer with glass bell jar cover; Germany, early 20th century; $150–220. ▶

Seven-inch sextant in brass with brass-fitted mahogany case; by Cail & Sons, Newcastle, England, ca. 1830; $450–600. Brass and copper instruments bring good prices, primarily due to their decorative quality. ▼

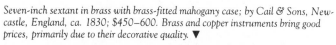

▲ Barograph in brass and cast iron in a glass and oak case; by M. W. Dunscombe, Bristol, England, early 20th century; $175–250.

Surveyor's compass in brass in hand-carved cherry- ▲
wood case; United States, early 19th century;
$700–850.

◀
Surveyor's wye level in brass; by Heller & Brightly,
Philadelphia, Pa., mid-19th century; $300–450.
Surveying instruments are attractive and interesting
collectibles.

Compound microscope in brass and glass; by Bausch & Lomb, ▲
Rochester, N.Y., early 20th century; $300–400. In original walnut
case.

Replica of a rare Scottish-design screw-barrel microscope in brass ▲
and iron; Edinburgh, Scotland, 20th century; $1,200–1,600.
Modeled on a ca. 1740 original made by William Robertson.

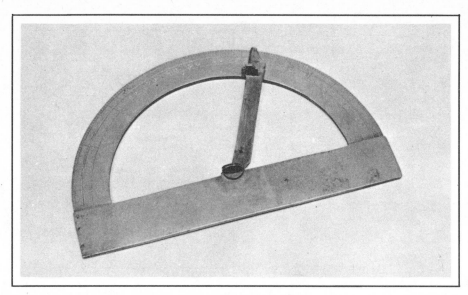

Protractor in brass; Europe, 19th century; $75–100. Drafting and mathematical instruments are a relatively untouched field. ◀

Scientific instruments; China, 19th century. Left: Diptych sundial incorporating a magnetic compass in wooden case; $85–125. Right: Two compasses in wood, one of them turned over to show the maker's signature; $150–200 each. ▼

266

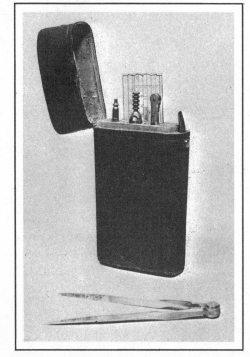

Sundial in pewter made for use on the New England coast; ▲ *United States, 19th century; $175–250.*

◀

Set of charting instruments for use in map work in brass in leatherette case; by Parker & Son, England, late 19th century; $90–130.

Set of drafting instruments in brass and iron in mahogany case;
▼ France, late 19th – early 20th century; $150–200.

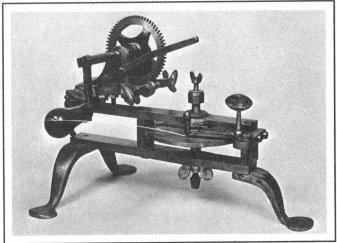

Clockmaker's wheel- ▲
cutting tool in iron
and brass; England,
late 18th century
$750–1,000. Serious
clock and watch collec-
tors are often interested
in tools used in the
trade.

▲ Set of maximum and minimum thermometers in
mahogany case; by C. F. Casella & Company,
London, England, late 19th century; $75–100.

▶
"Winshurst" machine in glass and metal on an
ebonized wood stand; France, 19th century;
$100–150. A type of experimental device.

267

13

Toys

It is difficult to imagine a world without toys, and archaeological discoveries indicate that playthings have existed in every well-developed culture. Not too surprisingly, the earliest of these artifacts are dolls. The tombs of Egyptian children have been found to contain tiny human figures made either of wood or of linen stuffed with reeds, and other doll-like objects have been uncovered from Greek and Roman sites and from the lonely backlands of South America.

Not all these figures were playthings. Doll-like objects have served a variety of religious and ritual purposes (the voodoo doll is but one example), and it is often impossible to determine the original use of such items.

It is clear, however, that Greek and Roman children played with dolls, for references to such toys exist, and dolls appear in paintings and illuminated manuscripts of the Middle Ages. The first such playthings to gain wide popularity in Europe were the so-called fashion dolls that were being made in Paris in the 1400s. Three hundred years later English and Dutch children were playing with carved wooden dolls that had high foreheads, painted features, and jointed limbs. Known in the British Isles as "penny woodens" (an allusion to their supposed cost), such dolls were sold throughout Europe.

Carved dolls were known in Japan during the 1600s. These figures, known as kokeshi, often had moveable heads but seldom had functional limbs. The Japanese have always been great doll makers, and the kokeshi were, by their standards, quite primitive. In fact, during the past two centuries they have produced many delicately carved or bisque-headed figures that are elaborately dressed in period costumes and that represent a level of great sophistication in the doll-maker's art.

Interestingly enough, the Chinese did not make dolls until the 1800s, and then they did so only for export, it being widely believed in China that the human figure was too sacred to be mimicked in this manner.

The greatest diversity in doll forms appears in Europe. Here the playthings were made of wood, of tin, of stuffed cloth, of composition (a mixture of sawdust, plaster, and glue), and of pottery. The most desirable of all were the porcelain-headed dolls produced in France and Germany during the nineteenth century. Perhaps the best-known makers are the Frenchmen Pierre Jumeau and Leon Bru. Their exquisite creations date from the late 1800s and may bring prices ranging into the thousands of dollars. The Germans, too, were masters in this field, exporting thousands of dolls to the United States during the 1880s.

Stuffed-cloth figures, perhaps the earliest of all playthings, remained popular throughout the nineteenth and into the twentieth century. Concerns such as the Arnold Print Works of Massachusetts produced printed cloth designs that could be cut up, stuffed, and sewn together. The teddy bear, inspired by President Theodore Roosevelt, became a best-selling toy in the hands of the German firm of Steiff.

Nor were dolls the only toys made of wood. Wooden pull toys in the shape of tigers and horses were found during excavation of ancient Thebes, and during the medieval era young boys trained for knighthood astride wooden hobbyhorses, toys which also appear on Chinese ceramics of the Sung period. During the past century a vast quantity of wooden toys has been manufactured, including the legendary Noah's Arks of Nuremberg and the lovable jointed circus figures produced by Albert Schoenhut, a German who settled in Pennsylvania.

Other popular wooden playthings include the rocking horse, jumping jacks and Jacks-in-the-Box, blocks, tops, and, of course, wooden dollhouses and their furnishings. It is interesting to note that the first doll or "baby" houses as they were known were large affairs mounted on stands and intended for the amusement of adults. It was not until the early 1800s that inexpensive wood or lithographed cardboard houses became generally available.

Among later developed toys none exceeded the popularity of those made of tin. Tin, which is thin sheet iron covered with rust-resistant melted tin, is an ideal medium for toymaking. It is lightweight, reasonably durable, and can be cut and shaped. Nevertheless, the first tin toys (doll furnishings) were not made until the late eighteenth century, and the business did not get underway in earnest until well into the 1800s.

The finest playthings in this medium were made in Germany, France, and the United States. Among the leading German manufacturers were Maerklin (a toy battleship made by this firm recently sold at auction for $25,000), Lehman, Hess, and Bing. Employing sophisticated methods of cutting and joining their toys as well as chromolithography, a form of decorative printing that had replaced the much slower process of painting toys by hand, the German manufacturers at Brandenburg and Goppingen turned out countless tin toys, some of which were powered by clockwork motors and all of which were attractively designed.

German tin playthings were exported to the far corners of the earth, but in North America they met formidable competition from the toy makers of the Connecticut River Valley. There, such firms as Stevens & Brown and Ives turned out everything from carousels to dancing dolls and replicas of every vehicle traveling the seaways and roads of North America.

During the present century two wars and attendant disasters seriously affected the German industry while American manufacturers turned their attention to other playthings. However, during the 1930s Louis Marx turned out many unusual mechanical character toys based on such popular comics and radio figures as Popeye, Mickey Mouse, and Dagwood Bumstead. The Germans, always quick to spot a market, also capitalized on this market, as did the Japanese, though their products were generally of lesser quality. Following the Second World War restored factories in both Germany and Japan produced excellent tin windup toys, and these are already attracting collector interest.

Toys have also been made of various other metals, including

pot metal, a mixture of tin and cast iron; lead; sheet steel; and cast iron. Iron came into use at a relatively late date but proved extremely popular, particularly in the United States. European manufacturers were making cast-iron wheels for their toys in the eighteenth century, but it was not until the 1850s that complete toys were made from this medium. At that time the American firm of J. & E. Stevens began to manufacture cap guns and "still" banks. These banks were in the shape of houses and human or animal figures. Within twenty years the even more popular mechanical banks had appeared. These were depositories designed so that insertion of a coin would cause a figure to take some action—tip his hat, say, or fall over. Though still banks were made in England and Germany, mechanical banks remained pretty much an American monopoly.

Much the same can be said of cast-iron toys. As industrialization swept the United States toy designers discovered that replicas of ships, fire engines, horse-drawn carriages, and buses attracted a great patronage. This had been true with tin, and it proved equally the case with cast iron. From 1885 until well into the 1930s American factories poured forth a vast quantity of cast-iron vehicles. Since their form made it impossible for them to be lithographed (printed decoration is applied to a flat surface only), they were carefully hand painted instead. Sturdy and realistic-looking cast-iron toys became a mainstay of the market.

Unfortunately the very popularity of such objects (certain banks and toys command prices in the thousands of dollars) has led to the manufacture of numerous reproductions. Cast from surviving original molds or through the use of authentic pieces, these reproductions are sometimes carefully "aged" and then offered as period pieces. Collectors making substantial purchases in this field should buy only from dealers who guarantee their wares.

Another category of metal playthings is that of lead soldiers, or military miniatures as they are now often called. The first of these popular toys were made of neither lead nor tin. Miniature figures in military regalia have been found in Tuscan and Egyptian tombs, but these are of wood or clay. Louis XIII of France once had an entire army cast in silver. However, as early as the sixteenth century the making of cast-tin soldiers was a major business in the city of Nuremberg, Germany.

These early figures were "flats"—they were cast in two dimensions with engraved details. Though by the late 1700s French and German manufacturers were producing tens of thousands of lead soldiers and some could boast of owning a thousand different molds for their production, they continued to make the flat figures until the early 1800s. Then the French firm of Mignot began to turn out three-dimensional examples, which were termed "solids." The solids were more realistic and they gradually took over most of the market, even though their weight and the greater amount of materials involved in their production made the cost of producing them objectionable. These problems were solved in 1893 when William Britain of London introduced hollow cast-lead figures. Britain's, along with Mignot, became the major twentieth-century producers in this field.

The great popularity of military miniatures has led to the use of other materials in their manufacture, including jigsaw-cut wood soldiers (often with lithographed decoration) rubber, cast iron, paper, and plastic. Since the end of the Second World War the latter material has largely come to dominate the entire field.

Prices for military miniatures, especially for matched sets, have risen steadily over the past decade, but they cannot compare with the prices asked in another area—toy trains. Unlike toy soldiers, of course, trains are of rather recent vintage. The first examples appeared in the 1830s and were really steam-driven miniatures, not toys. But by mid-century true toy trains were available. They were of two types. The first were the "carpet runners," which were large, unpowered trains that could be pushed or pulled around the room. Then in 1856 the American toy manufacturer George W. Brown developed the first clockwork-driven train. The Europeans had, in the meantime, perfected steam-driven toy locomotives, but these were heavier and much more expensive than Brown's little tin engine.

Though tin windup trains didn't run on rails until the German firm of Maerklin came out with standardized tin-plate tracking in 1891, they were immensely popular and widely made in both North America and Europe. Besides Brown, the major American manufacturers were the Ives firm and Lionel; European competitors included Maerklin and Bing of Germany and Rossignol of France.

Then late in the nineteenth century the electric train appeared on the scene. Ives made them and so did the Lionel Corporation, which eventually became the major American producer. In Europe Maerklin was joined by Karl Bub of Nuremberg and Hornby of England. Today there are thousands of train enthusiasts, and early rolling stock may cost as much as a full-size train did a hundred years ago!

On a more placid (and less expensive) note, we should take note of the many interesting table or board games that have appeared over the past few hundred years. Some, such as checkers and Parcheesi, are, in fact, far older, dating at least to the medieval period. But most collectors today concentrate on the many board games that appeared during the nineteenth century. These are all basically alike in that they involve a trip or chase about a course laid out on a board with the player's progress being determined by a cast of dice, turn of card, or spin of a dial.

The greatest of all such pastimes is Monopoly, which has sold millions of copies and been translated into several languages. But earlier games, such as The Mansion of Happiness and Prefectures of France attract more collectors. Board games were produced in large numbers both in the United States and in such European countries as France, Germany, and England. Collectors seek out those examples that have the most attractive covers and board layouts, with graphics a determining factor in desirability.

There are also a number of wheeled toys available. Doll carriages, in both three- and four-wheeled varieties, may be found as well as wagons, scooters, and miniature cars. Most of these are powered by a peddle arrangement, but the French produced several miniature gasoline-driven versions of contemporary autos during the 1920s, and these are highly desirable (and highly expensive) acquisitions.

Toy collecting is one of the most active fields in the antiques and collectibles world. Prices in certain areas, such as dolls, tin toys, and mechanical banks, are reaching remarkable levels, and these prices are being accompanied by the advent of fakes and reproductions. However, it is still possible to begin a collection with a modest outlay, especially in such areas as board games and paper playthings. In all cases, however, buy the best. Damaged or heavily repaired toys are seldom a good investment.

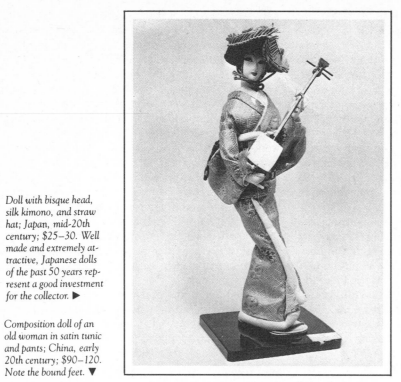

Doll with bisque head, silk kimono, and straw hat; Japan, mid-20th century; $25–30. Well made and extremely attractive, Japanese dolls of the past 50 years represent a good investment for the collector. ▶

Composition doll of an old woman in satin tunic and pants; China, early 20th century; $90–120. Note the bound feet. ▼

Doll with leather boots, painted wooden face, and fur-trimmed pants; Eskimo, 1890–1910; $80–95. Dolls of this sort were often made for sale or barter to white traders. ▼

Dolls in bisque, each less than 4 inches tall, in Chinese dress; Japan, 1920–30; $25–35 each. ▶

Doll with bisque head and shoulders, painted features, and leather body; Germany, 1870–90; $400–500. The delicate features of these bisque dolls make them a great favorite with collectors. ◄

Doll with bisque head and ball-jointed composition body; by Viola, early 20th century; $175–225. ▼

► *Doll with bisque head, soft body, and patent-leather shoes; by Armand Marseille, Germany, late 19th–early 20th century; $250–300. A German manufacturer, Marseille made dolls for local distributors such as Borgefelt as well as for French firms.*

Doll with bisque head and forearms and body in kid; Germany, late 19th–early 20th century; $275–350. As with many dolls, this one's costume is not original. ▼

Doll with bisque head with wood-and-composition ball-jointed body; by George Borgefelt, Germany; early 20th century; $350–400. ▼

Doll with bisque head and composition body; France, 20th century; $300–350. Marked "Unis," this doll was part of an international doll series. ▶

Artist's model doll in painted wood; France, 1870–90; $150–175. ▼

Doll with bisque head with wood-and-composition body and blond mohair wig; France, early 20th century; $750–875. Blonds are relatively uncommon among European dolls. ▼

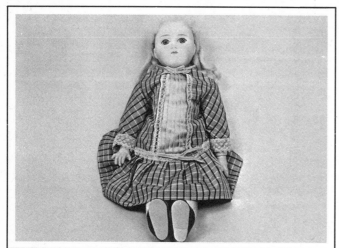

Crèche doll in carved and painted wood with silk clothing; Italy, early 19th century; $250–350. Pieces such as this were meant to be admired, not played with. ▼

Articulated wooden mannequin of the sort used to display fashions; Europe, late ▲ *18th–early 19th century; $250–325.*

Doll in stuffed velvet with painted features; by Chad Valley, England, 1925–35; $150–175. ▶

Kewpie doll in bisque; by Heubach, Germany, 20th century; $150–200. Though only 5 inches tall, this doll is big with collectors. ▼

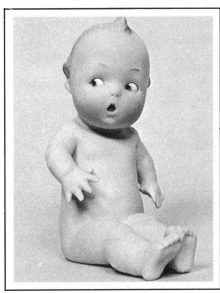

Ventriloquist puppets in painted wood and composition; by Berndt, Germany, ▲ *1920–30; $175–250 each. Left: Herby. Right: Kayo. German manufacturers frequently reproduced American comic characters.*

Doll in felt with swivel head, jointed hips and shoulders, and painted features; by Lenci, Italy, 1925–35; $350–425. Lenci is the Rolls-Royce of stuffed toys. ▼

Fisherman doll with sculptured stockinette face and paper body; Italy, 20th century; ▲ *$75–110.*

273

Stuffed toy cat in printed fabric; probably by Arnold Print Works, United States, 1890–1900; $50–60. ▼

Dollhouse in lithographed paper and wood in the Victorian style; by R. Bliss. United States, late 19th–early 20th century; $250–300. Marked Bliss examples are a must with dollhouse enthusiasts.
◄

Doll in bisque with matching celluloid baby; by Heubach Kopplesdorf, Germany, ca. 1931; $275–325. This doll was issued as a souvenir to the Paris Colonial Exposition of 1931.
▼

Hand puppets; by Steiff, ▲ *20th century. Left: Jocko the monkey; $65–75. Center: Snobby the poodle; $75–85. Right: Gaty the alligator; $80–90. Steiff was the world's most important producer of soft toys during the 20th century.*

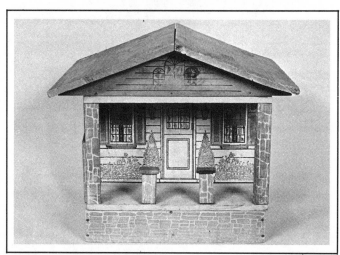

Dollhouse in lithographed paper and painted wood; United States, late 19th century; ▲ *$60–75. Lithography made possible the production of inexpensive dollhouses in large quantities.*

◄

Doll in fiber body; by Seminole Indians, southeastern United States, 20th century; $45–55.

Player piano in wood with plastic keys and metal gears; by Schoenhut, United States, 1920–35; $75–95. Better known for his jointed toys, Schoenhut was an early manufacturer of children's musical toys. ▼

Eagle gas stove in cast iron with skillet in green and white; United States, 1930–35; $45–60.
◄

Bathroom set in cast iron in black, cream, and green paint; by Tootsie Toy Manufacturing Company, United States, 1920–30; $60–75 the set. ▼

Child's tea set (part of a 13-piece set) in the Brown Calico pattern; by Stafford-shire, England, 1840–50; $300–350 the set. Sets of this quality are not considered toys. ▼

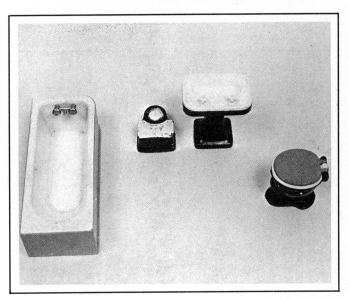

Child's porcelain tea set (part of a 32-piece set); Germany, 1890–1910; ▲
$145–225 the set.

Toys in cast iron; United States, 1930–40. Left: Royal gas stove; $30–35. Right: ▲
Rocking chair; $10–13.

275

Chicken in painted pottery; Mexico, early 20th century; $20–25. Hand-formed toys like this were once a common sight in every country. ◄

Pecking bird toy in polychrome wood; Russia, ca. 1890; $50–65. Hand-cut and painted toys of this type are common in eastern Europe. ▼

Figure in painted pottery; Japan, 1930–40; $45–55. Figures of ▲ rural fishermen, farmers, and artisans are still made in Japan and offer an interesting specialty to the discerning collector.

Kokoshi dolls in polychrome wood; Japan, late 19th century; $140–180 the pair. Early Japanese folk toys are relatively rare. ▼

Toy in the form of a moose in hand-carved and painted wood; Scan- ▲ dinavia, 20th century; $20–25.

Minnie Mouse dolls in wood; Germany, ca. 1928. Left: About 8 inches tall; $200–250. Right: $100–150. Cartoon dolls generally bring substantial prices today.

Dog pull-toy in papier-mâché with jointed legs; Europe, 1920–30; $50–70. Papier-mâché was a popular medium for inexpensive toys during the late 19th and early 20th centuries. ▲

Jointed horse in painted wood; by Schoenhut, United States, early 20th century; $80–100. This toy is part of the famous Schoenhut circus set-up and could support a clown on its back. ▶

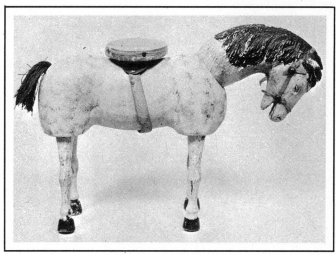

Circus toys; by Schoenhut, United States, 1910–20. Left: Donkey in painted wood; $75–95. Right: Clown with painted features and cloth costume; $90–110. ◀

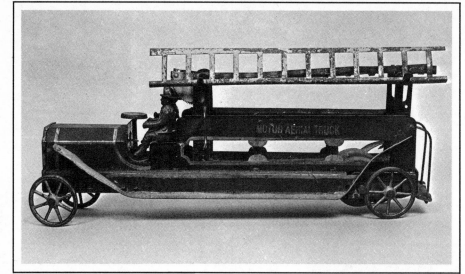

Fire truck in tin plate, called Motor Aerial Truck; probably Germany, 1925–30; $175–250. Lightweight, inexpensive, and easily decorated, tin was long a favorite material for toy manufacturers. ◄

Friction-powered touring car in tin plate painted yellow; Europe, ca. 1890; $175–225. Like many early motor cars, this one resembles a horseless carriage. ▼

Dump truck in tin plate; probably England, 1920–30; $75–100. This large vehicle is similar to the so-called strong toys produced by Chad Valley and other English makers. ▼

Fire truck in sheet metal and aluminum with logo of Los Angeles Fire Department; by Miller Ironson Corporation, California, 20th century; $100–150. ▼

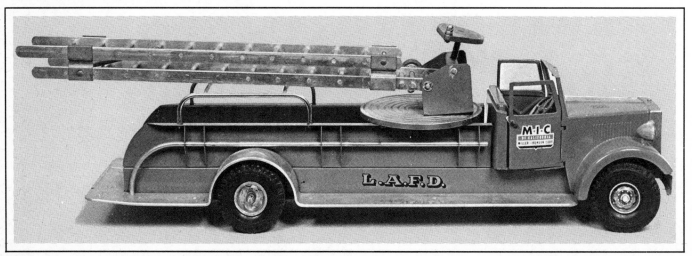

Antiaircraft gun in tin plate painted green and red; United States, 1930–40; $75–100. Once popular, guns such as this model emitted a loud "pop" with a strip of paper passed through a compressor. ▶

Windup toys in lithographed tin; by Marx, United States, 1935–45. ▲ Left: *B.O. Plenty*; $100–150. Right: *Dopey from the Snow White story*; $60–90. Marx was the leading maker of mechanical tin toys during the 1930s and '40s.

Windup battleship in tin with original lithographed finish; by Arnold, Germany, 1945–52; $90–120. Though still common, occupied Germany and Japan tin toys represent an excellent investment. ▶

Windup bus in tin plate; by Tri-Ang, England, 1940–50; $150–175. Pieces in ▲ mint condition, such as this one, always bring premium prices.

Windup penguin in tin with lithographed decoration; France, mid-20th century; $25–30. Though never a major producer, France did turn out some copies of American and German windup toys. ◀

Rare clockwork figure in tin of clown playing a xylophone; by Wolverine Manufacturing Company, United States, 1930–40; $250–300. ◄

Clockwork musical toys in tin, composition, felt, and cloth; by Schuco, Germany, 1945–52. Left: Monkey; $80–100. Right: Clown; $90–110. ▼

Windup robots in lithographed tin; Japan, 1950–60. Left: $35–45. Right: $25–30. Japan produced many interesting tin clockwork toys during the post–World War II era. ▼

◄
Windup vehicles in lithographed tin; by Marx, United States, 1950–60. Left: Tractor; $20–25. Right: Tank; $30–40. Late Marx toys are inexpensive and will increase in value.

◄ Battery-operated beer-drinking monkey in lithographed tin; by Liemar, Japan, 1950–60; $75–100. Though known in the 1930s, battery-operated toys have come into their own in the past 35 years.

◄ Battery-operated toy clown fiddler; by Alps, Japan, 1950–60; $150–200.

Battery-operated toy in lithographed tin, "Cragstan ▲ Crapshooter"; Japan, 1950–60; $60–75.

Army Supply Train (part of a set including engine and 12 cars) in lithographed tin and cast iron; by Marx, United States, 1930–40; $250–350 the set. Trains in general are very popular with collectors, and rare examples such as this are particularly sought after. ◄

Engine and tender in cast iron and tinplate; by Lionel Corportion, United States, mid-20th century; $300–350 the complete set. Lionel is one of the leading names among train manufacturers. ▼

Push-pull toy of Professor and Mama Katzenjammer in cast iron with original polychrome paint; Germany, 1925–30; $900–1,100. ▶

Horse roll toy in cast iron; by Ives, Connecticut, ▲ *1870–80; $700–800. Early cast-iron toys, most of which were made in the United States, bring exceedingly high prices.*

Roll toy horse-drawn ice wagon in cast iron in red, white, and yellow; United States, 1920–25; $135–165. ▶

Bell toy of horse and rider in cast iron in red and silver; United States, 1900–10. $125–155. Bell toys, which jingled when pushed or pulled across the floor, were a popular amusement for the young. ◀

Toy autos in pot metal;
England or United
States, 1930–40;
$12–18 each. ◄

Still banks in cast iron. Left: Charlie McCarthy;
United States, marked 1938; $75–90. Right: Lion;
▼ England, late 19th century; $150–200.

Still bank in lithographed
tin; by Morrison, United
States, 1910–25; $250–
300. This bank comes
with its original box, a
plus for any serious
collector. ◄

Rare mechanical bank in
cast iron; United States,
ca. 1898; $1,500–2,000.
A coin placed in the can-
non can be fired and will
knock down the ship's
mast. ▼

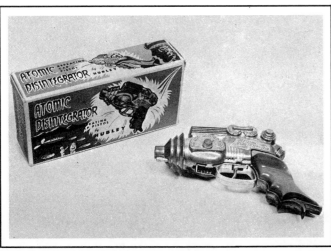

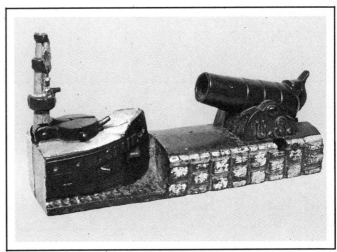

◄
"Atomic Disintegrator" in pot metal with silver paint;
by Hubley Toy Company, United States, 1930–40;
$125–150. Hubley was one of the great names in
early 20th century toy making.

Group of "flats," more or less two-dimensional soldiers, in lead; made in Chile from a German mold, mid-20th century; $8–10 each. The molds for military miniatures are often used for long periods of time.

Toy soldiers in lead; by Mignot, France, early 20th century; $22–28 each. These fully formed figures are of the type known as solids.

Hollow-cast lead soldiers; by Britain's, England, 1945–55; $10–15 each. Cast-iron tank; United States, 1925–30; $60–75. ▼

Extremely rare set of signaling boy scouts in hollow-cast lead in original box; by Britain's, England, 1925–35; $300–400 the set. ▼

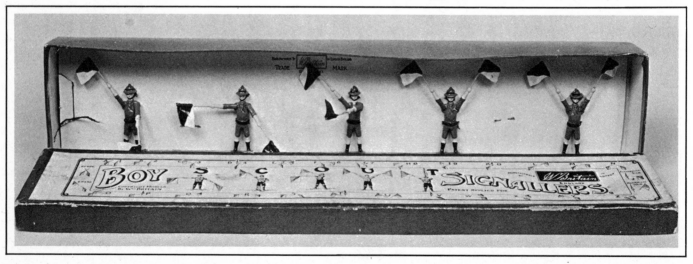

Speedboat in wood and metal, the Auto-Rameur; by France & Etranger, France, 1910–20; $250–300. Clockwork boats such as this were a common diversion for both adults and children during the early 20th century. ▶

Mammoth Circus with hollow-cast lead figures in original box; by Britain's, England, 1945–55; $1,000–1,500. A complete Mammoth Circus is practically unobtainable. ◀

Speedboat in wood and metal with windup motor and naval patrol officer with cloth costume and bisque head; Germany, 1920–25; $300–400. ◀

Military miniatures in the material known as Elastoline; Germany, 1935–45; $40–50 the set. ▶

▲ Horizontal steam engine in copper and cast iron in red and black paint; United States, 1920–25; $85–135.

Metal construction set; by Meccano, England, 1930–40; $30–40. Though popular with children, construction toys have never caught on with adults. ►

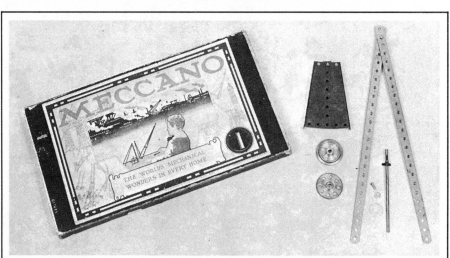

Building blocks in stone in blue, cream, and iron red; Germany, 1890–1900; $80–100. ◄

Pegboard puzzle in wood; Europe, early 19th century; $45–60. ▶

Picture puzzle in lithographed paper on cardboard; by McLoughlin, United States, copyrighted 1887; $90–110. McLoughlin produced a variety of games, puzzles, and other paper toys. ▼

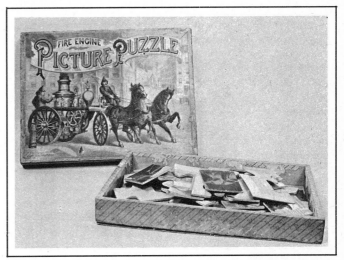

▲ *Picture puzzle in lithographed paper on cardboard; United States, 1910–20; $150–175. Rare and attractive puzzles bring good prices.*

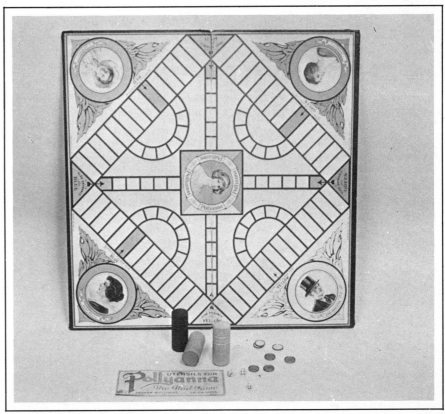

▶

Pollyanna, The Glad Game, board game; by Parker Brothers, Salem, Mass., 1900–20; $60–75. Board games are increasing in popularity. Like this one, most are made of attractively lithographed paper on cardboard.

14

Woodenware and Basketry

Objects made of wood or basketry materials are found throughout the world. Even the Eskimos, many of whom live in treeless areas and depend on driftwood for their timber, carve wooden boxes, toys, and household implements. In localities blessed with more arboreal growth wood has been used for making nearly everything imaginable.

In Africa, where most areas enjoy an abundance of trees, skilled carvers have worked for untold generations. Even the most simple objects, such as spoons and knife handles, are carved in elaborate geometric patterns, and larger pieces, such as eating and serving bowls and the bins in which grain is stored, are so heavily carved they are true works of art. This is understandable in light of the fact that until recently work and religion were intertwined in Africa, and the stylized figures on tools and everyday objects were talismanic—the carving on tool handles or on grain containers represented deities whose intervention would make the work go better or protect the food.

The religious significance of carving is common in primitive societies and may, in part, explain the extraordinarily high quality of the handwork. The crafts of Polynesia present a further example. The natives of Polynesia, a vast region of tiny islands scattered amid endless seas, lack nearly every raw material other than wood and stone. From the stone they have made idols and weapons; from the wood have come remarkable tools and utensils, some carved in the shape of native birds and turtles, others painstakingly decorated with complex openwork designs and polished to a high luster with leaves rich in silicic acid. War clubs and other implements of destruction have been patterned in the same way and stained red, yellow, and blue with natural dyes.

Another notable area of woodenware-making is the northwest coast of North America, where tribes of Indians and forest Eskimos have manufactured everything from giant war canoes and totem poles to ritual dance masks. All these pieces—from Africa, from the South Pacific, from North America—have a common characteristic: they are shaped in a highly sophisticated and abstract manner. Almost all the designs are based on natural forms—plant or more often animal—but in nearly every case these natural forms are reduced to their bare essentials, abstracted in such a way that they become part of a total composition that is essentially curvilinear or geometric. It was this remarkably "modern" style that, early in this century, drew Western artists and collectors to what they came to call primitive art. Today, collector enthusiasm in this area is so great that some tribes devote themselves to producing inferior replicas of the earlier pieces for sale to tourists and crafts dealers.

Looking at the remarkable beauty of nineteenth-century woodencraft, it is often difficult to believe the primitive way in which the pieces were made. In most cases the pieces were roughed out of a fallen timber with a stone or metal ax. They were then hollowed out where necessary by burning the wood away, bit by bit, and were decorated by chipping out tiny bits of wood or incising lines in the surface. Finishing and polishing involved long hours of work with stone or bone scrapers, sand, oil, and leaves. The end result might represent months out of a craftsman's life, but these were months gladly given, for in such societies the craftsman held a social position appropriate to his skills: indeed, in some instances he was regarded as a link between the people and their gods.

In western Europe, too, there were traditions of religious carving, and they lingered for a long time. At one time religious figures carved from wood adorned every church and were customarily worked into the decorative scheme of more secular objects as well. For the most part, however, the majority of collectible European woodenware is more worldly in conception. It is, nevertheless, often extremely well made and attractive.

A great variety of woodenware is spread from Scandinavia to the Iberian Peninsula. In the north both carving and burned-in decoration took second place to rosemaling ("rose painting"), a technique through which the whole surface of an object, be it house beam or saltbox, was covered with stylized floral and leaf motifs in bright colors. Rosemaling was practiced for the most part in Norway, with the custom spreading from there to the rest of Scandinavia and even to North America. Pieces decorated in this manner are among the most prized of all woodenware.

The making of staved objects—things like barrels and drinking vessels composed of curved wooden sections, or staves, held together with wood or metal hoops—was also popular in the north. Indeed, the designs of silver and pewter drinking vessels of the period often imitate the earlier staved wooden tankards.

In other areas people drank from containers that had been hollowed out by hand from pieces of solid wood. A good example is the Italian *grolla*, a massive gobletlike vessel with elaborate exterior carving, which was reserved for toasts on feast days and similar special occasions. Carving was a special Italian gift, and Italian craftsmen turned out delicately engraved spoons for the ladies and shepherd's staffs that bore the signs of the zodiac.

Many of the Italian carvers were themselves shepherds, for the long days alone in the mountains allowed time for the work. This was true also in Spain and Portugal, where these solitary whittlers shaped such things as the famous ox yokes of Portugal's Alentejo district and the mortars, spoons, and baking molds that come from the southern regions of Spain. This area was long held by the Moors, and the Islamic influence is evident in the geometric devices favored in decoration. Due to their relative isolation and, until recently, somewhat backward industrial development, both Spain and Portugal continued to produce high-quality wooden objects well into this century, and this area remains a happy hunting ground for sophisticated collectors.

The industrial nations of western Europe also have a long tradition of wood carving, though the better examples from these locales date from before 1900. In Germany the medieval custom of giving brides small trinket or storage boxes led to the production of chip or "bride's" boxes—covered oval containers made from thin strips of hardwood that were steamed until pliable and then bent into shape and fastened with wooden pegs or nails. Some of these vessels were decorated with incised figural decoration, but the majority bore painted representations of human figures—perhaps the bridal couple or an important historical personage. Brought to the United States by Germanic immigrants these boxes became the canvases on which appeared the stylized forms of such American heroes as George Washington and General Lafayette.

English woodenware is similar to Continental woodenware. In England we find butter molds carved with floral and animal devices, gingerbread forms, which might consist of a piece of wood as large as six by fourteen inches carved with a dozen different homely images, and knitting needles the handles of which were shaped in human form or covered with hearts and other love tokens. While most of these woodenware objects are not of great age, some few of them date to the seventeenth century.

France, too, had its woodenware traditions. In the south, close to the Spanish border, are found carved animal yokes and milking stools similar to Iberian examples, as well as remarkably complex necklaces carved from a single piece of wood. In the north, Brittany produced engraved spoons that were inlaid with wax or mother-of-pearl and were held in such high regard that they were customarily worn on the waistcoat like a pocketwatch.

In eastern Europe painting largely replaced carving as the preferred form of decoration for woodenware, and from Austria to Poland and Russia peasant craftsmen turned out a variety of brightly colored objects, such as spinning wheels, wall boxes, walking sticks, and even picture frames. Most of these were made from cheap, softwood, but their gay decorations have made them a popular tourist item.

Settlers in North America brought their woodworking traditions with them and adapted them to the native woods and local conditions. English customs prevailed in New England, with boxes, watch holders, and other small objects being painted to imitate wood grain or bearing tiny figural designs. In areas where the Dutch and Germanic peoples settled, the so-called Frisian carving (essentially geometric designs cut out in a triangular pattern known as notch carving) was dominant. The resemblance of such work to contemporary European examples has led to confusion and even misrepresentation of types.

Other influences were at work in other areas of the United States. Carving in the French style was done in Louisiana; rosemaling appeared in the north central states; and in the southwest Spanish-American craftsmen practiced Iberian techniques. Probably nowhere else in the world is it possible to find such a blend of techniques as in North America, and nowhere else is the enthusiasm for collecting so great.

Woodworking reached an especially high level of development in China and Japan. In China teak, camphorwood, and various hardwoods were used in the manufacture of elaborately decorated combs, painted and gilded lanterns, and a variety of boxes. These boxes were both carved and inlaid with substances such as mother-of-pearl, pewter, and porcelain. They became very popular export items during the late nineteenth century and, though diminished in quality, this trade continues to the present day.

Chinese craftsmen also produced many painted pieces, such as dishes, bowls, umbrella handles, and the like. The Japanese also made such items, though they made them primarily for sale overseas. For their own purposes the Japanese preferred much plainer items. They specialized in bamboowork, creating tiny, delicate dippers (hishaku) for use in the tea ceremony as well as needle cases, brush holders, and the cages in which singing crickets were kept. Perhaps the most famous of the Japanese woodenwares are the powerfully carved inro (medicine boxes) and the netsuke (the toggles used to secure inro to a sash or belt). Usually no more than two or three inches long, such pieces are blessed with a wealth of detail. Human and animal figures, monsters, flowers, and even mountains are to be found—often carved in such small scale as to require a magnifying glass for examination. Small wonder that earlier and better examples may now bring thousands of dollars at auction.

Like the making of woodenware, basketmaking has been practiced on a worldwide basis and the quality and quantity of construction varies greatly. Among the finest examples of the craft are the remarkable coiled and woven baskets produced by the Indians of the American West. Made from grass, roots, and branches that are carefully plaited and woven and dyed with natural colors, these pieces range in size from tiny, thimblelike containers to three-foot-tall grain storage baskets. Some of these baskets are so tightly woven that they are capable of holding water. Indian baskets are customarily decorated with stylized animal figures and complex geometric designs. Collected since before 1900, they now bring prices ranging up to four figures.

Chinese and Japanese basketry is also of high quality. Here the favored materials are bamboo and rattan, a vine that can be split into long, easily woven strands. Best known of the rattan ware are the round sewing baskets decorated with brass coins and "Peking glass" that have been made in China for over a hundred years. Also seen are the three-tiered "lunch baskets," which can be separated for serving a meal. These highly polished receptacles are especially favored, even today, by the Japanese.

African basketry appears in greater variety but is not as well known as other examples. In the arid areas of the north baskets are made of roots or grass, while lush jungle areas yield bark, vine, and reed containers. All are highly collectible and have been made for centuries. In fact, conical baskets of water rush have been found in pre-Christian Egyptian tombs.

In Europe basketmaking has largely died out, but good late-nineteenth- and early twentieth-century examples may still be found. Among these are the coiled straw bread rising, storage, and grape gathering vessels made in Germany and southern France. The technique of manufacturing such rye-straw containers was also brought to the United States, where similar forms were made from Pennsylvania to Texas. The shoots of the common willow tree were also employed in European basketry. The French made baby cradles from this substance for a long time, while in Bavaria it was made into market baskets embellished with paint and woven leather. Splint, the split core of ash or hickory trees, was utilized in Spanish cheese baskets and in French animal muzzles and English vegetable baskets. In short, nearly every available substance from mulberry vines to leather was tried out by the European and American basketmakers.

Woodenware and basketry collecting remain today as two of the only areas in which the novice or not-too-well-to-do enthusiast can gain a foothold in the antiques world at a modest expenditure. A great variety of objects is available. Many types are currently of limited interest to most collectors and are, therefore, relatively easy to obtain at reasonable prices. Perhaps most important of all, there are no antiques that reflect so well the everyday life and aspirations of common people throughout the world.

Lidded box in wood with incised geometric designs; Ba Kuba, Congo, late 19th–early 20th century; $175–250. African artisans have produced a variety of wooden vessels. ▼

Woodenware; Africa, early 20th century. Left: Ax with metal blade; Ba Kuba, Congo; $60–90. Right: Spoon with handle in form of a human head; Dan; $45–65. ▼

Food bowl in hand-hewn wood; Africa, early 20th century; $90–120. Plain, undecorated ware such as this is still readily available from dealers in African artifacts. ▶

Granary door in carved and decorated wood; Africa, late 19th century; $300–350. Doors of this sort are uncommon today and of great interest to collectors. In their day, they served a mundane purpose— keeping thieves and rodents from valuable supplies. ◀

Storage vessel in wood in geometric form with geometric decoration and touches of red paint; Kaffir, early 20th century; $225–285. A remarkably modern-looking vessel of the sort that influenced European Art Deco designers.

◄
Door latch in carved wood with incised decoration and two-piece lock surmounted by anthropomorphic figures; from the Dogon region of Mali, late 19th century; $150–200.

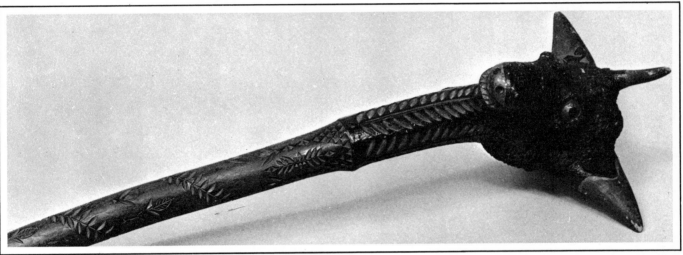

▲ Carved and painted war club with head in the form of a goat and incised decoration; Fiji, late 19th century; $200–300. Less common than African pieces, Melanesian wooden objects are popular with collectors.

Storage or eating vessel on wood base in the form of three ▲ anthropomorphic figures; Africa, early 20th century; $70–95. The crude carving indicates a late date for this piece.

Drinking cup in carved wood with repairs in leather; ▲ Africa, 1500–1700; $200–300. This piece is very rare.

War club in carved rootstock with incised decoration; West Polynesia, late 19th century; $150–200.

House post in the form of a human figure in carved ▲ wood; Borneo, late 19th–early 20th century; $175–250.

Eating bowl in carved wood; by Eskimo, Alaska, early 20th ▲ century $90–120. Due to a shortage of wood, the Eskimos have produced only a limited number of wooden objects.

Sewing box in carved and incised driftwood; by Eskimo, Alaska, late 19th century; $200–275. The decoration on this piece resembles the decoration on Eskimo scrimshaw. ▼

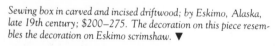

Large horn spoon with incised decoration; by Ameri- ▲
can Indian, Northwest Coast, U.S.: $200–250.

Box in wood with decoration painted and inlaid
in bone; Persia, mid–19th century; $60–80.
Highly detailed work such as this is typical of
Near Eastern craftsmen. ▼

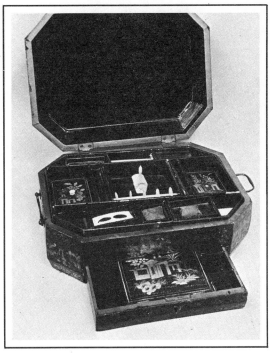

Box or carrying case for a bronze mirror in wood and ▲
lacquerware; Japan, 19th century; $50–75. An un-
usual form found only in the Orient.

Sewing box in black lacquer with gilt decoration and ▲
various compartments and carved ivory spools, bob-
bins, etc.; Japan, late 19th century; $250–325.

Mortar and pestle in carved wood with incised geometric decoration; Europe, early 19th century; $35–50. Though of some age, such pieces are relatively common and seem to be of little interest to most collectors. ▶

Arrow quiver in wood and black ▲ lacquer decorated with gold leaf; Japan, 19th century; $1,500–1,800. An extremely rare and well-preserved object.

Bowl with dragon motif in carved and painted polychrome wood; China, mid–19th century; $150–200. The Chinese have long made substantial quantities of woodenware for export. ▼

Carpenter's line holder in teakwood with elaborate carved decora- ▲ tion; Japan, late Edo period 1830–50; $160–210.

Baker's peel in wood; France, early 20th century; $50–65. Peels were used to place baked goods in the oven and to remove them when they were done.

Carved woodenware; France or Spain, 19th century. Above: Grain scoop; $45–55. Below: Large spoon with hook-carved handle; $25–30.

Large bowl in carved oak burl; Europe, 19th century; $250–350. Produced by an abnormal tree growth, burl is hard and has an attractive grain. It will also take a high polish.

Lidded storage box in softwood with decoration in brown and yellow paint; Germany, late 19th century; $75–95. A typical example of peasant decoration.

Mustard pot in wood with wire handle; England, mid-
to late 19th century; $55–70. Lathe-turned pieces
such as this were often made in small woodenware
factories. ▼

Wall match holder in carved wood with incised decoration; Europe, early 20th century; $20–25. ▼

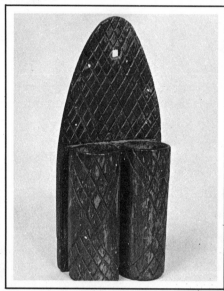

Sander in turned lignum vitae; England, mid–19th ▲
century; $30–40. The sand in this saltshakerlike ob-
ject was poured on wet ink to blot it.

Pair of miniature storage, or "bride's boxes"; early
20th century. Left: In boxwood with carved decoration; Italy; $30–45. Right: In birch with straw bind-
ings; Germany; $25–35. These are novelty pieces. ▼

Tape loom in wood; Europe, ca. 1800; $200–250. Tape looms were used to weave such things as belts, suspenders, and neckties. ▼

Two pieces of carved horn; probably Scandinavia, late 19th century. Left: Large ▲ *scoop or dipper; $50–65. Right: Drinking glass with brass bindings; $60–80. Horn was often carved like wood and served the same purposes.*

Group of bowls in wood; United States or Europe, mid-to late ▲ *19th century; $30–75 each. Many shallow chopping and mixing bowls were made in the United States, but few deep bowls, such as the one at left.*

Box in wood and straw work; England, mid–19th century; $60–75. The bulk of ▲ *decorative straw work came from the British Isles.*

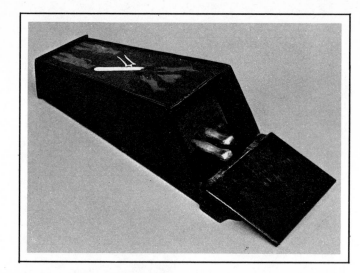

Knife box in walnut inlaid in bone and fruitwood with figures of Hessian soldiers and dogs; England, late 18th century; $600–750. Once found in every fashionable dining room, knife boxes are now rare.

Tea caddy in mahogany with elaborate molded top, bone escutcheon, and two interior compartments; England, late 18th–early 19th century; $550–700. ◄

Small storage box in mahogany with fruitwood inlay in the Neo- ▲ classic style; probably France, early 19th century; $90–120. A variety of boxes was used for storage of personal belongings during the 1800s.

Handled sewing box in birch with silk lining; made in a Shaker ▲ community, United States, late 19th century; $85–110.

Sewing box painted black and gilded in imitation of lacquerware with reverse-painted glass panel; France,
late 19th century; $300–375. A typically lavish ex-
ample of Victoriana.

Storage box in wood composed of inlay in light and ▲
dark wood on a pine carcass; United States, mid-19th
century; $125–150.

◄

Rare lift-top storage box in pine in the form of a book;
United States, mid-19th century; $200–275. Only a
few pieces of this sort are known.

299

Wall sconces in elaborately carved wood with gilt decoration; France, late 19th century; $120–170. These Victorian candleholders indicate a high degree of ▼ carving skill.

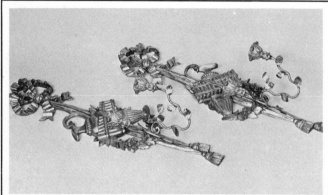

Carpenter's toolbox in pine; Canada, early 20th ▲ century; $40–55. Toolboxes like this may range in length from 2 to 4 feet.

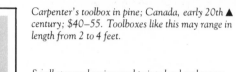

Small storage box in wood painted red and green; Guatemala, mid-20th century; $10–15. Boxes such as this are still sold to tourists. ▼

Ballot box in pine with original red paint; United States, 1840–50; $65–85. Ballot boxes were employed not only in local political contests but in many ▼ club and secret-society elections as well.

Pair of candleholders in carved pine; Spanish-▲
American, United States, late 19th century;
$200–300.

Regency period pail in mahogany with brass binding ▲
and brass liner; England, early 19th century;
$750–1,000. An uncommon and very sophisticated
piece of woodenware.

Objects in turned wood; England or United States, ▲
late 19th century. Left: Sander in walnut; $20–25.
Center: Bank in maple; $25–30. Right: Toothpick
holder in pine in old red paint; $20–25.

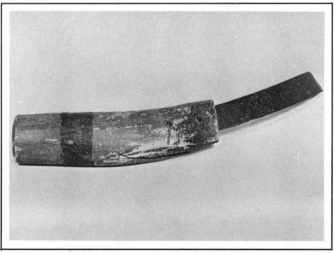

◀
Farrier's knife in carved wood in blue and black paint
with a steel blade; Canada, early 20th century;
$30–35. Paint was often added to give a distinction to
otherwise ordinary objects.

Candle lantern in painted wood and tin with glass panes and wrought-iron handle; United States, early 19th century; $225–275. Early lighting devices bring high prices. ▼

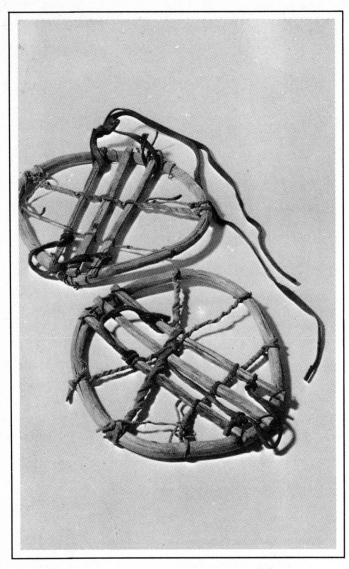

Pair of snowshoes in ▲ oak and leather; United States, late 19th century; $125–150.

▲ Unusual master salt in oak burl with geometric decoration; probably Spain, early 19th century; $200–275. For centuries the position of the master salt indicated the status of those at the table.

302

Musical instruments in wood; mid–20th century. ▲ Left: Thumb piano; West Africa; $20–25. Right: Flute; Yugoslavia; $12–15.

Compartmented storage basket in reed, woven grass, and wood; Africa, early 20th century; $95–135. This basket can be divided to provide several smaller baskets ▼ and trays.

Large tray in split and woven cane with geometric ▲ design in black on a white ground; Mombasa, Kenya, 20th century; $50–60. Trays were often used in food sorting and preparation.

Storage box in pine with brass ring finial and original green paint; United States, mid–19th century; $60–75. ▼

Unusual seed-pod-shaped food preparation basket in ▲ woven grass and willow; Ethiopia, early 19th century; $70–95.

Pair of lidded storage baskets in woven grass; Central Africa, early 20th century; $100–135 each. Even today basketry is important to the African economy. ▼

Storage basket in woven grass, bark, and rush, in ▲ conical form with matching top and unusual handle construction; North Africa, early 20th century; $80–120.

Large storage or carrying basket in untrimmed willow; Bangla- ▲ desh, mid-20th century; $65–95. A plain and undecorated but extremely appealing basket.

Basket in concentric woven grass stained blue and black; China, ▲ early 20th century; $45–60. Chinese baskets are often decorated with glass beads and brass coins.

Bread baskets in woven rye straw; Germany, late ▲
19th–early 20th century; $20–30 each. Rye-straw
basketry is common in much of central Europe.

Bread basket in woven willow in green paint; France,
early 20th century; $25–35. French artisans made
many things from willow, including cradles. ▼

Large storage basket in grass and willow decorated ▲
with geometric designs in red and blue dye; Philippines,
dated 1905; $100–135.

◄
Burden basket in split ash; central Europe, early 20th
century; $50–70. Note the extemely simple
construction.

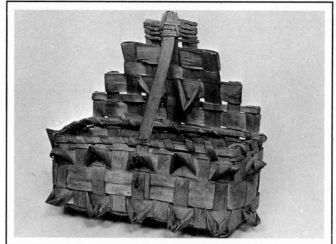

Loom basket in splint with curlicue decoration and traces of red paint; by Micmac Indians, Canada, early 20th century; $55–70. Making baskets for sale to tourists is an important part of this tribe's economy.

Covered basket in machine-cut ash splint stained red and green and decorated with curlicues; by Micmac ▼ Indians, Canada, early 20th century; $25–35.

Figure in woven rice straw, split bamboo, and cloth in bright paint; Indonesia, mid-20th century; $35–50. ▼

► Basketry in coiled multicolored grass and roots; by Hopi Indians, United States, early 20th century. Left: Covered carrying basket; $70–95. Right; Tray; $40–55.

Sewing basket in the form of a turkey in pine needles and pieces of pinecone; by Coushatta Indians, United States, 20th century; $40–50. A novelty piece from Louisiana. ▼

Basket in coiled grass and roots with geometric designs in brown against a lighter background; by Pima Indians, United States, early 20th century; $150–200. ▼

Basket in finely woven bark and grass with central star motif and ▲ *various human and animal figures; by Apache Indians, United States, late 19th century; $600–700. The American Indians are among the best basket-makers in the world.*

Covered basket in tightly woven root and straw; by Indians, ▲ *Northwest Coast, United States, early 20th century; $110–140. Indian baskets generally bring high prices.*

307

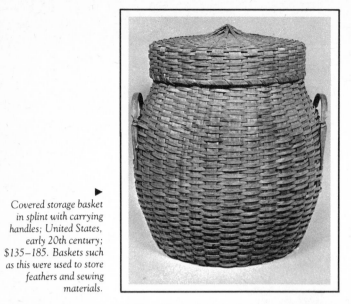

Covered storage basket in splint with carrying handles; United States, early 20th century; $135–185. Baskets such as this were used to store feathers and sewing materials.

Carrying basket in splint painted white; United States, early 20th century; $35–45. Baskets such as this were made by rural craftspeople.

Covered basket in coiled grass; by Indians, Northwest Coast, United States, early 20th century; $75–95.

Pair of baskets in reed and splint with wooden handles and bottoms; Nantucket Island, United States, early 20th century. Left: $250–300. Right: $400–500. A fad for these baskets has led to remarkably high prices.

Carrying basket in ash splint; United States, late 19th century; $70–95. This is the sort of basket used in shopping and in carrying vegetables from the fields. ◄

Group of small berry pickers' baskets in splint; United States, early 20th century; $20–25 each. Baskets of this sort have long been used in picking wild fruit. ▼

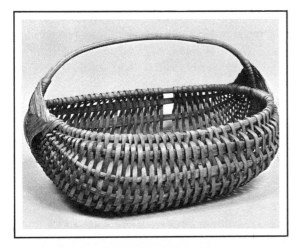

Carrying basket of the type known as a buttocks basket in rough ▲ splint and hickory; United States, early 20th century; $75–100.

Covered storage basket in splint decorated with stamped designs ▲ in red and yellow; United States, early 20th century; $80–120. Such so-called potato stamping decoration was used by both whites and Indians.

309

Appendix of Terms

Agata glass An ornamental glass, in shades from white to rose, with a mottled but glossy surface. Agata was widely made in nineteenth-century glass factories.

Amberina glass An ornamental glass, in shades from pale amber to ruby, produced primarily in American and English factories during the nineteenth century.

Amish An American religious society centered in Pennsylvania and Indiana and well known for its colorful geometric pieced quilts.

Art Deco A stylistic period (1910–40), named after the 1925 Parisian Exposition Internationale des Arts Décoratifs, characterized by furniture and accessories that blended eighteenth-century rococo forms with early twentieth-century materials and concepts of factory design.

Beaker A large drinking vessel with a wide mouth and sloping, cylindrical sides. Beakers can be found made of precious metals, glass, or ceramics.

Bed warmer A circular brass or copper pan with hinged, decorated lid and a long handle. Filled with charcoal or hot coals, it was used to warm beds.

Bisque (biscuit) Porcelain or pottery that is unglazed but fired. During the nineteenth century, bisque porcelain was used to imitate marble.

Black light A fluorescent light that will reveal most repairs and additions when shone upon a painting or a piece of glass or pottery. New material will fluoresce a lighter color than original material.

Blowpipe A long, hollow, metal tube used in glassmaking. The glass blower picks up a glob of hot glass on the end of the tube, and by blowing through the tube he can expand the glob to create a glass vessel.

Bohemian glass A colorless potash-and-lime glass made in central Europe and customarily embellished with elaborate cut or enameled decoration.

Brazier A metal pan designed to hold burning charcoal to warm a small space in a room. These heating devices were most common in Asia and southern Europe.

Brocade A woven silk multicolored fabric in which the pattern or figure appears in relief against a lighter background.

Brooch An ornamental metal, glass, or gemstone pin fitted with a clasp so that it can be worn on the breast or shoulder.

Bullion Unworked bulk gold or silver, usually in the form of bars or dust.

Cabinetmaker A craftsman trained to make furniture, particularly case pieces, such as sideboards, chests of drawers, or cupboards.

Calligraphic decoration Linear figural patterns based on a form of handwriting known as Spencerian script. The somewhat

flowery decoration is characterized by floral and animal forms.

Character toys Wooden, tin, or rubber toys of the period 1920–40 that are in the form of radio, movie, or stage luminaries such as Dick Tracy or Charlie Chaplin.

Chromolithography A color printing process involving the use of various plates or stones, each containing a different color. Books, prints, and toys have been made or decorated using this process.

Console table A side table the top of which is supported at the front by two legs and at the back with two brackets, or consoles, which are attached to a wall.

Crystal glass A brilliant colorless glass that has a high percentage of lead oxide. The term *crystal* refers to its resemblance to natural rock crystal, or quartz.

Embossing The process of creating raised decorative patterns on the surface of metals, paper, or leather.

Enameling The technique of applying opaque or translucent enamel colors to the surface of a piece of glass or metal.

Engine-turned decoration Designs or patterns made on ceramics or metals by cutting into their surfaces with tools while they are turned on a lathe.

Filigree work Decorative work in fine wire of silver or gold that is soldered to a base in various intricate and elaborate designs.

Flagon A large drinking vessel with a handle and spout and sometimes a lid. Flagons are made of metal, glass, or ceramics.

Flint glass An English glass made first with burned flint, later with lead oxide, and characterized by remarkable clarity and brilliance.

Flying buttress In architecture, a supporting or bracing structure, usually in the form of a band of stonework, joining an abutment to a wall.

Foot warmer A tin or soapstone box, often enclosed within a wooden frame, that was filled with hot coals or charcoal and used to warm feet.

Foundry A commercial establishment in which metals such as iron or bronze are cast.

Gilding The process of decorating pottery, glass, or metal with gold either as dust or in a solution that might be simply painted on the object, applied in combination with mercury, or painted and then fired at a low temperature.

Guild An organization of workingmen practicing the same craft and adhering to certain rules of membership, apprenticeship training, and quality of work produced.

Hallmarks Figural devices, names, and numbers stamped on gold, silver, or pewter, that indicate the piece's maker and the place of manufacture or attest to the object's quality and purity according to the requisite guild or governmental agency.

Incised decoration Decoration produced by cutting a design into the surface of an object. In ceramics this is done while the piece is rubber-hard, just prior to firing.

Inlay The process of inserting materials of a contrasting color or material into spaces cut in a solid object, such as a piece of wood.

Jack-in-the-box A toy consisting of a spring-mounted head enclosed within a lidded box. When the box is opened, the head springs out.

Jardiniere A piece of pottery or furniture designed to hold growing plants or flowers.

Jumping jack A string-mounted, jointed wooden toy. Pulling on the string makes the figure hop and move about.

Lacy glass A variety of pressed glass characterized by lace and beadwork decorative patterns that often cover the entire surface of the piece. Lacy glass was most popular during the period 1830–60.

Lost wax process An ancient technique of bronze casting wherein a wax replica of the object to be made was melted and replaced in the mold by the hot bronze.

Master salt A large metal, ceramic, or wooden saltcellar from which smaller saltshakers were filled. Traditionally, the master salt sat before the owner of the house.

Mechanical bank A toy bank, usually of cast iron, that performs some action when activated by the insertion of a coin. In the well-known Tammany Bank, for example, a coin placed in the figure's hand would be swiftly deposited in his pocket.

Metal A technical term from glassmaking for the molten glass as it comes from the furnace. In this state it is flexible and can be shaped.

Molds Molds are hollow wooden, plaster, or metal forms into which metal, glass, or ceramics may be poured while in a liquid state. Once hard, these materials retain the shape of the mold.

Nef A large ornamental table decoration, usually in the form of a sailing ship, that held knives, salts, and other tablewares. Nefs were so expensive that they were owned by only the wealthiest medieval nobles and merchants.

Papier-mâché A mixture of pulped paper and glue that can be cast in molds and, when hardened, painted and decorated with mother-of-pearl and gilding. It has been used to make trays, boxes, and furniture.

Paste The cut or colored glass used in the making of imitation jewelry.

Patterns In pottery and porcelain decoration, the patterns are the colored-tissue-paper designs that are applied to unbaked ceramics. Upon firing, the paper is destroyed, and the color adheres to the piece.

Peking glass Peking glass is brightly colored opaque glass, usually in the form of beads or small vessels, produced in and around Peking.

Pendant A small metal, glass, or ceramic ornament, as jewelry, that is usually hung from a chain and worn about the neck.

Period (style) A time interval during which furniture and certain decorative objects share a recognizably characteristic style of manufacture and design, such as the neoclassic period. The term also refers to pieces that were made during such a period, as a Chippendale period chair.

Pottery Nonvitrified earthenwares, such as majolica or Rockingham. In most cases the objects are kiln-fired, though in a primitive society they may be baked in the sun.

Reproduction A piece of furniture or a decorative accessory made in the style of a specific design period; an imitation of an earlier piece, whether intended to deceive or please.

Still bank A small repository for coins, usually of iron, tin, or ceramics and often in the form of a building, person, or animal. The name reflects the fact that such banks are not mechanical (see Mechanical bank).

Style of When discussing antique reproductions (pieces made to imitate examples made during a specific historical period) such pieces are said to be "in the style of" the period imitated.

Tankard A tall, sometimes lidded, drinking vessel made of wooden staves, metal, or pottery and used primarily for beer drinking.

Tapestry In textiles, a hand- or machine-woven fabric that is identical in appearance on both sides. The typical tapestry subject matter is a religious or mythological scene.

Tea caddy A small compartmented box or case to hold tea. Usually made of wood, but various metals, tortoiseshell, or papier-mâché may also be used.

Totem pole A large pole, carved and painted with various stylized birds and beasts, that traditionally adorns the area in front of a northwest coast Indian home.

Transfer printing The technique of using colored-tissue-paper designs to decorate porcelain and pottery. See Patterns.

Translucence A characteristic of porcelain: the fact that light may be seen through the wall of a ceramic vessel when it is held up to the light.

Trivet A metal stand designed to keep hot objects (such as a kettle) from damaging wooden surfaces (such as tabletops). The typical form is triangular with three legs.

Veneer Thin sawn or machine-cut slices of attractively grained wood that are glued or pegged onto the surface of ordinary wood to create a richer effect.

Votive figures Carved figures of wood that serve a religious purpose, such as the santos of Mexico and South America. Many votive figures are important pieces of folk art.

Bibliography

Furniture

Aronson, Joseph. *The Encyclopedia of Furniture*. New York: Crown Publishers, 1965.

Bishop, Robert, and Coblentz, Patricia. *Furniture, Prehistoric Through Rococo*. New York: Smithsonian Institution, 1979.

Hayward, Helena. *World Furniture, A Pictorial History*. New York: McGraw-Hill, 1965.

Hinckley, F. Lewis. *A Directory of Antique Furniture*. New York: Bonanza Books, 1953.

Joy, Edward. *The Connoisseur Illustrated Guides, Furniture*. New York: Hearst Books, 1972.

Kates, George N. *Chinese Household Furniture*. New York: Dover Publications, 1948.

Ketchum, William C., Jr. *Furniture, Neoclassic Through Modern*. New York: Smithsonian Institution, 1981.

Silver

Fales, Martha G. *Early American Silver*. New York: Funk & Wagnalls, 1970.

Fletcher, Lucinda. *Silver*. London: Robis Publishing Company, 1973.

Holland, Margaret. *Silver*. New York: Derby Books, 1973.

Honour, Hugh. *Goldsmiths and Silversmiths*. London: Weidenfeld & Nicolson, 1971.

Hughes, Bernard and Therle. *Three Centuries of English Domestic Silver*. New York: W. Fred Funk, Inc., 1952.

Hughes, Graham. *Modern Silver Throughout the World*. London: Studio Vista, 1967.

Taylor, Gerald. *The Connoisseur Illustrated Guides, Continental Gold and Silver*. London: 1967.

Wardle, Patricia. *Victorian Silver and Silver Plate*. London: Jenkins, 1963.

Virtu and Cloissoné

Chu, Arthur and Grace. *Oriental Antiques and Collectibles*. New York: Crown Publishers, 1973.

Clark, H. G. *Pictorial Potlids*. London, 1970.

Ellenbogen, Eileen. *English Vinaigrettes*. London, 1967.

Harrison, Hazel, ed. *World Antiques*. Secaucus, N.J.: Chartwell Books, 1978.

Hughes, G. Bernard. *English Snuff Boxes*. London, 1971.

Kelley, Austin, P. *The Anatomy of Antiques*. New York: The Viking Press, 1974.

Ricketts, Howard. *Objects of Vertu*. London: Barrie & Jenkins, 1971.

Jewelry

Armstrong, Nancy. *Jewelry*. London, 1973.

Bradford, Ernle. *Four Centuries of European Jewelry*. London, 1967.

Fregnac, Claude. *Jewelry From the Renaissance to Art Nouveau*. London: Heidenfeld, 1965.

Hughes, Graham. *Modern Jewelry, An International Survey*. London: Studio Vista, 1968.

_____. *The Art of Jewelry*. London: Studio Vista, 1966.

Peter, Mary. *Collecting Victoriana*. New York: Frederick A. Praeger, 1968.

Bronze

Chu, Arthur and Grace. *Oriental Antiques and Collectibles*. New York: Crown Publishers, 1973.

Fry, Roger, et al. *Chinese Art*. London: B. T. Botsford, Ltd., 1945.

Ishizawa, Masao, ed. *Pageant of Japanese Art: Sculpture*. Rutland, Vt.: Charles E. Tuttle Company, 1958.

Mackay, James. *The Animaliers, Animal Sculptures of the 19th and 20th Centuries*. London: Ward Lock, 1973.

Savage, George. *Concise History of Bronzes*. London: Thames & Hudson, 1969.

Metalwares and Weapons

Alexander, William, and Street, Arthur. *Metals in the Service of Man*. London: Hammondsworth, 1972.

Coffin, Margaret. *American Country Tinware, 1700–1900*. New York: Galahad Books, 1968.

Kaufman, Henry J. *Early American Ironware*. New York: Weathervane Books, 1976.

Mackay, James. *Turn-of-the-Century Antiques*. New York: E. P. Dutton, 1974.

Michaelis, Ronald. *British Pewter*. London: Woodbridge, 1978.

Perry, Evan. *Collecting Antique Metalware*. London and New York: Hamlyn Publishing Company, 1974.

Wills, Geoffrey. *Collecting Copper and Brass*. London, 1962.

Pottery and Porcelain

Bemrose, Geoffrey. *Nineteenth Century English Pottery and Porcelain*. London: Faber, 1952.

Cox, Warren. *The Book of Pottery & Porcelain*. New York: Crown Publishers, 1944.

Hillier, Bevis. *Pottery and Porcelain: 1700–1914*. London: Wedenfeld, 1968.

Honey, W. B. *European Ceramic Art*. London: Faber, 1952.

Ketchum, William C., Jr. *The Pottery and Porcelain Collector's Handbook*. New York: Funk & Wagnalls, 1971.

Palmer, Arlene M. *Chinese Export Porcelain*. New York: Rutledge Books/Crown Publishers, 1976.

Wynter, Harriet. *An Introduction to European Porcelain*. New York: Thomas Y. Crowell, 1971.

Glass

Ash, Douglas, ed. *Dictionary of British Antique Glass.* Levittown, N.Y.: Transatlantic Arts, 1976.

Buckley, Wilfred. *European Glass.* Boston: Houghton Mifflin Company, 1926.

Gardner, Paul V. *Glass.* New York: Smithsonian Institution, 1979.

Mariacher, Giovanni. *Italian Blown Glass from Ancient Rome to Venice.* New York: McGraw-Hill, 1961.

Newman, Harold. *An Illustrated Dictionary of Glass.* New York: Thames & Hudson, 1978.

Polak, Ada. *Glass: Its Traditions and Its Makers.* New York: G. P. Putnam and Sons, 1975.

Van Salden, Axel. *German Enameled Glass.* New York: Crown Publishers, 1971.

Primitive and Folk Art

Andrews, Ruth, ed. *How to Know American Folk Art.* New York: E. P. Dutton, 1977.

Boas, Franz. *Primitive Art.* New York: Dover Publications, 1955.

Buehler, Alfred, et al. *The Art of the South Sea Islands.* New York: Crown Publishers. 1962.

Bush, Lewis. *Japanalia.* New York: David Mackay Company, 1959.

Douglas, Frederic H., and D'Harnoncourt, Rene. *Indian Art of the United States.* New York: The Museum of Modern Art, 1969.

Hansen, H. J., *European Folk Art.* New York: McGraw-Hill, 1968.

Lipman, Jean, and Winchester, Alice. *The Flowering of American Folk Art.* New York: The Viking Press, 1974.

Textiles

Bishop, Robert, and Safford, Carleton L. *America's Quilts and Coverlets.* New York: Weathervane Books, 1974.

Eiland, Murray L. *Oriental Rugs, A Comprehensive Guide.* Boston: Little, Brown and Company, 1977.

Ketchum, William C., Jr. *Hooked Rugs: A Historical and Collectors's Guide.* New York: Harcourt, Brace Jovanovich, 1976.

Leitch, Gordon B. *Chinese Rugs.* New York: Dodd, Mead & Company, 1928.

Morris, B. *History of English Embroidery.* London, 1954.

Swain, Margaret H. *Historical Needlework.* London: Barrie & Jenkins, 1970.

Timepieces and Scientific Instruments

Baillie, G. H. *Watches: Their History, Decoration and Mechanism.* London: Methuen, 1929.

Burton, E. *Clocks and Watches, 1400–1900.* London: Praeger, 1967.

Chapius, A., and Jaquet, E. *Technique and History of the Swiss Watch.* Boston: American Horologist and Jeweler, 1956.

Daniels, George. *English and American Watches.* London: Abelard-Schuman, 1967.

Distin, William H., and Bishop, Robert. *The American Clock, A Comprehensive Survey, 1723–1900.* New York: E. P. Dutton, 1976.

Tyler, E. J. *The Craft of the Clockmaker.* London, 1974.

Ullyett, K. R. *British Clocks and Clockmakers.* London: Collins, 1947.

Toys

Eaton, W. M. *Dolls In Color.* New York: Macmillan, 1975.

Hertz, Louis H. *The Toy Collector.* New York: Funk & Wagnalls, 1969.

Jacobs, Flora Gill. *A History of Dolls' Houses.* New York: Charles Scribner's Sons, 1965.

Ketchum, William C., Jr. *Toys.* New York: Smithsonian Institution, 1981.

King, Eileen. *The Encyclopedia of Toys.* New York: Crown Publishers, 1979.

Mackay, James. *Childhood Antiques.* New York: Taplinger Publishing Company, 1976.

Pressland, David. *The Art of the Tin Toy.* New York: Crown Publishers, 1977.

Woodenware and Basketry

Bobart, Henry H. *Basketwork Through the Ages.* Oxford, England: Oxford University Press, 1936.

Earle, Alice M. *Home Life in Colonial Days.* Stockbridge, Mass.: Berkshire Traveler, 1974.

Hansen, H. J., ed. *European Folk Art.* New York: McGraw-Hill, 1967.

Hothem, Lar. *North American Indian Artifacts.* Florence, Ala.: Books Americana, 1978.

Ketchum, William C., Jr. *American Basketry and Woodenware.* New York: Macmillan, 1974.

Pinto, Edward H. *Treen and Other Wooden Bygones.* London: G. Bell and Sons, 1969.

Woodstock, A.S. *Basketry.* Independence, Mo.: Herald House, 1960.

Index

316

Acknowledgments

Marylou Alpert, Croton-on-Hudson, New York
Donna Bartells, New York, New York
Ruth Bigel Antiques, New York, New York
Cintra Huber, New York, New York
Aaron Ketchum, New York, New York
James Lyons, New York, New York
Myers & Elman, New York, New York
Phillips Galleries, New York, New York
Plaza Auction Galleries, New York, New York
Barbara Rohrs, New York, New York